# Writing Effective Policies and Procedures

# Writing Effective Policies and Procedures

## A Step-by-Step Resource for Clear Communication

## Nancy Campbell

### AMACOM
### American Management Association

New York · Atlanta · Boston · Chicago · Kansas City · San Francisco · Washington, D.C.
Brussels · Mexico City · Tokyo · Toronto

This publication is designed to provide accurate and authoritative
information in regard to the subject matter covered. It is sold with
the understanding that the publisher is not engaged in rendering
legal, accounting, or other professional service. If legal advice or
other expert assistance is required, the services of a competent professional person should be sought.

Library of Congress Cataloging-in-Publication Data

Campbell, Nancy, 1949–
    Writing effective policies and procedures : a step-by-step
  resource for clear communication / Nancy Campbell.
      p.  cm.
  Includes bibliographical references and index.
  ISBN-10: 0-8144-7960-X
  ISBN-10: 978-8144-7960-5
    1. Management—Handbooks, manuals, etc.  2. Business writing.
I. Title
HD38.15.C36   1997
658.4'53—dc21                       97-40744
                                        CIP

Printing number

25  24  23

# Contents

## 5  Is There a Certain Format I Should Use?  134

### Tools and Resources for Chapter 5  155

## 6  How Do I Get Them to Read This?  205

## 12   We're Thinking About Going On-Line                                    **372**

What It Means to Go On-Line        372
The Advantages and Disadvantages of Going
    On-Line        373
The Case of External Users        376
Designing an On-Line System        378
Chapter Summary        378

### Tools and Resources for Chapter 12                                        **381**

# Introduction

WHY THIS BOOK IS IMPORTANT

This book is important because clear policies and procedures have a profound effect on an organization. Systems operate properly. People operate properly. We all get the information we need clearly and quickly.

WHY YOU ARE IMPORTANT

As a writer of policies and procedures, you are therefore an important person in the lives of your readers. You can ease the way for them. You can reduce their frustration. You can save them tremendous amounts of time. You can help them eliminate mistakes, increase efficiency, and save money. All this with the supposedly simple act of writing a good policy or procedure.

WHAT YOU MUST DO

In reality, though, policy and procedure writing isn't so simple. You must be both a word master (for accuracy) and a word miser (for brevity). You must become a design expert (for readability). You are sometimes a lawyer (for risk avoidance) and occasionally a psychiatrist (for cooperation). You are always a craftsperson, shaping your document to meet the needs of your readers (for clarity and speed).

HOW THIS BOOK HELPS YOU DO IT

This book is a realist's guide to accomplishing all this. Discussions are brief and to the point. At the end of each chapter is a section called Tools and Resources. It contains samples, forms, guidelines, and tip sheets for you to use in writing, communicating, and implementing your own policies and procedures.

Mark this book up. Make notes in it. Copy and use its forms, guidelines, and tip sheets. This book is a workhorse.

Anyone can write a good policy or procedure using this book. Whether you've been doing it for five days or for twenty-five years, this book gives you the tools to write policies and procedures that meet the needs of both reader and organization.

HOW TO
SURVIVE THE
PROCESS

You'll face many challenges in creating your document. Time is short. Pressure is high. You must cope with changing circumstances and changing minds. You may have to fight to get the resources you need. But in the end it's worth the effort.

When the frustrations of the process loom large, focus on this simple fact: Your readers' lives will be easier and your organization will be improved because of what you've done.

Then take yourself to lunch.

I wish you good writing.

# Acknowledgments

This book is dedicated to all those who have ever been asked to put together a policy or procedure as if it were the easiest thing in the world to do.

With special thanks to R. P. Campbell, who offered valuable comments and assistance; to Adrienne Hickey, who exhibited great patience under unusual circumstances; to Mary Heideman, who started this project; and to all the AMACOM editors whose assistance and suggestions considerably improved this work.

# Writing Effective Policies and Procedures

# 1

# What's a Policy, What's a Procedure?

Policy and procedure writing is about clear communication. It's making sure that people have the information they need to do what they're supposed to be doing. With the right information and enough of it, both organization and reader function properly.

## Why You Need Policies and Procedures

You need policies and procedures for the simple reason that you can't do much without them. If a company didn't have any, daily operations would become chaotic and users frustrated. Policies and procedures are nothing more, and nothing less, than the way an organization operates.

They tell the reader what the organization wants done, why it wants it done, and how to do it. The policies deal with the "what" and "why." The procedures deal with the "how." And while we often talk about them in the same breath, there are important differences between the two. For a discussion of those differences, see the Summary Comparison of Policies and Procedures (1-1) at the end of this chapter.

## Policies

Policies are guidelines that regulate organizational action. They control the conduct of people and the activities of systems.

A policy is actually a type of position statement. It explains the organization's stand on a subject and why there's a rule about it. It tells the reader how the organization intends to operate.

Your organization is free to operate any way it chooses as long as it doesn't violate any laws. This, however, means that the organization must make clear, conscious decisions about its own standards and principles of operation.

These decisions become the organization's policies. Do you want to achieve a zero-defect rate? Will you be available to customers twenty-four hours a day? Will you extend credit to first-time buyers? Should you offer day care to employees?

Your organization can be generous or conservative. It can impose rigid rules or create flexible guidelines. The choices it makes are the basic rules—the policies—that readers are expected to abide by.

---

### A Special Note About Policies

The skill at the heart of good policies is not writing. It's decision making. If the organization doesn't have a clear sense of what it wants to do, the writer will be severely limited. There's only so much that can be done with confusing or incomplete information. Policymakers must do their jobs before writers can do theirs.

Start with a clear decision, then proceed with good writing.

---

## Ambiguity in Policies

Many writers are uncomfortable with policy statements because they're often broad, general, and ambiguous. "It is our intent to provide the best customer service in the industry." Is that a policy statement? Certainly. It influences the way employees do their jobs. But it is also ambiguous, not telling employees *how* to provide the best customer service.

A policy can be a philosophy, a mission, or a general objective. Anything that establishes a guideline for users is a policy, whether called by that name or some other. Examine your organization's mission statement or objectives, and you'll probably find some policies in them.

Ambiguity is necessary in policy and procedure writing. In fact, it's often desirable: You can't pin down everything in quantifiable or statistical terms.

When, where, and how much ambiguity is appropriate depends largely on the subject matter. An inventory procedure, for example, is much more definable than an ethics policy. However, the degree of ambiguity is also influenced by three other factors:

1. Users' ability to understand and deal with the policy. How well will they cope?
2. Managers' ability to understand the policy and willingness to enforce it. How much training will they need?
3. The intensity of the issue and the organization's commitment to it. How closely does the organization wish to control the matter?

On the other hand, policies can also be quite specific: "It is our practice to bill within thirty days of delivery" or "Any accident involving more than $50 in damage will be considered a serious infraction." These precise guidelines are policies that are intended to regulate the user's conduct.

---

### APPROPRIATE AMBIGUITY

Ambiguity is part of a policy and procedure writer's life. When used at appropriate times and in an appropriate manner, it's both necessary and desirable. It's also legal. Learn to be comfortable with it.

---

## Procedures

If policies are the organization's guidelines, procedures are its workhorses. A procedure is the normal method of handling things. It's a protocol for implementation, the "how to."

Procedures supplement the policy guidelines with specifics and complete the information users need. It's not sufficient to say, "It is our policy to provide the best customer service in the industry" and stop there. Users need to know what that means. How do I provide the best service? Do I give customers whatever they want? Am I supposed to give them nothing but make them feel good about it? Is there a dollar limit on action I can take? Is there a certain amount of time I should spend on a problem and no more?

Procedures are action oriented. They outline the steps you expect people to take and the sequence in which to perform those steps. They also frequently point out the consequences of failure to comply, such as damage, loss, injury, or discipline. Clearly stated consequences help users understand (1) the seriousness of the matter and (2) their responsibility for it.

**Example 1-1.** An ambiguous procedure.

---

QUALITY CONTROL PROCEDURE #E-105
FOLLOW-UP ON EQUIPMENT FAILURE

1. Call the customer within three hours after receiving the Failure Report from the Warranty Service Department.
2. Determine the nature of the reported problem by getting details of the equipment failure. Use the questions on the attached list.
3. Using this information, along with information from the Warranty Service Department, assess whether the equipment failure was due to customer negligence or a mechanical defect.
    a. If the problem appears to be due to mechanical defect, refer the case to the Engineering Officer.
    b. If the problem appears to be due to customer negligence, contact the assigned Account Executive.
    c. If the origin of the problem is still unclear, refer the case to your supervisor immediately with all the applicable records.

---

## Ambiguity in Procedures

Procedures are usually very specific, but they can contain ambiguous elements. In fact, although ambiguity is usually less frequent in procedures than in policies, it can be just as important.

For example, the procedure shown in Example 1-1 gives the impression of being precise, but in reality it contains a lot of ambiguity. The third step, which instructs readers to assess the reason for the equipment failure, actually requires them to use their own best judgment based on the information they've obtained from the customer. And all of the subsequent steps call for a professional judgment on the part of the user.

## The Importance of Subjectivity

Determining what and how much ambiguity is appropriate in a policy or procedure can be difficult. And the reason is simple: It makes most of us uncomfortable because it requires subjectivity.

For years many of us have been told to "be objective." The theory is that being objective is the only way to be fair and professional. From a practical standpoint, subjective judgments are tough to explain and difficult to enforce. From a legal standpoint, they're hard to defend and create inconsistencies. So we work hard to avoid subjectivity and try to make our policies and procedures completely objective.

The problem is that all that well-intentioned advice about being objective isn't correct. And again, the reason is simple: Being completely objective isn't possible.

Writers and decision makers are all humans, not robots. So are users and readers. We can't possibly "program" people the same way we do computers, with page after page of technical data only. At some point, we have to call on the reader to use sound business judgment within the limits of the policy or procedure.

In addition, many of the basic decisions our organizations make about how they operate are highly subjective. One manager thinks twenty-four-hour customer service is the only way to go, but another thinks it's a waste of money. Both have facts to back up their positions. Why do they feel so strongly? Because their best judgment tells them it's a good way to do business.

The fact is that total objectivity isn't workable. Some subjectivity is frequently required. What's more, it's often precisely what people are paid for: to exercise sound professional judgment.

The key to appropriate ambiguity and successful use of subjectivity is the phrase *professional judgment*. You don't want readers to use their own personal standards to interpret policy directives or procedural steps. Instead, you want to ensure that they exercise sound business judgment.

As a policy and procedure writer, then, your job is to determine:

1. Which of your subjects legitimately require users to exercise some subjective judgment
2. How much subjectivity is called for
3. What standards or parameters should be used as a basis for making that judgment

Use the Subjectivity Checklist (1-2) at the end of this chapter to achieve the proper balance of objectivity and subjectivity on each project.

## When You Need Policies and Procedures

Never create a policy or procedure just to have one or because it seems like a good idea. Policies and procedures should *accomplish* something.

Organizations sometimes get the idea that they "should" have a policy or procedure and go into a writing frenzy. But if you don't stop to

---

TOTAL OBJECTIVITY ISN'T THE ANSWER

Think about this: If you could boil your organizational policies and procedures down to objective facts and statistics only, you wouldn't need people. You could program computers to do it all and fire the staff. Not likely to happen anytime soon.

Your real goal is to find the proper balance between the objective elements and the subjective elements in each policy and procedure.

---

question what you're trying to accomplish, you'll end up with a lot of paper no one reads.

And sometimes policies and procedures are unthinking reactions to an incident. A user makes a mistake and someone says, "Let's have a policy in case it ever happens again." Why? Ask yourself a few questions before you jump into the writing fray:

- Has such an incident ever happened before?
- Is it really likely to happen again?
- Is this an isolated, once-every-twenty-years occurrence?
- Are the consequences of the mistake so serious (financially, legally, or operationally) that you need to be sure it never happens again?

There are certain areas where it's commonly agreed that policies and procedures are always necessary, such as personnel, health, or safety. In general, you need a policy or procedure whenever there's a need to control, direct, or inform.

The process of creating policies and procedures is about clear communication, so ask yourself what it is that users should be informed about. Look at your own situation and determine what makes sense. You need a policy or procedure for any issue that (1) is important or (2) benefits from clarification.

## What's Important

Important issues are those that have a substantial impact on either the audience or the organization. Just remember that these two groups often have radically different perspectives on the same subject.

For instance, safety is a very important issue to an organization that cares about its employees and wants to comply with the law. Yet employ-

---

Overload Alert

There's a real danger in creating a policy or procedure for everything: People ignore them. There are too many policies and procedures, and they all start to sound alike. The user goes on overload.

Avoid the tendency to overdo it. Ask yourself whether users really need or want to know about something before you begin writing.

---

ees often treat safety policies and procedures casually, believing that they already act in a sufficiently safe manner.

On the other hand, employees might react very strongly to a change in the organization's smoking policy. Yet management may view it as a minor and almost unimportant change.

For the organization, important issues are generally those that affect:

- Efficiency
- Resources
- Schedules
- Customers
- Finances
- Image or reputation
- Health and safety
- Productivity
- Marketing
- Staffing
- Liability and other legalities

For users, important issues are those that affect their personal circumstances or well-being, such as:

- Benefits
- Hours
- Working conditions
- Job security
- Stress
- Satisfaction
- Status
- Personal principles
- Personal goals
- Family

Consider both sides of the issue, and don't underestimate perceptions. If users perceive that a policy or procedure will affect them negatively—or take something away from them—it becomes important to them.

## What Needs Clarification

Certain issues require clarity even if neither your audience nor your organization would consciously consider them important. Policies and procedures are needed if the subject matter:

- Is lengthy
- Is complex
- Is routine but nonetheless essential to successful operations
- Affects the reader's ability to function
- Affects the reader's status
- Affects the reader personally
- Involves significant change or high volumes of change

Much of this is simply a matter of retention. Long, complicated policies and procedures are hard to remember. Change is hard to adjust to. Some rules aren't used very often, and routines tend to create carelessness. At some point, readers need a reference or, if nothing else, a reminder.

See the lists of common policy and procedure topics at the end of this chapter. There is a Health and Safety topic list (1-3), a Personnel topic list (1-4), and an Administrative topic list (1-5).

## Written vs. Unwritten

It's perfectly all right to leave some policies and procedures unwritten. It's both normal and necessary. Writing down everything people are supposed to know and do is impossible. And since most people already have enough paper and enough rules as it is, it's also undesirable. If you can leave it unwritten, do.

Unofficial rules often work better anyway. Think about some of your own. Is it understood that customers can call anytime, even with a minor problem? Does everyone just know that the real billing deadline is twenty-four hours prior to the official cutoff? Is it a given that spouses are included in company functions?

We all have these types of unwritten rules, but they're such a built-in part of our daily lives that they're almost unconscious. Many are related to matters of organizational culture, such as dress and hygiene, but you may want to leave others unwritten as well.

Consider leaving a policy or procedure unwritten when:

▪ It involves organizational culture and norms (e.g., socializing, meetings, hours, and dress).

▪ It cannot be consistently enforced. For example, "Don't discuss your salary with other employees." Enforcement of such a policy is lenient at best. The problem is that once users realize enforcement is lax, they think the same is true of *all* the rules.

▪ It is potentially offensive or intrusive (e.g., body odor, clothing styles, and dating). These are real issues, but writing them down turns into a minefield. It's less disruptive to deal with them informally.

▪ It simplifies. Everyone understands the rules, they work well without formalizing them, and it's one less piece of paper.

On the other hand, you should always put a policy or procedure in writing if the issue is one of:

▪ Accountability
▪ Clarity
▪ Consistency
▪ Critical importance
▪ Documentation
▪ Health or safety
▪ Legal liability
▪ Licensing or regulatory requirements
▪ Serious consequences

---

### DON'T TRY TO FORMALIZE EVERYTHING

Can you imagine trying to write out every single standard, rule, or instruction your organization needs to function every day? It would take years—and long before you finished, you'd have to start over because of all the changes. Don't even try.

---

## When to Write the Unwritten Rules

Sometimes the unwritten rules that have been working well informally begin to break down. This happens most frequently as (1) the organization grows, (2) change increases, and/or (3) complexity arises.

You can tell when it's time to put it in writing because certain clues crop up. Are questions common? Do people seem confused? Are people interpreting the policy or procedure in unique ways, such as wearing dirty jeans and ratty T-shirts on casual Fridays? You're courting trouble if you ignore these signals. It's time to write it down when the organization encounters:

- Accidents (involving injury or noninjury)
- Changes (lots of them, or a few significant ones)
- Complaints (internal or external)
- Confusion
- Cost overruns
- External events or trends that have an impact (such as smoking issues)
- Frequent questions
- High waste factors
- Inconsistency
- Misunderstandings
- New laws or regulations
- Sensitivity or volatility
- Stress or frustration
- Unique interpretations of unwritten policies or procedures

## What to Include in Policies and Procedures

This is very hard to define because it depends almost entirely on your audience and your reason for writing the policy or procedure. For instance, if you're developing a particular policy or procedure because of a new law, the legal requirements dictate what information to include. If you're revising it because it's out-of-date, current practice or technology determines the content. If you're writing for customers instead of employees, their needs take precedence.

You must make a judgment based on your audience and your purpose. Look at what readers *need* to know, then look at what they *want* to know.

---

NEEDS VS. WANTS

What readers need to know and what readers want to know are two different things. The first is required, the second is interesting. Consider both.

---

### What Readers Need to Know

This is information readers must have to comply with the policy or procedure. It includes the requirements, such as actions, steps, parameters, or limits. It also usually includes logistics, such as who's covered, eligibility criteria, deadlines, and enforcement.

If you believe readers need to know a certain thing, ask yourself why. What will they actually do with the information? Don't just assume that they "should" know it. A lot of irrelevant information finds its way into documents because we assume that people need to know something.

However, it's not always easy to determine whether readers legitimately need to know something. When it's unclear, stop and ask yourself, "Who says so?" Then ask, "Why?" There are a great many people who may be saying that readers need to know something. Some are internal, such as the CEO, and some are external, such as the courts. It may be an accrediting agency or the users themselves.

If you can't identify anyone who's saying so, then ask yourself, "Why do they need the information?" They may need it to:

- Eliminate confusion
- Get the job done
- Get the job done faster or better
- Increase understanding or comprehension
- Make the job easier
- Make the job safer
- Reduce errors or waste
- Reduce frustration

If you can't identify who's saying that readers need to know something, and you can't identify why they need to know it, they probably *don't* need to know it.

## What Readers Want to Know

This is information that may not be necessary in a technical sense but is significant for your readers. It's important for one reason: because it captures readers' interest.

If you don't catch readers' interest, they quit reading. Their attention wanders. The material seems dull because it's only what someone else wants them to know. There has to be something in it that interests *them*.

All of us, if we're honest, are more attentive to things that do something for us. Your readers are the same. Generally, they're interested in what a policy or procedure does (1) *to* them or (2) *for* them. Here are some of the common questions readers have and what you can do about them:

- *"Why am I being required to do this?"* Give the reasons.
- *"What will this do to me? For me? Will it make my life easier or harder?"* Describe the effects.
- *"Will I get enough training, time, money, and staff to do what's required?"* Identify the resources.

- *"What do I do if I don't understand or get stuck?"* Outline the assistance available.
- *"Will I have a chance to voice my concerns and problems? Will they listen to me?"* Describe the feedback mechanism.
- *"What if it doesn't work?"* Designate a correction process.
- *"Will I be blamed if this goes wrong? Will I end up holding the bag?"* Assign the responsibility.

---

### WIIFT

The writer's motto should be WIIFT: What's In It For Them. If you can answer that question—tell readers what the policy or procedure will do *to* them and *for* them—you've got their attention.

---

## Level of Detail

Every policy and procedure writer struggles with the level of detail, because there is no magic formula for how much to include. The general rule is that the level of detail must be both sufficient and appropriate to your subject and your audience.

*Sufficient* usually means the right type of information and the right quantity. *Appropriate* usually means fitting for the topic and the audience.

If the subject is complex, level of detail should be high. The same is true if mistakes carry serious financial, safety, operational, or legal consequences.

The audience is a key factor. Are people experienced or inexperienced? Trained or untrained? Receptive or hostile? Audience analysis is part of your basic planning process.

Use the Level of Detail Checklist (1-6) at the end of the chapter to assess whether the level of detail in your draft is appropriate.

## Manuals and Handbooks

If you have more than a few policies or procedures, it's convenient to gather them together into a reference book of some sort. The purpose is organizational. It's faster and easier for readers to find the material.

Many writers are concerned about the title of the book. Should it be called a manual, handbook, or user's guide? All the names are used, and from a practical standpoint they're essentially interchangeable.

There is, however, one potentially significant legal difference that involves distribution and content questions. *Manual* implies restricted circulation, and *handbook* implies general distribution. It may sound insignificant, and in many cases it is, but it can also create a contractual issue. For a discussion of this legality, see Chapter 3.

Information that's organized encourages readers to use it more frequently and with greater care. Even if you have a small number of policies and procedures, a handbook can serve as an organizing tool and central reference.

## Chapter Summary

- Policies and procedures are often discussed and used as if they're the same, but there are important distinctions between them. Policies regulate and control organizational actions, whereas procedures are the customary methods of handling things.

- Policies can be either ambiguous or specific. Procedures can contain some ambiguity but are usually more specific and detailed than policies.

- It's acceptable, even desirable, to have unwritten policies and procedures, since it's impossible to write everything down. But be alert to the signs that the informal, unwritten rules are no longer working.

- A policy or procedure should always *accomplish* something. Never have a policy or procedure just to have one or because it seems like a good idea.

- Address issues that readers need to know about and want to know about. Assess what's sufficient and appropriate for your topic and audience, and include the appropriate level of detail.

- Consider having a handbook or manual for speedy reference and access.

# Tools and Resources
# for Chapter 1

## 1-1: SUMMARY COMPARISON OF POLICIES AND PROCEDURES

| | *Policy* | *Procedure* |
|---|---|---|
| Definitions: | ☐ A general guideline to regulate organizational action and conduct.<br>☐ A philosophy, standard, or criterion that helps users exercise good judgment and discretion in the management of daily affairs.<br>☐ A definite course or method of action selected from among alternatives and in light of given conditions to guide and determine present and future decisions *(Webster's Ninth New Collegiate Dictionary)*. | ☐ The customary method of handling things.<br>☐ A particular way of doing things.<br>☐ A set of steps that must be followed to achieve the desired results.<br>☐ A protocol. |
| Function: | ☐ Tells who, what, why. | ☐ Tells how. |
| Synonyms: | ☐ Rule<br>☐ Standard<br>☐ Principle<br>☐ Philosophy<br>☐ Guideline<br>☐ Goal<br>☐ Mission | ☐ Instruction<br>☐ Protocol<br>☐ Step<br>☐ Process |
| Purpose: | ☐ Regulates, directs, and controls actions or conduct.<br>☐ Sets criteria that allow users to regulate their own conduct in an appropriate manner. | ☐ Tells users how to implement the requirements.<br>☐ Tells users how to achieve the necessary results. |

*(continues)*

## 1-1:  SUMMARY COMPARISON OF POLICIES AND PROCEDURES (*continued*)

| | *Policy* | *Procedure* |
|---|---|---|
| Nature and Scope: | ☐ Ranges from broad philosophies to specific rules. Often imprecise and intangible. | ☐ Tangible, precise, exact, specific, and factual. Succinct and to the point. |
| Type of Writing Required: | ☐ Usually expressed in standard sentence and paragraph format. | ☐ Best expressed using special formats such as playscripts, flowcharts, and lists. |
| What to Include: | ☐ What the rule is.<br>☐ Why it exists.<br>☐ When it applies.<br>☐ Whom it covers.<br>☐ Enforcement.<br>☐ Consequences.<br>☐ Emergency contacts and references.<br>☐ How to get help or interpretation. | ☐ Actions.<br>☐ Conditions for action.<br>☐ Alternatives.<br>☐ Emergency procedures.<br>☐ Consequences.<br>☐ Warnings and cautions.<br>☐ Help sections.<br>☐ Examples.<br>☐ Graphics.<br>☐ Forms.<br>☐ Who is responsible. |
| Examples: | ☐ "Our inspection program is intended to ensure a zero-defect rate."<br>☐ "Our goal is to provide the best customer service in the industry."<br>☐ "It is our practice to bill within thirty days of delivery."<br>☐ "All employees are expected to conduct themselves in a civil, courteous manner at all times." | ☐ "1.  Locate Part A.<br>  2.  Locate Part B.<br>  3.  Insert A into B.<br>  4.  Turn handle.<br>  5.  Tighten screw."<br>☐ "—Call the vendor.<br>  —Explain the delay.<br>  —Determine whether any special problems are created by the delay."<br>☐ "To request vacation time, fill out Form VR-1 and submit it to your |

☐ "We provide one week's vacation after one year of employment and two weeks' vacation after five years of employment."

supervisor. This must be done at least one month before the desired time off."

## 1-2: SUBJECTIVITY CHECKLIST

Ambiguous policies and procedures require users to exercise discretion and sound judgment. The question is whether the organization has provided the support and information necessary to help them do that. If you can meet the test of the questions in this checklist, your use of subjectivity and ambiguity is probably appropriate. Answer the questions carefully. Inappropriate ambiguity causes practical and legal problems.

1. Given the nature of this particular topic, does it make sense to leave some ambiguity?

   ☐ **Yes**   ☐ **No**

2. If so, how much? _____

   _____

   _____

3. What would happen if we eliminated the ambiguity? _____

   _____

   _____

4. Have we identified as many objective, tangible factors/steps as possible?

   ☐ **Yes**   ☐ **No**

5. What potential mistakes or problems could result from the ambiguity? (Consider operational, financial, legal, health, safety, quality, and customer concerns.) Explain. _____

   _____

   _____

   _____

   _____

   _____

   _____

6. How potentially serious are those mistakes or problems? _____

   _____

   _____

   _____

7. Have we provided ways for the user to get help or answers when needed?

☐ **Yes** ☐ **No**

8. If not, what can we do to help the user? _____

_____

_____

9. We are requiring users to exercise discretion and good judgment. Have we provided sufficient information, training, and resources for them to do that?

☐ **Yes** ☐ **No**

10. If not, what additional resources are needed? _____

_____

_____

11. Have we identified the type of experience, education, or background that a user must have to understand the issue and exercise sound judgment?

☐ **Yes** ☐ **No**

12. If so, what are they? _____

_____

_____

13. Have we identified, as clearly and specifically as possible, the bases for the judgments to be made?

☐ **Yes** ☐ **No**

14. Have we made it clear that judgments are to be based on professional and business standards, not on personal preferences and biases?

☐ **Yes** ☐ **No**

15. Have we set limits or boundaries beyond which users cannot go?

☐ **Yes** ☐ **No**

16. Have we made it clear that the individual will be held accountable for the judgments made and the actions taken as a result?

☐ **Yes** ☐ **No**

## 1-3: COMMON TOPICS—HEALTH AND SAFETY

- ☐ Safe workplace
  - ▪ General duty of care
  - ▪ Management commitment
  - ▪ Employee involvement
  - ▪ Enforcement
  - ▪ Discipline
- ☐ Emergency action plans
- ☐ Hazard communication
- ☐ Hazard elimination
- ☐ Personal protective equipment
- ☐ Energy control
- ☐ Electrical safety
- ☐ Bloodborne pathogens
- ☐ Violence in the workplace
- ☐ Safe work practices
- ☐ Record keeping
- ☐ Training
- ☐ Self-assessment and inspection
- ☐ Maintenance

## 1-4: COMMON TOPICS—PERSONNEL

- ☐ Attendance
  - ▪ Absenteeism
  - ▪ Tardiness
- ☐ Benefits
  - ▪ Educational
  - ▪ Life insurance
  - ▪ Medical and dental
  - ▪ Profit-sharing plan
  - ▪ Retirement program
- ☐ Discipline
  - ▪ Standard procedure
  - ▪ Exceptions to standard procedure
  - ▪ Gross misconduct
- ☐ EEO and nondiscrimination
  - ▪ Disability
  - ▪ General nondiscrimination
  - ▪ Sexual harassment
- ☐ Employee relations
  - ▪ Complaints
  - ▪ Grievances
  - ▪ Union agreements
- ☐ Leaves of absence
  - ▪ Family and medical leave
  - ▪ Funeral
  - ▪ Holidays
  - ▪ Jury duty
  - ▪ Maternity
  - ▪ Military duty
  - ▪ Paid versus unpaid
  - ▪ Personal
  - ▪ Short- and long-term disability
  - ▪ Sickness
  - ▪ Vacation

- ▪ Voting
- ▪ Abuse of leave
- ☐ Pay
  - ▪ Wage and salary system
  - ▪ Overtime
  - ▪ Incentives and bonuses
  - ▪ Payroll deductions
  - ▪ Salary reviews
  - ▪ Commissions
  - ▪ Garnishment
- ☐ Performance evaluations
  - ▪ Annual or periodic
  - ▪ Salary reviews
  - ▪ Special cases
- ☐ Recruiting and hiring
  - ▪ Orientation
  - ▪ Promotions
  - ▪ Relocation
  - ▪ Transfers
- ☐ Separations
  - ▪ Retirement
  - ▪ Resignation
  - ▪ Layoffs
  - ▪ Termination
  - ▪ Severance pay
- ☐ Substance abuse
  - ▪ Alcohol
  - ▪ Drugs
  - ▪ Other substances
  - ▪ Rehabilitation
- ☐ Working conditions
  - ▪ Break periods
  - ▪ Health and safety issues
  - ▪ Work hours

## 1-5: COMMON TOPICS—ADMINISTRATIVE

- ☐ Confidentiality
- ☐ Dress code
- ☐ Emergencies
  - ▪ Administrative
  - ▪ Physical or medical
  - ▪ Customer
- ☐ Employment-at-will
- ☐ Ethics
  - ▪ General
  - ▪ Gift policies
  - ▪ Conflicts of interest
- ☐ General conduct practices
- ☐ Office parties and company functions
  - ▪ Alcohol use
  - ▪ Holiday parties
  - ▪ Recreational outings and picnics
- ☐ Open-door policies
- ☐ Smoking
- ☐ Suggestion programs
- ☐ Telephone use
- ☐ Use of company property

## 1-6: LEVEL OF DETAIL CHECKLIST

There are no precise standards as to how detailed a policy or procedure should be. The general rule is that the level of detail must be both sufficient and appropriate for your audience and your subject. *Sufficient* usually means the right type of information and the right amount of it. *Appropriate* usually means fitting for the topic and the audience.

1. Does it give the user sufficient information to complete the required action?

   ☐ **Yes**  ☐ **No**

2. Does it provide sufficient information to guide the user in exercising good judgment and discretion?

   ☐ **Yes**  ☐ **No**

3. Is the information of the right type, considering both subject and audience?

   ☐ **Yes**  ☐ **No**

4. With this information, can the audience do what we want them to do?

   ☐ **Yes**  ☐ **No**

5. Is the level of detail appropriate to the subject? (An ethics policy may not need the same detail as an inventory procedure.)

   ☐ **Yes**  ☐ **No**

6. Is the level of detail appropriate to the type of audience—its experience, knowledge, and size (e.g., novice versus expert, customers versus employees)?

   ☐ **Yes**  ☐ **No**

7. How comfortable is the audience with the subject?

   ☐ **Very**  ☐ **Somewhat**  ☐ **Little**  ☐ **Not at all**

# 2

# Where Do I Start?

It's simple but true: Start at the beginning. Plan this project as you would any other important project.

Many policy and procedure writers develop a list of areas to be covered and simply start writing. It's a mistake. You're missing a lot of important information, and that reduces your ability to write both accurately and well.

If you want your document to be effective, don't skip the preliminaries. (The actual writing of your document comes in Chapter 4.)

## The Four Steps of Development

We hear a lot about planning, but the trouble is that it means so many different things to so many different people. It's like talking about flying: To a stunt pilot it means one thing, to a fighter pilot it means quite another.

In policy and procedure writing, we usually talk about the development process instead of the planning process. It's the preparation prior to drafting, and it has four steps:

1. Planning
2. Analysis
3. Research
4. Prewriting

How long you spend on each step, and how in-depth you get, depends to a great extent on you. You may just think things through carefully and make a few notes, or you may develop thick schedules and charts. It's largely a matter of your experience and comfort level.

However, it's also a matter of the document type and length. Creating an entire quality assurance manual requires more preparation than revising a petty cash policy. The lengthier and more complex the project, the more planning, analysis, research, and prewriting you have to do. See the Development Summary (2-1) at the end of this chapter for an overview of the four steps.

## Each Step Is Necessary

Even though you may be under tremendous time pressure, go through each step at least briefly. A short plan, an analysis of the project basics, research of key issues, and a quick outline (which may be part of the prewriting step) are essential in even the most difficult writing situations.

Be sure, too, that you go through the steps in the proper order. Outlining before you research only wastes time and could cause errors or omissions. Start at the beginning and proceed in sequence.

## The Steps Are Nothing New

These steps are straightforward and familiar. Most of us use the skills every day of our working lives without even being aware of it. As a writer, you need to bring them to the forefront and use them consciously.

The rest of this chapter is a description of each of the four steps: planning, analysis, research, and prewriting.

## Step 1: Planning

You must develop a plan, however brief. And in most cases, the plan should be in writing.

It may not be necessary to do a formal plan if your project is simple and you're the only writer. But what about those complex projects or working with a team of writers? Policy and procedure projects rarely turn out to be simple.

Tight deadlines and time pressures can tempt you to bypass planning. If time's a problem, keep your plan simple. Stay with basics such as the tasks, sequence, and deadlines. Don't get complicated, but do make a plan. It's hard to stay focused without one. See the Planning Tip Sheet (2-2) at the end of this chapter for an overview of this step.

## Setting Schedules

For simple projects, you may find that all you need in the way of a schedule is a piece of paper. List the steps, indicate who's responsible

---

### THE DISCIPLINED WRITER

A written plan is a discipline that all good policy and procedure writers use. It:

- Focuses your thinking
- Organizes your time
- Keeps the project on track
- Can be revised as project conditions change

---

for each one, and put a time estimate beside each. It doesn't require mathematical precision, just a reasonable estimate.

For lengthy or complicated projects, such as manuals and handbooks, create a time chart. Pick a technique you like or develop one of your own.

Milestone charts and Gantt charts are common techniques. Both are bar charts that show time frames for each step. They can also include other factors, such as personhours, assignees, or overlapping and simultaneous steps, and they're easy to update as project demands change. See the sample milestone chart in Example 2-1.

**Example 2-1.** Example of a Milestone chart.

| | May | June | July | August |
|---|---|---|---|---|
| Tasks | 7 14 21 28 | 4 11 18 25 | 2 9 16 23 30 | 6 13 20 27 |
| 1. Interview operators; review outline. | △ SAM 14 days ▽ | | | |
| 2. Review information and clarify questions. | △ | ROB 30 days ▽ | | |
| 3. Draft the report. | | △ NANCY & ROB ▽ ??? | | |
| 4. Review and revise. | | △ ALL 4 weeks ▽ | | |

Project: _____

Use the Sample Scheduling Form (2-3) at the end of this chapter to start the scheduling of your project.

Whether your scheduling is simple or complex is determined by the nature, length, and complexity of the project. Just don't skip it. Without a schedule of some sort, you're bound to miss your deadline.

---

### A Helpful Hint If You're Under Extreme Time Pressure

Do a brief plan that identifies key steps and deadlines. Don't be tempted to bypass the written plan. It will take more time to backtrack and cover forgotten steps than to take an hour of planning time up front.

---

## Using a Team

Consider who should be involved in the project. What kind of expertise is called for? What skills are needed?

The project may be such that a team of writers can work faster, cover more territory, and be more thorough than you alone. The size of the project may be too great, or the subject matter too complex, for a single writer. The time pressure may be too intense.

Team writing has all the benefits and disadvantages of any team activity. You can get more work done, and it can be done faster. On the other hand, you can waste a lot of time in discussion and meetings.

Success depends on good organization and clear communication. Make conscious decisions about how the team will operate (central authority versus consensus). Decide what size is appropriate (two writers or ten).

---

### Working With a Team of Writers

- Select members with appropriate backgrounds or expertise.
- Meet or talk regularly.
- Establish ground rules.
- Agree on assignments and responsibilities.
- Establish a monitoring system.
- Agree on deadlines.
- Develop a team style guide.

---

The real key to team writing is absolute clarity in communication. Inform all members about schedules, deadlines, responsibilities, and changes. Talk through issues. If you don't, you'll end up with ten different ways of doing things.

## Being Realistic

Once you've drafted a plan, ask yourself how realistic it is. Have you squeezed time frames for certain steps to fit the deadline? Will it work? Have you listed the people responsible with the assumption that they'll be able to meet that obligation? Such assumptions can be costly.

Consider whether there are any unresolvable conflicts. Check with management to see if it anticipates any new projects that could conflict with this one.

And then identify your potential "brick walls." Is there a possibility that the production department could miss its review deadline because of a sudden spurt of orders? Has one of the key players been sick a lot recently? Decide how probable these events are and develop a backup plan.

A written plan helps you anticipate trouble before it hits. Many good policy and procedure writers have been known to throw up their hands and say, "What's the use?" That common frustration is largely avoidable with realistic planning.

---

PLANNING IN A NUTSHELL

Schedule your tasks, organize your time, and anticipate difficulties in advance. Then keep your plan flexible to meet changing project demands.

---

## Step 2: Analysis

Analysis is a realistic look at the audience, the assignment, the context in which it's been made, how much and what types of research are required, and the conditions under which you'll have to work. Identify all pertinent factors that influence the project. See the Analysis Tip Sheet (2-4) at the end of this chapter for an overview of this step.

## Nature and Reasons

Begin with an analysis of the "what" and the "why" of the project so that you understand both its nature and the reasons behind it.

First look at who requested the project. Was it you? Your boss? A manager? An employee? A customer?

Then examine the reasons for the request. Has the requester recognized a need no one else is aware of? Does he or she have information that others don't? Has a specific problem or special event occurred? Did someone realize that an update was overdue? Does someone have a pet issue?

And finally, look at the nature of the project. Is it technical or nontechnical? Simple or complex? Sensitive or not? Time-tested or a complete change?

---

### A HIDDEN INFLUENCE

Be alert for hidden influences—that is, hidden political agendas—that can influence the nature of the project. Does someone think this will be a quick fix? Is the project just part of a larger issue? Politics do play a role in policies and procedures, and some of what you write may be highly controversial.

---

## Goals and Results

Be sure you understand the goal of the finished policy or procedure. What is the desired end result? What is supposed to happen, or not happen, if this document is successful?

The desired result may be a decrease in accidents on the shop floor. Maybe the goal is to make it faster and easier for customers to use your product. The goal may be to maintain quality, expedite billing, cut equipment costs, or increase client satisfaction ratings. Get specific.

If you're not clear what the goal of the project is, now is the time to go back to the requester for more information. You can't help readers understand the importance of the policy or procedure if you don't understand it yourself.

---

THE GOLDEN RULE

Never write a policy or procedure just to have one or because it sounds like a good idea. A policy or procedure should always have a defined result. It should *accomplish* something.

---

## Audience

The more you know about your audience, the better the choices you can make in the content, wording, format, and design of the document.

Is your audience experienced, inexperienced, or a mixture of all levels? Are they technical people or laypeople? What is their educational level? What types of policies and procedures are they used to? Are there any particular sensitivities?

Think about their preferences and expectations. What formats and designs are they accustomed to? What do they want to see and know? What do they need to know?

Also think about the attitude they'll bring to the document. Will they be receptive or hostile? Eager or reluctant? Rigid or flexible? Fearful or confident? Users have a relationship with the document that affects how they read, and you need to know what that is.

You should also distinguish between "users" and "readers." The first group has to use, or implement, the information. The second scans or reads for general awareness and knowledge. Write primarily for your hands-on user group.

## Conditions of Use

The conditions under which users read affect the way in which you write and format your document. Will they use it on a shop floor or in a standard office environment? Indoors or outdoors? While covered with grease and dirt? In poor light, or when they're tired at the end of shift?

Will they use it during emergencies or daily operations? Will they need the information yesterday or eventually? Will they have to do troubleshooting? All this affects what you write, how you present it, and how you format it.

## Topic and Urgency

Look at the type of subject matter and its urgency level. Is it an operational item or an emergency item? A financial matter or a personnel matter? An installation issue or a repair issue?

Be sure to distinguish between urgency and immediacy. A policy or procedure can be immediate without being urgent: It might be necessary to submit a form quickly (immediate), but the form itself may be relatively minor (nonurgent).

## Impact

Examine the impact of the document on the organization. Is the issue of great importance or a routine matter? Is the document used frequently or infrequently? What are the consequences of noncompliance? Could inappropriate action or lack of action pose a financial, legal, operational, or safety threat?

Perhaps the topic is sensitive or controversial. Should it even be put in writing? See Chapter 1 for a review of unwritten policies and procedures.

## Project Conditions

Be realistic about the conditions under which you'll be working. Has sufficient time been allotted? Do you have adequate staff and resources for the project? Is information readily available? If not, what shortcuts or compromises will you have to make?

Being overly optimistic now only causes trouble later. Look at your situation honestly. Do you need more time or help? If so, don't be afraid to ask for it.

---

ANOTHER HELPFUL HINT IF YOU'RE UNDER EXTREME TIME PRESSURE

Skip the analysis of who requested it and why, as well as the detailed analysis of the project's nature. Focus on topic, project conditions, timing, and audience. Then move on to the research step.

---

## Requester Updates

If your analysis reveals any serious flaws in the process, inform the requester. You may have to go back to the decision-making stage or revisit the schedule. Discuss the possibility of additional time, staff, or resources. Ask for help and advice.

On occasion, writers have to fight for the resources to do the job. Does the requester want an entire quality manual done in three months? Something's got to give. If it isn't the deadlines, it may be accuracy. You must make the trade-offs, and their consequences, clear to the requester.

# Step 3: Research

When you reach this phase, you're taking the first real action on matters of content. How much research you need and what types are determined by the analysis you've just completed in step 2. Look at the nature, length, complexity, and conditions of the project, and then make an appropriate decision. Only you can determine how much research you can and should do. See the Research Tip Sheet (2-5) at the end of this chapter for an overview of this step.

## Starting With the Difficult Areas

Start with the most difficult, complex information, since it takes the longest to study and decipher. It's tempting to do the easiest research first, but resist the urge.

Tackling the toughest areas first gives you time to ask questions, get clarification, and resolve misunderstandings. If you leave them until last, significant parts of the research just won't get done.

There is, however, one time when you may in fact do the easiest research first: when it's the only information available. Don't waste time sitting around waiting for other information to become available. Do what you can, when you can.

## Meeting With Content Experts

Content experts can be your best friends. Interview them in person or by phone, survey them, or write them a letter. But use them.

Interviews are the best means of getting critical information from these people fast. That's especially true when you already have a good working relationship with the experts and can easily solicit their input

---

### REVISITING THE SCHEDULE

Schedules aren't set in stone. They must respond to changing conditions. Analysis may uncover a surprising complication, or research may reveal an unexpected issue. Update the schedule after completing each of the other steps.

---

and help. If you don't know the experts well, you may need to invest some time in developing reasonable working relationships.

## Meeting With Others

Don't stop with content experts. Talk to anyone who holds information. For instance, longtime employees who have seen it all may have important insights on what has worked, what hasn't, and why. Talk to anyone who has information.

Talk to internal people: users, enforcers, approvers, interested parties and affected departments, line personnel, staff personnel, technical people, laypeople, experienced hands, new hands.

Talk to external people: customers, industry and trade associations, reference librarians, professional organizations or societies, others in the industry.

---

### START TALKING TO USERS NOW

Now is the appropriate time to involve your users in the process. Ask them what problems they've been having and how they've dealt with them. Get their suggestions and comments. Who knows what's going on out there better than the users?

Involving people early on gives you two advantages:

1. You get valuable insight and information.
2. It reduces complaints and resistance later on.

---

## Interviewing

Observe the normal etiquette of informational interviews. Have a list of prepared topics and questions so you don't waste time. Inform the interviewee fully about your reasons for requesting the interview.

Explain the project, its nature, and its time frame. Few people go out of their way to provide information without understanding why it's being requested.

And always take notes—always. This is the wrong time to prove that the memory course you took actually works. Accuracy is the issue, so leave nothing to chance. And as a courtesy, explain to the interviewee that you'll be taking notes and why.

If you're doing a large number of interviews or the subject is a complex one, use a standard form for notes. You'll need to collate all the information into one document when the interviews are finished, and a form speeds that process. See the Sample Interview Note Form (2-6) at the end of this chapter for a form you can use to collect your notes.

Your notes, in whatever form, are the foundation of your document's content. They're also documentation if operational or legal questions arise later. So take notes carefully and accurately.

## Soliciting Information in Writing

It's sometimes necessary to request information in writing because circumstances, such as time or distance, won't permit direct individual interviews. Draft a memo or letter requesting input, or use a survey or questionnaire.

Keep the memo, letter, or survey as short and simple as possible. Include a reasonable deadline for return, a contact name and number, and the reason for the request. Then follow up on those that aren't returned.

Remember, though, that written requests are generally less effective than personal interviews. They often go in the to-be-done later stack, never to resurface. Response rates can thus be quite low.

---

### A SPECIAL NOTE ABOUT TALKING TO CUSTOMERS

Customers have information that's critical to your project. Your success in getting their information depends largely on how good your relationship with them is.

Do they trust you? Feel comfortable talking to you? Believe your request is genuine? Have faith that something will come of it and their time won't be wasted? If your relationship is good, the information you get can be extremely valuable.

---

## Reading and Studying

Sometimes interviewing or surveying is not sufficient or not possible. Explore books, articles, or trade publications that contain current, relevant material. Use the plethora of specialized databases available, especially for technical content.

Look through organizational files. They may contain memos or letters outlining problems and possible solutions.

Review suggestion forms or comments made during meetings. Prowl through departmental files. And don't forget your current policies and procedures. Have there been any comments about or reactions to them in the past?

An excellent source many writers overlook is libraries. Most reference librarians will do a topic search that is amazingly thorough and absolutely free. You can use local libraries, university libraries, and the Library of Congress, which has millions of documents and is on the Internet.

Get on the Internet, too. Check out the World Wide Web. There are vast resources of information out there. Use them, and they'll strengthen both your document and your reputation as a careful writer.

## Being Realistic and Disciplined

You seldom have time to locate everything that's out there on a given subject. Don't try. Concentrate on the critical information and fill in lesser information as you can.

---

AND ANOTHER HELPFUL HINT IF YOU'RE UNDER EXTREME
TIME PRESSURE

Be realistic. You don't have time to locate every fact. Pick the top three or four items and concentrate on those. Notify the requester of any potential troublespots caused by insufficient research time.

---

## Step 4: Prewriting

Prewriting is the missing link between the preparatory steps you've just taken (planning, analysis, and research) and the actual drafting of your document. It organizes the material and speeds drafting.

Once the research is done you have lots of information, and the temptation now is to sit down and start writing.

Don't. You'll find yourself more worried about the mechanics of writing than about content or accuracy. Instead, ask yourself this question: "How do I convey this information to the reader in the clearest, most logical way possible?"

You need to organize the material before you start drafting. Don't get caught up in concerns over wording or format until you have:

- Accurate, complete content
- Good organization
- Logical flow

See the Prewriting Tip Sheet (2-7) at the end of this chapter for an overview of this step.

## Content

First and foremost, be sure you have all the information that's necessary or relevant to the reader.

All policy and procedure writers know how easy it is to overlook one minor detail, such as what type of wrench to use or whose signature to get. You're dealing with a mountain of information and some of it can get lost.

The solution is to use a process called mind-mapping. Originally a project management tool, it's now used for virtually any project that requires a thorough, organized approach.

A mind-map is a simple way to get all possible content concerns out on the table before you start to write. It's essentially a "brain dump" in which you make quick notes of any issues that come to mind on a given topic. See the Mind-Mapping Instruction Sheet (2-8) at the end of this chapter, which outlines the steps involved and gives an example.

Mind-mapping is critical because starting with an outline can lead to omissions and errors.

Most outlines are in a list format, and they're usually numbered. But what if you write down "1. Inspections," and then decide that it isn't really number 1 on your list? You cross it out. Later, when you get further down the list where "Inspections" really belongs, you've forgotten about it.

Your structured and creative thinking processes are in conflict. Which one wins? The structured side. It pushes the creative side into the background. Content becomes a secondary issue.

**Example 2-2.** A mind-map and the outline it led to.

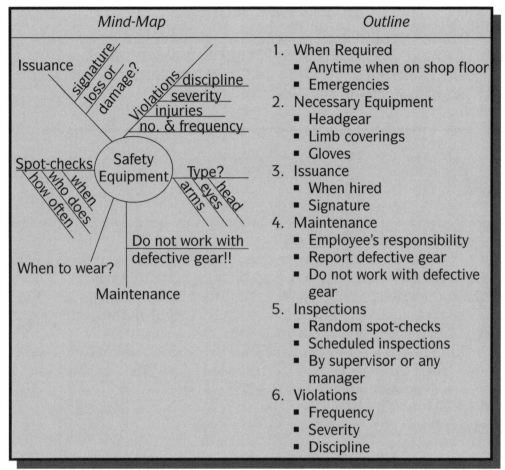

| Mind-Map | Outline |
|---|---|

1. When Required
   - Anytime when on shop floor
   - Emergencies
2. Necessary Equipment
   - Headgear
   - Limb coverings
   - Gloves
3. Issuance
   - When hired
   - Signature
4. Maintenance
   - Employee's responsibility
   - Report defective gear
   - Do not work with defective gear
5. Inspections
   - Random spot-checks
   - Scheduled inspections
   - By supervisor or any manager
6. Violations
   - Frequency
   - Severity
   - Discipline

Mind-mapping reverses this process. It's totally random and eliminates the rigid visible structure of the outline. Instead, you record your thoughts and knowledge at random. Then you can put the information in whatever order or sequence you wish.

Start with a mind-map. Then proceed to an outline. See Example 2-2 for an example of a mind-map and the outline it led to.

It's imperative that you pin down issues of substance before you worry about wording and grammar. Too often, writers finish a draft only to realize, "Oh, no. I forgot to mention. . . ." This is less likely to happen if you do a mind-map.

Mind-maps are easy to do, but they get results. This book, for instance, began life as a mind-map and couldn't have been done without one.

---

WHY MIND-MAPPING IS CRITICAL

Traditional outlining sets your creative side (content) at war with your structured side (organization). The structured side usually wins, and the result is errors and omissions. Mind-mapping reverses this process and allows you to focus on content issues first.

---

## Organization

Once you've identified what information should be included, it must be placed in the proper sequence.

Create an outline from your mind-map. A quick writer's trick is to place each item from the mind-map on a separate sticky note, then arrange and rearrange the order as appropriate. You can change the flow and the topic/subtopic groupings as much you like. This technique is fast, it's easy, and it gives your material a logical layout.

Outlines can be done using key words, phrases, sentences, or paragraphs. Start with a key word or phrase outline, then expand into a sentence or paragraph outline if needed.

## Flow

As you arrange your sticky notes, be careful to put the material in a sequence or flow that's logical *to the reader.* What seems to flow smoothly to you as a writer may seem disjointed and confusing to a user.

Ask yourself the following questions:

- Will this make sense to the readers, considering when and how they'll use the information?
- Will this be the order in which readers will use the information?

---

ONE MORE HELPFUL HINT IF YOU'RE UNDER EXTREME
TIME PRESSURE

Do a ten- to fifteen-minute data dump. Set it aside for at least an hour, then review it for additions and omissions. Construct a key word outline and begin drafting.

---

# Chapter Summary

▪ Preparation is the foundation of the writing process. It's usually referred to in policy and procedure writing as the development process and includes four steps: planning, analysis, research, and prewriting.

▪ Planning is necessary in some form on all projects to keep the writer focused. Analysis reveals vital information about the project and the audience. Research uncovers vital information about the subject. And prewriting, which is the missing link between preparation and drafting, organizes the material.

▪ How much preparation you do is up to you. But you should always do some, no matter how brief, and it should usually be in writing. Skimming over the preliminary work causes errors and omissions, as well as frustration and wasted time.

# Tools and Resources
# for Chapter 2

## 2-1: DEVELOPMENT SUMMARY

Here is a summary of the four steps of development.

1. *Plan:*    In writing, break your project down into its various phases:

   ☐ Analysis ☐ Formatting
   ☐ Research ☐ Reviewing
   ☐ Prewriting ☐ Editing
   ☐ Drafting ☐ Getting approval

   Establish reasonable timeframes for each phase, then revise as necessary. Revisions usually continue throughout the project.

   If you're under extreme time pressure, create an abbreviated plan, but don't skip it.

2. *Analyze:*    Scrutinize everything that affects the project or the subject matter:

   ☐ Project scope ☐ Audience
   ☐ Project nature ☐ Usage
   ☐ Goals ☐ Urgency
   ☐ Conditions ☐ Sensitivity
   ☐ Organizational impact ☐ Potential obstacles
   ☐ Availability of    and delays
      resources, information

3. *Research:*    Start with the difficult or complex issues. Interview content experts and other holders of information. Solicit input in writing where appropriate.

   Read and study files, trade publications, articles, specialized databases, and suggestion forms. Consult libraries.

4. *Prewrite:*    Organize and outline the information from your research. Start with a mind-map or random list, then create a key word or sentence outline.

   Be sure the flow and sequence of ideas makes sense from the *user's* point of view.

## 2-2: Planning Tip Sheet

### Purpose

☐ Planning organizes the project. A written plan helps the writer focus on and monitor the project as well as anticipate problems.

### When to Do It

☐ On all projects. For small projects, keep it simple (a task list with time estimates). For larger projects, develop time charts (Gantt or Milestone charts).

### How to Do It

1. Break the project down into individual phases.
2. Break each phase down into tasks or steps.
3. Identify who is responsible for each step.
4. Estimate how much time each step requires.
5. Consider using a team of writers.
6. Identify potential problems that can throw the schedule off.
7. Develop a backup plan or strategy.
8. Revisit the schedule from time to time during the project.
9. Develop a strategy to deal with changes to the project.
10. Stay flexible to meet changing conditions.
11. Use task lists for simple projects.
12. Use Gantt charts, Milestone charts, or similar devices for more complicated projects.

### Where to Go

☐ Colleagues or others with experience in (1) the subject, (2) the writing process, or (3) similar projects
☐ The team of writers, if using one
☐ The project requester

## What to Cover

☐ Phases
☐ Steps
☐ Substeps
☐ Overlapping steps
☐ Simultaneous steps
☐ Deadlines
☐ Critical subdeadlines
☐ Time estimates for each step and substep
☐ Potential roadblocks
☐ Strategy for dealing with roadblocks
☐ Staffing levels
☐ Responsible parties
☐ Overall project time frames

## 2-3: SAMPLE SCHEDULING FORM

### SCHEDULING CHART

| Task | Time Frame | | | |
|------|---|---|---|---|
|  |  |  |  |  |
|  |  |  |  |  |
|  |  |  |  |  |
|  |  |  |  |  |
|  |  |  |  |  |
|  |  |  |  |  |
|  |  |  |  |  |
|  |  |  |  |  |
|  |  |  |  |  |
|  |  |  |  |  |
|  |  |  |  |  |
|  |  |  |  |  |
|  |  |  |  |  |
|  |  |  |  |  |
|  |  |  |  |  |
|  |  |  |  |  |
|  |  |  |  |  |
|  |  |  |  |  |
|  |  |  |  |  |

## 2-4: ANALYSIS TIP SHEET

**Purpose**

☐ Analysis identifies factors that help the writer make better choices in the wording and design of the policy or procedure.

**When to Do It**

☐ On all projects except minor revisions, routine updates, or routine adjustments that are legally mandated.

**How to Do It**

☐ List all the relevant factors.
☐ Ask probing questions in each area.
☐ Brainstorm with yourself for answers.
☐ Write down what you know.
☐ Identify missing information.
☐ Brainstorm with colleagues.
☐ Get clarification from project requester.

**Where to Go**

☐ Operating personnel
☐ Project requester

**What to Cover**

☐ How the assignment originated
☐ Reasons or purpose behind it
☐ Desired result of the policy or procedure
☐ Nature of the topic
  - Subject
  - Sensitivity
  - Technical content
  - Urgency
  - Immediacy
  - Legalities
  - Complexity

*(continues)*

## 2-4: ANALYSIS TIP SHEET (*continued*)

☐ Project conditions
- Timeframes     • Resources                          • Imposed limits
- Staffing       • Availability of information

☐ Nature of the audience
- Readers vs. users                  • Experience level
- Attitudes                          • Background and training
- Preferences                        • Internal vs. external
- What they need to know             • What they want to know
- Customary methods and formats
- Conditions under which they'll
  use it

## 2-5: RESEARCH TIP SHEET

### Purpose

☐ Research identifies all the relevant information on the subject of the policy or procedure. Ensures the accuracy and completeness of the content.

### When to Do It

☐ On all projects. How much you do is determined by the size, complexity, and timing of the project, as well as the availability of information.

### How to Do It

☐ Interview in person or by phone.
☐ Send written requests for information (memo, survey, questionnaire)
☐ Discuss in meetings.
☐ Hold informal conversations.
☐ Read and study.
☐ Start with the hardest items first.
☐ Be disciplined enough to know when to stop.

### Where to Go

☐ Content experts
☐ Experienced users
☐ Enforcers
☐ Approvers
☐ Technical experts
☐ Other departments
☐ Trade associations
☐ Libraries
☐ Customers
☐ Other organizations
☐ Files, suggestion forms, meeting minutes
☐ Existing policies and procedures
☐ Any information-holder, internal or external
☐ Specialized databases
☐ Professional organizations

### What to Cover

☐ Legalities
☐ Regulatory requirements
☐ Personnel matters
☐ Health and safety issues
☐ Technological issues
☐ Operational areas
☐ Cost factors
☐ Equipment information
☐ Industry standards
☐ Competitive practices

## 2-6: SAMPLE INTERVIEW NOTE FORM

**Interview Notes**

**Project:** _____

**Interviewee:** _____

**Interviewed by:** _____  **Date:** _____

**Topic(s):** _____

## 2-7: PREWRITING TIP SHEET

### Purpose

☐ Prewriting organizes content in the clearest, most logical manner. The main purpose is to gather the content together without being distracted by the mechanics of writing (grammar, spelling, composition, format). A transitional step between preparation and drafting.

### When to Do It

☐ On all projects except the most minor revisions or extremely simple new issues. Should always be done before the first draft.

### How to Do It

1. Do a preliminary data dump (e.g., mind-map, random list).
2. Set it aside for a period of time, then review.
3. Eliminate unnecessary or irrelevant information.
4. Add missing information.
5. Review with colleagues if possible for additions and deletions.
6. Organize information into related groups and subgroups.
7. Place sections in logical order.
8. Create a key word or sentence outline.
9. Expand to a sentence or paragraph outline if needed.

### Where to Go

☐ Colleagues with experience or content knowledge
☐ Outside technical experts
☐ Users and readers

*(continues)*

## 2-7:   PREWRITING TIP SHEET (*continued*)

**What to Cover**

- [ ] Responsibility
- [ ] Technical matter
- [ ] Exceptions
- [ ] Emergencies
- [ ] Operational issues
- [ ] Maintenance issues
- [ ] Customer concerns

- [ ] Costs
- [ ] Staffing
- [ ] Equipment
- [ ] Scope
- [ ] Forms
- [ ] Approvals
- [ ] Legal and regulatory issues

- [ ] Time factors
- [ ] User questions
- [ ] Implementation
- [ ] Noncompliance
- [ ] Internal impact
- [ ] External impact

## 2-8: Mind-Mapping Instruction Sheet

People sometimes learn mind-mapping and say, "It's too simple!" But that's precisely why it works. It can be done manually or on a computer. Here are the steps:

1. Get a blank sheet of paper.
2. Draw a circle or square in the middle.
3. Write the topic inside the circle or square.

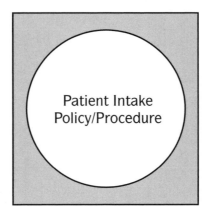

Patient Intake
Policy/Procedure

4. Think about the topic.
5. Record anything and everything that occurs to you on "branches" (lines that extend out from the center or from other lines).
6. Work quickly, recording your thoughts as fast as you can write.
7. Ignore neatness, spelling, grammar, punctuation, and other standard writing criteria.
8. Set the mind-map aside for a while. Talk to colleagues about the topic. Then add anything you left out.

*(continues)*

## 2-8:  MIND-MAPPING INSTRUCTION SHEET (*continued*)

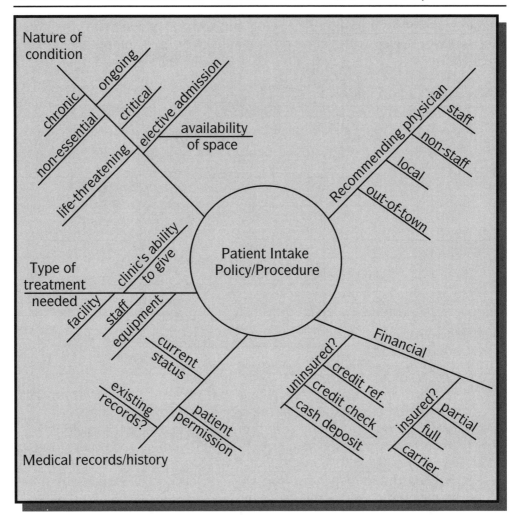

A good mind-map often takes only ten or fifteen minutes, though a complex procedure may take much longer.

The key to a mind-map is to write down everything you're thinking about. Don't self-censor, and don't worry about the mechanics of writing. Once you have all the content issues in front of you, you can decide what to include and what to exclude. Then and only then are you ready to organize the material and worry about flow and sequence.

# 3

# Isn't There a Law Somewhere?

As an organization, you can produce whatever goods or services you wish. You can hire, discipline, and fire employees. You have the right to tell people what to do and how to do it. You have the right to set the rules.

However (and this is a big however), these rights are not absolute. Health and safety laws, employee and consumer rights, liability law, and contract law all impose certain restrictions on how organizations operate. The courts hold you responsible for what you do, what you say you'll do, and what you tell others to do.

So as you draft your policies and procedures, stop for a moment and consider: You'll get your organization sued if you're not careful.

## A Basic Overview

Don't despair—you don't have to be a lawyer to write policies and procedures that are in line with the law. But you do have to be familiar with the restrictions imposed by both statute and case law (accumulated court decisions in individual cases).

A detailed description of all the legal issues that affect policies and procedures would take hundreds of pages, and only your lawyer would read it anyway. What follows, then, is a brief overview of the central issues and legal precepts. At the end of the chapter, in the Legal Tip

---

A FRIENDLY REMINDER

Don't believe all those lawyer jokes you hear. Your attorney can be your best friend in a policy and procedure project.

---

Sheet (3-1), is a detailed outline of the content considerations and writing techniques that will minimize your legal risk.

Pursue specific questions in depth with your legal adviser. You may be concerned about liability if your product instructions are in error or about the conditions under which you can dismiss someone. The areas in which you need to develop special knowledge are dictated by your particular business needs.

---

A PRACTICAL TIP FOR WRITERS

Your lawyers are critical to your process and may at times request specific wording, but be wary of having them actually write your policies and procedures. Remember that they're legal experts, not operational or management experts. They provide necessary and valuable legal assistance, but you are the expert in managing and operating your organization.

---

## What You Can and Will Be Sued For

Most of us don't think about our policies and procedures as creating legal risk. But consider the possibilities. You can and will be sued if:

- Procedures used by customers or employees are unclear, imprecise, or poorly worded.
  *An instruction says, "Before adjusting the valve in the engine, be sure it is shut off." Does "it" refer to the valve or engine? Confused, a user reaches into a running engine and injures his or her hand.*

- Your policy or procedure violates some law or legal precept, intentionally or unintentionally.
  *You have a clearly written layoff policy that's based on length of service. Unfortunately, all the people who get laid off just happen to be women—and you are accused of gender discrimination.*

- The wording of your policies and procedures restricts the organization's ability to act.
  *In an effort to show that the organization deals in good faith and is not arbitrary, your employee handbook reassures employees that "termination will be made for cause only." You then try to fire an employee without cause under your employment-at-will provision.*

- You have written policies and procedures but don't use them or don't enforce them consistently.

  *Your attendance policy says that employees are permitted a maximum of three late arrivals per quarter, but as a practical matter managers allow most people more than that. Then a manager fires an employee for having four tardinesses, citing the policy.*

- You fail to state who is responsible for or what the consequences of noncompliance are.

  *Your product instructions clearly tell users to change the hydraulic fluid after every 500 hours of operation, but they don't say that failure to do so invalidates the warranty and makes the user solely responsible for resulting problems.*

- Your policies or procedures are incomplete, in improper order, or inaccurate.

  *Your procedure tells the user to "turn the handle to the left," when it should read "turn the handle one-half rotation to the left. Do not overrotate." A user turns the handle too far and is injured.*

---

### A SPECIAL OBLIGATION

There are two special barriers that may prevent users from understanding your policies and procedures: language barriers and literacy problems. As the issuer, you have a special obligation to make every reasonable effort to communicate clearly.

For literacy problems, be sure the document is written at an appropriate reading level. For language barriers, you may need to translate the document. In either case, you can work with the affected users and explain verbally. Check with your attorney on specific situations.

---

## Types of Violations

You cannot violate the law, act in a careless manner, or break a promise. The first is known as a tort, the second is a type of tort called negligence, and the third is called a breach of implied contract.

### Torts

A tort is simply a wrongful act, one that violates a duty imposed by law, and is grounds for a civil action.

For instance, you face court challenges based on torts if your operational policies and procedures violate safety regulations or pollution laws, if your administrative policies and procedures violate fiduciary laws or fraud statutes, or if your personnel policies and procedures violate civil rights laws or "public policy."

Public policy protections play a special role in personnel policies and procedures. The term *public policy* refers to actions that may not have any direct statutory protection but are generally recognized as being in the public interest. Jury duty, for example, is considered a public policy necessity; as such, it is a protected activity. Likewise, many states protect whistle-blowing. Forcing people to commit perjury is a similar violation. All are common claims and grounds for a lawsuit.

> **Example:** *A supervisor informed police that a coworker was selling stolen merchandise, and the supervisor then cooperated in the subsequent police investigation. The supervisor was fired for carelessly involving the police instead of reporting the situation to the company for internal handling.*
>
> *When the supervisor then sued, the employer argued that it should be able to exercise discretion and sound business judgment in looking at how management employees handle such matters. The court disagreed, saying that "public policy . . . favors citizen crime-fighters." The supervisor was allowed to sue. Even if the employer had had a policy that reserved its right to exercise its own business judgment and review the actions of its managers, it would not have been sufficient because of the public policy issue.* Palmateer v. International Harvester *(1981).*

Few organizations knowingly create policies and procedures that violate the law, but check the legalities before you start to write a particular document.

## Negligence

Negligence is a type of tort that's especially important in policy and procedure writing. It's the failure to exercise reasonable care in instances where such care is a duty under the law.

Let's assume that your organization produces high-end road-grading equipment. In a hurry to market a new machine, you publish poorly written operating procedures that contribute to a loss of business, damage, injury, or even death. Your organization has been negligent.

Negligence claims tend to affect procedures more often than policies, but they can arise in either case. They have always been a major issue when it comes to product liability and operating procedures. You are obligated to give clear, complete, and reasonable instructions for installation, operation, maintenance, and repair.

---

### THE FORGOTTEN POLICIES AND PROCEDURES

We all tend to overlook them: the informal and unwritten rules. They're such a built-in part of our daily lives that we're largely unconscious of them. But they can still constitute an officially sanctioned way of doing things, and the courts hold you accountable for them.

An example of an informal rule is when the departmental manager sends out a brief memo or e-mail giving directions to the staff. An example of an unwritten rule is when the whole department uses a procedure for years, but no one ever gets around to writing it down.

Rules that are unconscious and uncontrolled spell legal trouble.

---

In the last few years, negligence has also emerged as a major issue in personnel policies and procedures. There are now numerous cases involving negligent hiring, negligent supervision, negligent retention, negligent firing, and even negligent reference checking.

> **Example:** *A company hires a serviceman who works unsupervised in customers' homes, but it doesn't check references before hiring him. He later robs and assaults an elderly customer in her home. The investigation reveals that he had a history of violence. The company, which does have a reference-checking policy, is found guilty of negligent hiring.*

The failure to have responsible policies and procedures, or the failure to communicate, follow, and enforce them, can lead to charges of negligence.

## Breach of Implied Contract

### What It Is

If you've never thought of your policies and procedures as a contract, think again. As laypeople, most of us think of a contract as an official, signed agreement between two parties. But that's only one type of contract, known legally as an express contract.

Most courts (it varies from state to state) also recognize what's known as an implied contract. In lay terms, this means that you said you would do something or would do it in a certain way. You committed yourself to the action either verbally or in writing.

Suppose your policy says that you'll follow a five-step progressive discipline procedure, then you fire several employees summarily. They claim that they were entitled to those five steps and that, by reneging on the procedure you promised them, you breached an implied contract.

---

### PROMISES, PROMISES

If you make a promise and then break it, you may be guilty of breach of contract. It's a unique type of contract known as an implied contract, and it can be either verbal or written.

If you say you'll do something, you may be creating an implied contract.

---

### Why It Is

Two companion court cases in Michigan (*Toussaint v. Blue Cross and Blue Shield of Michigan, Ebling v. Masc Corp.,* 1980) opened the door to implied contract claims. Both involved dismissals in which the employees claimed that promissory policy statements were made, guaranteeing job security and/or a fair review of problem performance. In one case, the promises were verbal. In the other, the organization referred the employee to the policies and procedures in the personnel manual.

The Michigan Supreme Court ruled that an organization's "stated policies and established procedures" can create a right to continued employment. The court also found that a contractual obligation exists if the organization creates policies and procedures, then leads employees to believe that they are:

- Established and official rules
- Fair rules
- Rules that are consistently, uniformly applied to all employees

### Where It Applies

Implied contract claims frequently involve disciplinary or termination matters and are of special concern in personnel policies and procedures.

---

IMPLIED CONTRACT VARIES IN EACH STATE

Since the decision in the Michigan companion cases, courts in most of the states have recognized the concept of implied contract in some form. A state-by-state list showing the current status in each state is at the end of this chapter in the chart of Implied Contracts on a State-by-State Basis (3-2).

---

**Example:** *A bank loan officer was fired after an audit found serious irregularities in a number of loans. However, the bank did not review the technical errors with the officer or follow the disciplinary procedures contained in its employee handbook. The court ruled that the procedures in the handbook were contractually binding and should have been followed.* Pine River State Bank v. R. Mittile *(1983).*

Implied contracts tend to have the greatest impact on handbooks and manuals, which are collections of (supposedly) well thought out and carefully crafted decisions about how you operate. Courts hold you responsible for your decisions and for your statements about them.

However, because an implied contract can also be verbal, the concept affects your unwritten policies and procedures as well. Virtually anything you do or say that could be construed as a policy statement is under scrutiny.

The Illinois Supreme Court ruled (in *Dudulao v. St. Mary of Nazareth Hospital*) that an employee handbook creates an enforceable contract if it meets the traditional criteria for a contract. These are: (1) promissory language, (2) communication of the policy, and (3) acceptance by the employee (that is, the employee continues to work under the policy).

But the court also said that the same was true of *any policy statement*. In other words, if you say you'll do it, you may have created a contract.

## Good Faith

Courts have also said that contracts, express or implied, may carry an assumption of "good faith and fair dealing."

**Example:** *An employee with eighteen years' service and satisfactory performance reviews was fired without adequate investigation or a fair hearing as provided for in company policies. The court ruled that dismissing an employee with a satisfactory record without legal cause violates the assumption of good faith and fair dealing implicit in a contract.* Cleary v. American Airlines *(1980).*

# Disclaimers

Because users and courts may see your policies or procedures as an implied contract, it's important to clearly dispel any such notion. This applies to both internal and external policies and procedures.

There are many different ways to word disclaimers, and you'll find several examples in the Sample Disclaimers (3-3) and the Sample Employment-at-Will Statements (3-4) at the end of this chapter. Your lawyers may have a set wording they want you to use, but in any case, have them review the final version.

Whatever wording you settle on, be sure it's strong, clear, and definite. You don't want any confusion in the mind of the user—or the court.

## Internal Policies and Procedures

Disclaimers protect you by declaring that the internal policies or procedures do not constitute a contract and may be changed anytime at management's discretion.

It's common to use a general disclaimer at the front of a handbook or manual. You can also use repeated disclaimers: Place a general disclaimer at the front, then put specific disclaimers in certain significant sections such as benefits, discipline, or hiring (which may involve employment-at-will). In each case, make it clear that the contents may change and are not contractual.

## External Policies and Procedures

If you're writing for external users or customers, warranty disclaimers and other disclaimers are a means of clarifying responsibilities or consequences.

Your disclaimer may state that the manufacturer is not responsible for consequences unless the established policy or procedure is followed in its entirety. Or it may state that the warranty is invalid if procedures are not properly followed.

# The Necessity of Updating

There's no law against having old policies and procedures. The problem is a practical one that can turn into a legal one.

Suppose your manual is five years old and no one follows the procedures anymore. Instead, new procedures have just "evolved."

Then a user injures herself and takes you to court, claiming that she was just following proper procedure. She arrives in court waving a copy of your official manual.

If you were the judge, what would you think?

If yours is like most organizations, update projects get pushed to the back burner. There's always something more important to do. Don't be fooled. Courts expect you to keep people informed of your current standards and rules.

## Manuals vs. Handbooks

Policies and procedures are frequently grouped together by topic into a handbook or manual. Another term heard with increasing frequency is "user's guide." From a practical standpoint, the terms are much the same. Which you use is a matter of preference or custom.

But from a legal standpoint, there can be an important difference.

The term *handbook* may imply information that is widely distributed to a general audience. The term *manual* may imply more detailed information that is restricted in circulation to a select audience and is considered confidential.

Information that is distributed to a general employee audience may create an implied contract with those employees. But confidential information intended for a select group doesn't necessarily create a contractual obligation to employees as a whole.

> **Example:** *A manager is fired. In the manager's manual there is a strongly promissory statement about firing for cause. He sues for breach of implied contract based on that statement.*
>
> *The court determines that the promissory statement is in the manual but not in the employee handbook. The manual, which is confidential and for distribution to managers only, does not constitute a contract because it is not intended for general distribution to all employees.*

If you have only one policy or procedure book, the term you use for it may be of little importance. However, if you do have separate documents covering the same subject, the handbook is usually the one that is for general employee distribution. The manual is usually the one that contains not only policies and procedures but detailed instructions on how to interpret, implement, and enforce them. It's distributed to a select user group only, such as managers, and all references to the manual are deleted from the general handbook.

The term *user's guide* is increasingly used to avoid the implication of any promises or contractual obligations. The title implies that the book contains guidelines, not absolutes, and that there may be changes or deviations. It's most often used for the policy and procedure books intended for general distribution.

Whatever term you use for the book that is distributed for general internal use, make sure it contains an acknowledgment statement to be signed by employees. See the Sample Acknowledgment Statements (3-5) at the end of this chapter.

---

### A Pop Quiz

Your safety policy says that goggles must be worn at all times on the shop floor. The policy is clearly written and you've had it for twenty years. But many people who will be on the floor for only a brief time, ten or fifteen minutes, don't bother.

You also conduct tours of the production area, and your policy requires that goggles be worn by all who take the tour. A disabled person is unable to wear them and is denied entry to the tour.

What do you think a court would say if someone complained?

---

## What the Courts Want You to Do

The courts don't want all of us to become lawyers or to spend half our time worrying about legal risks. What they do want is for organizations to:

1. *Operate in a safe, reasonable, and fair manner.* Develop policies and procedures that are accurate, complete, and responsible. Observe the rights of employees and customers. Operate in good faith. Deal fairly.

2. *Communicate your policies and procedures clearly.* Tell people what they're supposed to do and how. Write succinctly, using clear language that's easy to understand. Make the policies and procedures easily accessible. Cover all appropriate and necessary topics. Communicate the consequences of noncompliance. Notify users of changes.

3. *Enforce policies and procedures.* It does no good to have policies and procedures unless you use them. Include enforcement provisions in your policies and procedures to show that you're serious, then use those provisions. If you deviate from a policy or procedure, be sure that you have

a good business reason for doing so and that you have reserved the right to discretionary action with proper wording.

Organizations are expected to behave fairly and to take all reasonable steps to protect themselves, their employees, their customers, and others they may deal with.

## How to Protect Yourself

Although there are no legal guarantees, you can minimize the risks of lawsuits or lost cases. There are two goals: to reduce your legal exposure, and to be in a good position to defend yourself if it becomes necessary.

Focus on two factors: content matters and writing techniques. Research the issues and call your legal specialist when you have questions. Err on the conservative side. Then devote enough time to your policies and procedures to be sure that:

1. The content is appropriate, sufficient, and accurate.
2. The writing is clear, understandable, and precise.

The specific writing techniques and content considerations that can help you avoid legal trouble are outlined in detail in the Legal Tip Sheet (3-1) at the end of this chapter. In general, they fall into six categories:

1. *Word your policies and procedures carefully.* Avoid promissory language. Use words with precision. Say what you mean and mean what you say. Qualify your statements so users and courts don't think that these rules were intended for all conditions or all times. Watch out for certain common words and phrases that can cause trouble.

2. *Check the content.* Be sure it's complete, accurate, and in the proper sequence. Be sure it doesn't violate any law, regulation, or legal precept. And be sure it's what you really mean to say.

3. *Reserve management's right to discretionary action.* Avoid boxing yourself in. Include statements that say management has the right to take alternative action if, in its judgment, such action is necessary. Check with your attorney for precise wording appropriate to your application. See the Samples of Discretionary Wording (3-6) at the end of this chapter.

4. *Preserve your right to make changes.* Use careful wording, but also state that management has the right to make changes as necessary. Use disclaimers.

5. *Consider the informal and unwritten rules.* A brief departmental memo, or a practice that's gone on informally for years, may still constitute an officially sanctioned way of doing things. Informal and unwritten rules tend to go unnoticed and uncontrolled.

6. *Use and enforce the rules.* Describe the consequences of noncompliance. Outline enforcement procedures and hold the enforcers accountable. Be consistent in application. If you deviate, be sure you have good business reasons for doing so and the discretionary right to do it.

---

COURTS HATE GUESSING GAMES

Courts rule based on what you said and did, not on what you *intended* to say or do. They can't read your mind. They can only interpret what you said.

---

## Chapter Summary

▪ Any policy or procedure—written or unwritten, formal or informal—can put you at legal risk. You may face a court challenge for a tort, which includes negligence of some type, or for breach of implied contract.

▪ To minimize legal risks, consider both the content and the wording of your policies and procedures. They must be accurate, complete, and thorough. They must be precisely worded and clearly written so that they are understandable and usable. They must also be communicated and updated.

▪ If you have more than one book of policies and procedures on the same subject, there can be a legal difference between a manual and a handbook. A handbook for general distribution may create an implied contract, whereas a manual for limited distribution may not.

▪ Be familiar with the statutes that affect you and with case law, which varies from state to state. Get legal advice as needed.

▪ Courts expect organizations to operate in a safe, reasonable, and fair manner. They also expect organizations to clearly communicate their standards of operation and keep them current.

# Tools and Resources
# for Chapter 3

## 3-1: LEGAL TIP SHEET

### Main Legal Issues

☐ *Torts:* Violations of law or legal requirements
☐ *Negligence:* A lack of due care, and one type of tort
☐ *Implied contract:* Promising to do something and then not doing it

### Documents Affected

☐ Handbooks, manuals, and user's guides
☐ Individual policy statements or procedures
☐ Informal memos or letters that constitute policy or procedure
☐ Unwritten policies and procedures

### Content Areas Affected

☐ Administrative
☐ Employment
☐ Financial and fiduciary
☐ Health and safety
☐ Operational
☐ Product and consumer
☐ Quality assurance

### What You Can Do to Minimize Risks

1. *Use disclaimers:* In clear language, explain that the policy or procedure is not a contract and may be changed anytime at management's discretion. Use a general disclaimer, then use additional disclaimers for specific policy or procedure areas to reinforce the message. When policies or procedures are meant for external use by customers or others, use warranty disclaimers and other statements to clarify responsibilities and consequences. See the Sample Disclaimers (3-3) at the end of this chapter.

*(continues)*

## 3-1:  LEGAL TIP SHEET (*continued*)

2. *Have an employment-at-will statement:*

   This is a type of disclaimer that should go in all personnel handbooks or manuals. It reserves the employer's right to terminate at will and the employee's right to quit at will. See the Sample Employment-at-Will Statements (3-4) at the end of this chapter.

3. *Preserve management's discretionary authority:*

   Use statements such as the following: "Management reserves the right to take alternative steps when it deems such action appropriate," or, "This policy is a guideline for _____. However, circumstances may arise in which we find it necessary to take other steps not specifically designated in this policy. We reserve the right to do so at our discretion and when we believe business conditions warrant." See the Samples of Discretionary Wording (3-6) at the end of this chapter.

   Statements such as these do not give management free reign to act irresponsibly. They do preserve your ability to deal with unusual or extreme situations without having to follow policies or procedures intended for use under "normal" conditions. Avoid boxing the organization in and eliminating needed discretionary action.

   These statements should appear in individual policies and procedures where appropriate to the topic, such as disciplinary matters or emergency procedures. A general statement to the same effect appears in your handbook's general disclaimer. Check with your attorney for specific wording.

4. *Use words with precision:*

   "Say what you mean and mean what you say" should be the policy and procedure writer's motto, for all the reasons listed in this tip sheet. Examine every statement to be sure it accurately reflects the subject's content and the organization's intent. Remember that courts rule based on what you said and did, not on what you intended to say or do.

5. *Avoid promissory language:*

The word *will* means that you are committed to that position or action. The word *shall* is the strongest legal commitment you can make. If you use them, mean them.

6. *Qualify your statements:*

If used correctly, the word *will* is a perfectly legitimate word to use. However, because it may be construed as a promise or contract, place a qualifier or restriction on your statements. Examples include words or phrases such as "usually," "in most circumstances," or "under normal operating conditions." (See number 7 below.)

7. *Watch out for weasel words, such as "perhaps," "maybe," or "almost":*

These words can be perfectly valid, but they often indicate an attempt to "weasel out" of responsibility, hence their name. However, they're also useful as qualifiers (see number 6 above). If you use these words, be sure you mean them.

8. *Watch out for words such as "can," "may," "must," "ought," "could," "should," and "might":*

These words are deceptively simple-sounding, but each has a specific meaning. Use them with precision: Say what you mean and mean what you say. Courts can't read your mind. They can only interpret what's been said. "Part A ought to fit into Part B" sounds suspiciously like negligence. "Must" mandates, "may" gives permission, and so on.

9. *Watch out for absolutes, such as "always" or "never":*

Absolutes permit no exceptions. If your policy contains the word *always,* you had better mean "always." All a good lawyer has to do is show that you deviated once, three years ago, and you're in trouble. Since you do want to preserve discretionary capability in many instances, think twice before using absolutes. They're most appropriate, even necessary, in health- and safety-related documents, e.g., "Never smoke near the oxygen tanks."

*(continues)*

## 3-1: Legal Tip Sheet (*continued*)

10. *Watch out for conditional phrases such as "If only . . .":*

Conditional words and phrases are more of that potentially promissory language. "As long as . . . " and "if . . . " imply a guarantee that so long as that condition is met, a certain result will occur. Like the other potentially promissory words, these are perfectly valid to use. Just use them with precision, and be sure that's what you mean.

11. *Create a complaint or review procedure:*

Courts like to know that there is a fair process for the resolution of conflicts or disagreements.

12. *Have a disciplinary procedure for those who violate the rules:*

If you don't enforce your policies and procedures, the courts may assume that you aren't serious. If you ignore them, why can't the user?

13. *Have a disciplinary procedure for those who fail to enforce the rules:*

Many organizations don't make it clear to enforcers (usually managers) that enforcement is a serious responsibility. Establish a policy that holds enforcers accountable as well as users.

14. *Communicate your policies and procedures:*

Tell people what they're expected to do and how they're expected to act. Court cases sometimes hinge on whether or not the user knew about the policy or procedure.

15. *Get a signed acknowledgment:*

The best way to prove that you did in fact communicate with users is to have them verify in writing that they received the information. With internal handbooks, the acknowledgment should state that the user has received, read, and understood the content, and agrees to abide by the policies and procedures. See the Sample Acknowledgment Statements (3-5) at the end of this chapter.

16. *Explain the consequences of noncompliance:*  One of the most important things users need to know is how serious improper action is. Could they be injured? Fired? Sued? Paid late? Courts have been known to find that even though an employee violated a policy or procedure, he or she was never told that being fired was a possibility. The punishment would be considered too severe under those circumstances. You might then have to reinstate the fired employee.

17. *Review your unwritten policies and procedures:*  An implied contract can be verbal. Unwritten policies and procedures are just as important in many ways as your more formal written ones. They're also easier to forget about. They can still be the basis of a lawsuit.

18. *Review your informal policies and procedures:*  Informal memos and e-mail messages circulate every day. These may in fact be directives or instructions that constitute a policy or procedure. The fact that it isn't officially part of your handbook or isn't called a policy won't interest the court very much. The court just wants to know whether that's what you really did or expected others to do. If it's how you really operate, it becomes your policy or procedure.

19. *Review everything:*  Since complications are always waiting in the wings, develop the legal version of peripheral vision. A good question to ask yourself is, "Is there anything in this issue that could blindside us?" Become familiar with your topic, research it, and stay current. Talk to your attorneys as needed.

20. *Don't assume anything:*  The mere fact that you have a policy or procedure is not in itself a legal protection. The policies and procedures must be consistently practiced and enforced. They must also be within the law. Your policy may state clearly that the safe use of the product is the sole responsibility of the user. But if the user can show that your organization produced or marketed the product

*(continues)*

## 3-1: LEGAL TIP SHEET (*continued*)

recklessly, your policy won't be much help. Courts hold you responsible for what you do, what you say you'll do, and what you tell others to do.

21. *Reserve the right to make changes:*

It's not always possible or desirable to explain everything in detail. You may need to keep the document to a reasonable length, or audience analysis might show that general summary information is more appropriate. For instance, your employee handbook might contain summaries of your benefits programs without detailing every single condition or limitation of each program.

If users don't know this, they may form unrealistic expectations or, worse, assume contractual rights. Courts have ruled in favor of organizations that have clearly stated that they have the right to modify (add, delete, change) their policies and procedures. It's an important practical and legal message, and it's usually part of a disclaimer.

You should also consider placing a separate statement in individual policies and procedures that are especially significant, such as those on discipline or safety. (Also see number 3 above.)

**Comments**

☐ There are some things organizations should never do with regard to policies and procedures:
1. Don't make illegal rules.
2. Don't condone illegal practices, written or unwritten.
3. Don't make rules and then violate them yourself.
4. Don't make promises you don't intend to make or can't keep.
5. Don't depend on your written policies and procedures as a sole defense legally. Cases are seldom that simple. Your past practices, your intent, and a myriad of other circumstances all play a part.

## 3-2: IMPLIED CONTRACTS ON A STATE-BY-STATE BASIS

The courts in most states recognize the concept of implied contract. This list indicates the current status on a state-by-state basis.

Note that this list is a general informational guide only. New court decisions or new legislation may change this information at any time. For specifics in your state and local jurisdiction, consult the relevant laws or get qualified legal advice.

| State | Recognizes Implied Contract | State | Recognizes Implied Contract |
|---|---|---|---|
| Alabama | Yes | Missouri | Yes |
| Alaska | Yes | Montana | Qualified recognition |
| Arizona | Yes | Nebraska | Yes |
| Arkansas | Yes | Nevada | Yes |
| California | Yes | New Hampshire | Yes |
| Colorado | Yes | New Jersey | Yes |
| Connecticut | Yes | New Mexico | Yes |
| Delaware | Yes | New York | Qualified recognition |
| District of | | North Carolina | No |
| Columbia | Yes | North Dakota | Yes |
| Florida | No | Ohio | Yes |
| Georgia | No | Oklahoma | Yes |
| Hawaii | Yes | Oregon | Yes |
| Idaho | Yes | Pennsylvania | Yes |
| Illinois | Yes | Rhode Island | No |
| Indiana | No clear ruling | South Carolina | Yes |
| Iowa | Yes | South Dakota | Yes |
| Kansas | Yes | Tennessee | Yes |
| Kentucky | Yes | Texas | No clear ruling |
| Louisiana | No clear ruling | Utah | Yes |
| Maine | Yes | Vermont | Yes |
| Maryland | Yes | Virginia | Yes |
| Massachusetts | Yes | Washington | Yes |
| Michigan | Yes | West Virginia | Yes |
| Minnesota | Yes | Wisconsin | Yes |
| Mississippi | Yes | Wyoming | Yes |

## 3-3: SAMPLE DISCLAIMERS

Disclaimers are an important way to protect your organization by stating that the policy or procedure is not a contract and may be changed at any time at management's discretion. Here are some sample general disclaimers for use in company handbooks or manuals. These are general disclaimers, but you should also consider specific individual disclaimers for certain high-profile subjects, such as discipline or benefits.

Note that these are examples only. Do not use the wording in these samples without the knowledge and approval of your attorneys. After all, they're the ones who will have to defend it in court. Whether you use your own or your attorney's recommended wording, be sure it's clear and understandable.

> We have prepared this handbook to help you understand how our organization works. You must read and observe the policies and procedures described in this book.
>
> This book is neither a contract nor a promise of employment. Neither is it a guarantee of a particular process under any particular set of circumstances. It is a summary of the standards by which we operate. We reserve the right to change these policies and procedures anytime, and we will notify you of such changes.

> The contents of this manual are presented as a matter of information only. You should not consider anything contained in it to be contractual or promissory. Changes may be made and enforced from time to time at the company's discretion.

> This handbook is for informational purposes. It is meant to acquaint you with the company's rules and methods of operation. It does not create contractual obligations of any sort for either you or the company, and it may be changed as conditions warrant.

## 3-4: SAMPLE EMPLOYMENT-AT-WILL STATEMENTS

An employment-at-will statement reserves the company's theoretical right to terminate an employee without reason, cause, or notice. It also reserves the employee's right to quit on the same basis. Such a statement, samples of which appear below, belongs in your personnel handbook or manual. However, remember that employment-at-will provisions should only be used in worst-case scenarios.

Note that the following are examples only and should not be used without the knowledge and approval of your legal advisers. They may have pro forma wording they want you to use. Be sure that whatever wording you use is clear and understandable.

> This handbook outlines the rules and regulations of our organization, which you are required to follow. You have the right to end your employment at any time without notice or cause, and the organization also has the same right.

> Your employment with the organization is at will, which means that either party may terminate the relationship at any time and for any—or no—reason. You may end your employment here without notice or reason, and we also have the right to end it without notice or cause.

> This organization employs at will. This means that you may leave the organization anytime you wish, without cause or notice. We also reserve the same right and may end your employment anytime without cause or notice.

## 3-5: SAMPLE ACKNOWLEDGMENT STATEMENTS

Court cases are sometimes lost when a user claims that he or she never received the policy or procedure. A signed acknowledgment is proof that you communicated your policies and procedures with users. Here are some sample acknowledgment statements to use with your handbooks or individual documents.

Note that these are examples only and should not be used without the knowledge and approval of your legal advisers. They may want to combine the acknowledgment with the general handbook disclaimer and/or the employment-at-will statement.

> I have received a copy of the _____ handbook/policy/procedure. I understand that it is my obligation to read and understand this material and to abide by the rules established by the organization. I also understand that I am governed by these policies and procedures and that the organization may change them at will.

> I have received the _____, which outlines both my obligations and my privileges as an employee of the _____ organization. I agree to familiarize myself with the contents of this book and to seek clarification of any item that I do not understand. I also agree to comply with the standards and rules outlined in this document.

## 3-6: Samples of Discretionary Wording

It's important to reserve the right to make changes throughout your policies and procedures. Separate statements, such as disclaimers, are necessary but not sufficient. Where appropriate to the topic, include clear wording in the policy or procedure itself. It needn't be long, just clear. You're building in flexibility. See the samples below. Always check wording with your attorney before final publication.

> We fully intend to observe the procedure as stated above. However, we also reserve the right to take alternative steps if we deem such steps necessary.

> The policy as stated below will apply in most circumstances. However, circumstances can vary greatly and management may sometimes require you to follow other guidelines or rules.

> This procedure is intended for use under normal operating circumstances. Other circumstances may arise that, in management's judgment, require a different approach. We reserve the right to take a different course when we believe it to be appropriate.

> This policy is a guideline only. Circumstances may arise in which we find it necessary to take other steps not specifically designated here. We reserve the right to do so at our discretion.

# 4

# What's the Best Way to Word This?

We've all been to school and sat through English class. You know about sentence structure, word order, grammar, and spelling. So why should you spend time on the details of language now?

Because some of the rules have changed.

## Technical vs. Narrative Writing

No, you weren't asleep in class. And no, the rules you learned in school haven't disappeared. It's simply that policy and procedure writing is a different type of writing with its own set of rules.

The writing most of us learned in school is called narrative writing, and its purpose is to impress the reader. It's usually descriptive and lengthy, and it is often complicated. It uses complex grammatical structures to show the writer's command of the language. This type of writing is common in letters and memos.

But when you deal with policies and procedures, you're using a form of technical writing. Its purpose is not to impress. Its sole purpose is to get a message across quickly and clearly.

Policy and procedure users aren't judging grammatical merit. They

---

CLARITY AND SPEED

Quit trying to impress the audience with your command of the language. There are only two criteria you have to remember: speed and clarity. If users clearly understand what's expected of them and can understand it fast, you have a successful document.

---

don't care about erudite vocabulary or sophisticated sentence structure. They're not interested in the fine points of language.

They're interested in the content. They want fast, clear information. And the secret to writing good policies and procedures is to give it to them—which means throwing out some of the old writing rules.

## The Old Rules

But it's hard to ignore old, engrained writing habits, such as don't use one-sentence paragraphs. Never start a sentence or a paragraph with "and" or "but." Use impressive vocabulary words. Use compound sentences and complex clauses.

The problem is that many of these rules boil down to this: Bulk counts. The more, the longer, the fancier—the better.

When you were in grade school, chances are that some teacher asked you to write an essay about your summer vacation. Only 200 words. Excited, you started yours: "I had a great time." But then you panicked. That's only five words. You had 195 more to go. What to do? Aha! Start padding. Take the simple, clear message and dress it up with more words: "I had a really, really, really great time on my summer vacation."

And so it went for most of us throughout school. Write so many words. Write so many pages. "Good" became synonymous with "long."

That was entirely appropriate back then. Our teachers were making sure we mastered the language and could engage in sophisticated narrative writing when needed.

But we unconsciously use the same approach today when we're writing a technical document such as a policy or procedure. The result is long, windy writing that's hard to read. We've all seen three-page policies that could have been clearly stated in three paragraphs.

And it's nothing more than habit. We're addicted to excess words and needlessly complicated grammar.

In the interest of speed and clarity, some of the old rules have got to go.

## The New Rules

The new rules are easily summarized: *Simple is good.* No more padding. No more complex sentence structures or fancy vocabulary. Kick the word habit. Be brief and clear. Get rid of pompous, stuffy language. Eliminate unnecessary verbiage.

Learn new habits. Be precise and keep it short. Use words carefully. Set a rhythm that keeps the reader moving. Be both a word miser and a word master.

The rest of this chapter highlights the central writing issues. At the end of the chapter is a Wording Tip Sheet (4-1) with a complete list of techniques. Review it every time you start to write.

---

### The Policy and Procedure Writer's Oath

I do solemnly swear to avoid excess verbiage, fancy phrasing, and long words and sentences. I will resist the temptation to display my grammatical mastery and linguistic skill. I will devote myself to the pursuit of short, clear messages. I will dazzle with speed and clarity.

---

## Being a Word Miser

Word misers—people who use only the number of words necessary—are on a mission. They want to get rid of every single word that doesn't mean something.

They dump pompous language and talk to readers (not down to them). They eliminate unnecessary adjectives and use clauses sparingly. They use short words, sentences, and paragraphs. They are merciless in the pursuit of the short and simple. How do you become a word miser? Follow the tips given below.

### Think in Ones

One word is better than two. Two sentences are better than three. Word misers look for the main idea in a sentence, phrase, or paragraph, then they ask whether the additional words in that grouping add anything that's important. Look at this sentence:

*Use the designated hammer.*

Do you really need the adjective "designated"? Maybe. But if there's only one hammer in the whole procedure, the word "designated" is just taking up space.

---

### PADDING ALERT!

Be on alert for padding that sneaks into your writing when you're not looking. Adjectives are a big problem, and prepositional phrases and extra clauses are dead giveaways. Here are two examples of padding:

*the proper, designated wrench*

*the designated wrench, which will be found in the proper toolbox in the storage room next to the adjacent workspace*

---

## Dump Pompous, Stuffy Language

Thinking like a word miser works wonders on windy, stiff language. Compare the following sentences:

*All rental car reservations must be made through our affiliated travel agency.*

*Reserve rental cars through our travel agency.*

The second is a vast improvement over the first. And it only took three basic word miser rules to make the message shorter and clearer: Use active voice, start with an action verb, and eliminate all unnecessary adjectives. A list of these rules comes later in this section.

## Speak to the Reader

One of the best word miser techniques is to ask yourself how you would say it if you were talking to the user in person. I don't know anyone who would actually say:

*Utilize available nonrail ground mode transportation systems.*

Yet we write it that way because it somehow sounds better (translation: longer). What it really means is this:

*Use trucks.*

But this somehow sounds too simple. The everyday language we use doesn't seem good enough for the printed page, so we dress it up. Complicated three-syllable words replace clear one-syllable words: "use" becomes "utilize," "start" becomes "initiate," "stop" becomes "desist." Flabby, excessive writing.

Dump this old habit fast. Simple, common language is exactly what you're looking for in most policies and procedures. Talk to readers out loud, then write down what you would say. Users don't take the *subsequent* step, they take the *next* step. They don't *initiate* a call, they *make* it.

---

### YOUR NEW LIFE AS A WORD MISER

The simplest way to start your new life as a word miser is to write it as you would speak it. You instinctively shorten, eliminate excess wording, and use active voice. Many of the important rules are natural in the spoken word.

---

## Follow the Word Miser's Rules to Live By

Certified word misers have a whole set of rules they live by, a credo for kicking the word habit. They're summarized below and detailed in the Wording Tip Sheet (4-1) at the end of the chapter.

Some of these rules may make you grind your teeth at first. Start a paragraph with the word "But"? Never! It's bad form. Maybe, but think how much faster and clearer it is for the readers. They're instantly prepared for what's coming (an exception or reversal).

Being a word miser is hard work. You have to set aside many of the

---

### THINK ACTIVE VOICE, PRESENT TENSE

The shortest, clearest, strongest message in the English language comes from using normal word order: subject, verb, object. It's called active voice.

Active voice cuts the number of words, reduces grammatical errors, and clarifies who does what. Add present tense, which gives a sense of immediacy, and you have a simple, powerful statement. Isn't the second sentence below stronger and clearer than the first?

> *All requests for leave, as provided for in the company handbook, will be submitted by the requesting employee to his or her supervisor for approval.*

> *Employees submit leave requests to their supervisors.*

---

writing habits you've used for years. You have to consciously question the use of every word and phrase. It takes time and effort. As Mark Twain once said, "I'm sorry this letter is so long. I didn't have time to write a shorter one."

---

### WORD MISERDOM

- Be vigilant. Watch for adjectives that sneak in and clauses that come out of nowhere.
- Be ruthless. Slash long sentences and paragraphs, and eliminate four- and five-syllable words.
- Show no mercy. This is a war on excess words.

---

## Be an Accurate Word Miser

Being a word miser is a lot of fun once you get the hang of it, but it can also be dangerous. You may cut too much—and in doing so, you may change the meaning.

For instance, consider which of these statements is the shortest and which is the clearest:

*Return the completed form in seven days.*

*Return the completed form in seven working days.*

It would be easy to eliminate the adjective "working" and think you've been a word miser. But you've also deleted critical information: There's a big difference between seven *calendar* days and seven *working* days.

Don't cut words mindlessly. Always ask whether a word or phrase adds any meaning. And if you can't be both brief and clear, always choose clarity.

---

### THE CASE OF BRIEF VS. CLEAR

Remember this simple rule: Never sacrifice clarity for brevity. A short, simple policy or procedure is easy to read, but it won't help the reader if it omits important information. *Clarity is your number 1 priority, brevity is number 2.*

---

### *The Word Miser's Rules to Live By*

1. Use common words and phrases.

   **by,** *not* **in accordance with**

2. Use one- and two-syllable words.

   **use,** *not* **utilize**

3. Get rid of windy phrases. See the List of Wordy Phrases (4-2) at the end of this chapter.

   **because** or **since,** *not* **in view of the fact that**

4. Get rid of redundancies. See the List of Redundancies (4-3) at the end of this chapter.

   **absolutely essential**

5. Get rid of empty phrases.

   **There is. . . .**

6. Eliminate all unnecessary adjectives and descriptions.

   **Employees may use rental cars,**
   *not*
   **Employees may engage a commercially hired rental car in the destination city for transportation purposes.**

7. Limit the number of clauses and phrases, and keep them short.

   **Use the wrench in the storage closet nearest to the machine,**
   *not*
   **Use the designated wrench found in the proper storage space in the adjacent storage closet that is located closest to the machine.**

8. Use short sentences (fifteen words maximum, twenty at the outside).

   *Rule:*     Fifteen words is preferable; twenty is maximum. In procedures, twelve is preferable and fifteen is maximum.
   *Example:* See item 7 above. The first example has eleven words, the second, twenty-two.

9. Use short paragraphs.

   *Rule:* One hundred words or less; forty or less in procedures.

10. Use one-sentence paragraphs.

    *Reason:* They're attention-getters.

11. Keep phrases and clauses short.

    *Rule:* Five words is preferable; ten is maximum.

12. Use transitions at the start of sentences and paragraphs to tell readers what's happening next. See the List of Transition Words and Phrases (4-4) at the end of this chapter.

    **and** or **also** to continue.
    **but** or **yet** to reverse.
    **because** to explain.

13. Use lots of lists.

    *Reason:* Lists shorten, clarify, and add white space.

14. Use active voice.

    **Start the truck,**
    *not*
    **The truck should be started.**

15. Use present tense.

    **The operator reports the breakdown,**
    *not*
    **The operator will report the breakdown.**

16. Start with an action verb.

    **Ask your supervisor,**
    *not*
    **The operator should ask the supervisor.**

17. Use standard word order of subject-verb-object.

    *Reason:* Inverting word order causes a more passive voice, misplacement, and extra clauses. It also lengthens.

    **Hold the bolt in place and tighten the screw,**
    *not*
    **While tightening the screw, the bolt should be held in place.**

## Being a Word Master

Being a word miser is only half the battle. You must also become a word master: someone who uses words with precision and respect. How do you become a word master? Follow the tips given below.

---

The Fun of Being a Word Miser

Oh, the joy of puncturing pompous language! Word misers get a secret thrill out of skewering policies and procedures like this:

*An employee using air transportation may be authorized by the supervisor to engage a rental car in the destination city for transportation when the cost is less than that of taxi fare or enables the traveler to accomplish company business in a more efficient manner.*

Whew! You could get depressed reading a document like this. It's a word miser's nightmare: a single sentence that's forty-five words long, has too many clauses and prepositional phrases, and has lots of unnecessary words. And some words are just silly. Who "engages" a rental car or takes "air transportation"? That policy is full of flab.

Apply the word miser's rules and look what happens:

*Any employee who travels by air may use a rental car if:*
 *a) it costs less than a taxi, or*
 *b) it allows more efficient conduct of company business.*
*Rental car use must be authorized by the employee's supervisor.*

What did we do? We used short sentences, a list, a few short prepositional phrases, common words, and a few essential adjectives. Voilà! Another word miser victory.

---

## Say What You Mean and Mean What You Say

Word masters understand that every word has a meaning, and most have multiple meanings. They're aware of the amazing number of possible misinterpretations in even the simplest statements, such as:

*Turn the handle to the left.*

Think about how many different ways readers can take that. One may yank the handle hard all the way to the left. Another may slowly rotate it one one-hundredth of an inch at a time. Which do you want them to do? Say precisely what you mean:

*Turn the handle slowly to the left until it stops. Do not force the handle.*

## Use Specific Language

Avoid vague words that invite varying interpretations. "Keep the acid cool." If you don't define what "cool" is, readers will define it for themselves. Be specific: "Keep the acid at 45°F."

This can be a bit tricky when you don't have a statistical measure to attach. Consider these two statements:

*The column may tilt if not anchored firmly.*

*The column must be anchored in concrete for stability.*

The first statement is vague because of the word "may." The second statement is specific because of the word "must." Choose your words precisely, with a conscious understanding of their meanings.

Be especially careful with so-called weasel words: *may, might, could, should, ought to, probably, usually.* We often use these common words interchangeably. Don't. Each has a precise meaning of its own.

---

### ELASTIC LANGUAGE

Vagueness isn't always bad. In fact, it's often desirable. It can make a policy or procedure more elastic, such as: "Supervisors may approve alternate schedules at their discretion."

The key is to use vague words only when you mean them. Never use them by accident or through force of habit.

---

## Developing a Rhythm

Word misers and word masters also develop one other skill: composing. They develop rhythm in their documents.

Rhythm is what keeps readers reading. It holds the attention and actually improves comprehension. And it comes from two sources: consistency and parallelism.

## Consistency

Remember the rule that said you should never use the same word ten times in a row? Forget that rule. It's the opposite in most policies and procedures. Varying your words often confuses the reader. Consider the following:

*Step 1. Turn the lever one stop to the right.*
*Step 2. Rotate the lever to the off position.*

How is "turn" different from "rotate"? Readers may waste valuable time and effort trying to figure out if there's a distinction.

Use the same word to describe the same action or object throughout the section or document. Pick a verb and stick with it:

*Step 1. Turn the lever one stop to the right.*
*Step 2. Turn the lever to the off position.*

Creativity doesn't count in policy and procedure writing. Consistency and clarity do.

## Parallelism

This is one of the most powerful writing techniques you'll ever master. And there's nothing mysterious or difficult about it. It simply means using the same grammatical format for like items. Consider this procedure:

1. *The part is removed.*
2. *Repair the part.*
3. *The part shall be replaced.*

It sounds strange and awkward, and the sole reason is that it's not parallel. The three steps use different grammatical constructs. They change from present to future tense, from passive to active voice and back again. Make them parallel and it's much easier to read:

1. *Remove the part.*
2. *Repair the part.*
3. *Replace the part.*

The procedure now has a rhythm that's easy to follow. And all we did was apply several word miser rules uniformly to each statement (use present tense, use active voice, start with an action verb).

## Being Correct

Even with all these techniques, it's still possible to lose the reader. Send out a policy or procedure with one error in grammar or usage, and that's all some people see. They circle the mistake and hang the document on the bulletin board so others can enjoy the joke.

Incorrect language in a policy or procedure isn't just an innocent little joke. It reduces the document's credibility (and doesn't do much for yours, either). It can cause confusion, misinterpretation, and mistakes.

So while we are setting aside some of the old rules, remember that we're not throwing them all out. Continue to observe the basics of good grammar. You must still be sure that:

- Subjects and verbs agree.
- Spelling is correct.
- Words are used properly. (Is it "affect" or "effect"?) See the List of Problem Words (4-5) at the end of this chapter.
- Pronouns are used properly. ("The operator starts the engine unless he or she sees signs of damage," not "The operator starts the engine unless they see signs of damage").
- Placement is correct. ("The engineer only operates the equipment.") See the Guidelines on Misplacement (4-6) at the end of this chapter.
- Gender-neutral language is used where appropriate. See the Guidelines for Avoiding Sexist Language (4-7) at the end of this chapter.

The good news is that you don't have to remember everything yourself. There are software programs, such as Grammatik, Right Writer, and Correct Grammar, that monitor grammar, spelling, and agreement for you. Many check fifty or more different grammar rules and remind you of the proper style for the document.

And all good writers keep some sort of style guide handy, such as *The Chicago Manual of Style* or Shipley and Associates' *Style Guide*.

## Considering the Reader

Writers have to understand the audience before the audience can understand the words. The audience analysis you did before you started writing (see Chapter 2) becomes a crucial factor in choosing the right words.

### Don't Assume Anything

One of the biggest mistakes writers make is to assume that readers will understand. And we don't even realize we've done it.

*Hammer the nail into the wall.*

Sounds simple enough, but this statement assumes that readers know which hammer, which nail, and which wall. It even assumes that readers know which end of the nail should be pointed toward the wall. You may be thinking, "Well, they certainly should know or they shouldn't be doing this." True. But "should" doesn't count in policies and procedures. All that counts is reality.

## Look at the Reader's Experience

Go back to your original audience analysis and look at experience levels. Will you have brand-new users with no experience? Will you have experts with twenty years of experience? Will you have both groups side by side?

The diversity of user experience poses a challenge, but the rule is simple: Visualize the least experienced user and write for that person.

## Use Jargon Carefully

We live in an age of jargon, with thousands of acronyms and abbreviations floating around. One policy statement started off like this:

*In accordance with the requirements of the ADA, we will make all reasonable accommodations.*

A reader sincerely wanted to know why the American Dairy Association had control over the company's accommodations. (The policy writer was thinking of the Americans with Disabilities Act.)

Don't presume that terminologies are common just because *you* know them. And don't get caught up in faddish language. Some readers like it, but it offends a lot of people. Consider these three factors when you use jargon:

1. It's dangerous to assume that all readers really are familiar with it. Analyze the audience carefully.

2. Jargon is often long and complicated-sounding, especially in technological subjects. It can be cumbersome and hard to read. If you can find a plainer way to say it, do.

3. Some jargon is just plain pompous. Legitimate words and phrases become fads. People think they sound better (translation: fancier). So words that have a specific application start showing up where they don't belong:

*We encourage employees to interface with other departments in the performance of this procedure.*

Sounds mysterious, unpleasant, and maybe even illegal. You don't really want employees to interface with other departments; you want them to *work* with other departments.

---

### Jargon Can Be Good

There's nothing inherently wrong with jargon. It's often useful. When all readers are familiar with it, it saves time and space. But *all* readers must be familiar with it. Not most, and not many. All.

---

## Distinguish Between Users and Readers

In the analysis step in Chapter 2, we noted that the audience usually contains two distinct groups: users and readers. Users have to implement the policy or procedure, while readers scan the document for general information. Users have to take direct action; readers don't.

The rule here is simple: Write for the user. It isn't that you're ignoring the readers. Their needs are important, but the users' needs must take precedence.

---

### Writing for the Boss

Writing for users sounds logical, but there's a hidden trap. One of the biggest groups of readers is management. And whom do we often write to please? The boss. We accidentally end up writing for readers instead of users. Take the boss into account, but remember that you need to write primarily for users.

---

## Calculate Reading Level

By some estimates, well over 50 percent of today's workforce reads below a ninth-year level. Education, experience, and language barriers are all factors, and you must consider them as you write.

The sixth- to eighth-year reading level is a reasonable range for many policies and procedures. It's the same reading level used by most newspapers and is good as a general guideline. However, you have to adjust the reading level up or down for your audience and material.

Reading level corresponds with simplicity and shortness. The shorter and simpler the words and sentences are, the lower the reading level. Most grammar software packages and many word processors assess the reading level for you with built-in formulas.

To calculate reading level manually, use the Gunning Fog Index. Developed more than three decades ago, it's a simple mathematical formula. Take a short sample paragraph, and count the number of sentences and long words. Then do a bit of quick math. The final figure tells you the reading level of the paragraph. The Fog Index formula and a sample calculation are at the end of the chapter in the Formula for Calculating Reading Level (4-8).

## Word Documents Carefully

Do as much as you can to avoid words that provoke unpleasant reactions. Avoiding words and phrases that are known to bother people increases receptivity and reduces resistance. See the List of Words That Turn People Off (4-9) and the Guidelines for Avoiding Negativity (4-10) at the end of this chapter.

# Using Special Techniques for Procedures

Procedures require special precision. A procedure that's misunderstood can result in injury, death, or severe damage. It can lead to decertification or loss of license. As a result, several special writing techniques have evolved to help produce the high level of clarity needed.

## Start With an Action Verb

This rule also applies in policies, but it has special significance in procedures. Procedure users don't want theory or background. They want the writer to tell them one thing: what to do. The verb answers that question and is the first thing readers want to see. Compare the following:

*As you begin, be sure you have Parts A and B in front of you.*

*Locate Parts A and B.*

Which would you rather read? The first sounds friendly, but it's a waste of time. The phrases at the beginning of the sentence hide the information the reader's looking for.

The Verb Bank (4-11) at the end of this chapter gives you a list of short, common, effective verbs to choose from when writing your procedures.

## Use One Action per Step

This is a vital rule in procedures. Steps that contain more than one action confuse the reader and bury the message.

*After locating parts A and B, insert B into A while turning the handle to the left and tightening the screw.*

There's just too much going on in this sentence. There are actually five different actions in one so-called step. How do you know? Look for the action verbs. In this case, there are four action verbs: locate, insert, turn, and tighten. But the first one (locate) has two different objects (part A and part B), so it's really two separate steps. If we break the procedure down into one action per step, it looks like this:

1. *Locate part A*
2. *Locate part B*
3. *Insert B into A*
4. *Turn the handle to the left*
5. *Tighten the screw*

Easier and faster all around. However, there are two special considerations:

1. You can occasionally have more than one action per step. Consider steps 1 and 2 in the example above. If there are hundreds of parts and it could be difficult to locate each one, separating steps 1 and 2 makes sense. But if there are only two parts—A and B—in the entire process, it makes more sense to combine them:

1. *Locate parts A and B*

When combining actions, be sure the combination is simple and logical.

2. You must be careful of the relationship between actions. The original procedure—"insert B into A *while* turning the handle to the left"— implies that these two things must be done simultaneously. When you break actions into separate steps, question the relationship between the steps to be sure you don't accidentally alter the meaning.

See the Formula for Calculating Readability in Procedures (4-12) at the end of this chapter.

## Assign the Action

Readers want to know who's responsible for each step. If the procedure is written for a single user, such as instructions on setting a VCR, there's no need to assign the action. Whoever starts the procedure is expected to finish it.

But if multiple actors are involved, it's critical to clarify the responsibility. Name names, or you'll end up with something like this:

### *Payroll Procedures*

1. *Verify the hours worked and send to Payroll.*
2. *Record the hours worked.*

Who does step 1? Who does step 2? If you don't assign the actions, everyone assumes that someone else is supposed to do it. The following works much better:

### *Payroll Procedures*

1. *Departments verify the hours worked and send them to the Payroll Department.*
2. *The Payroll Department records the hours worked.*

---

### A Special Caution

Watch out for pronouns. They're perfectly legitimate to use, but they often cause confusion:

*Departments notify supervisors of new regulations. They are responsible for implementing and enforcing the procedures.*

Who is "they"—the departments or the supervisors? The best strategy is often to avoid pronouns and stick with proper nouns.

---

## Pack a Sentence

Readers tend to remember two things best: the first and last things they see. That's how memory functions. Therefore, the two most powerful positions in any sentence are the beginning and the end.

Packing a sentence is simply the technique of packing the punch where it does the most good in a sentence. Key words are placed first and last. This technique is meant for use in special cases, such as warnings and cautions. Consider these two warnings:

> *Warning:* Operation with wet hands can cause a shock hazard due to moisture seeping inside.

> *Warning:* Operation with wet hands may allow moisture to seep in and cause a shock hazard.

The first example starts with wet hands and ends with moisture seeping inside. But the power word, the one you want readers to remember, is "shock"—and it's hiding in the middle of the sentence, right where people are most likely to forget it.

The second example turns that around and leaves the reader with the important idea: a shock hazard.

## Choose the Right Format

It isn't easy to remember all these new habits, so choose a format that uses them by design. Playscript is the best and clearest format for most procedures involving more than one person or department. But outlining and lists can also work well. Let a good format help you fight the battle for clarity and brevity. The various formats are discussed, with examples, in Chapter 5.

## Chapter Summary

- Policy and procedure writing isn't like the writing most of us learned in school. It's a form of technical writing, and its purpose is to get the message across quickly and clearly. So a lot of the writing rules are different: no more long paragraphs, complicated sentence structure, or fancy vocabulary. You're after simplicity.

- Become a word miser, and eliminate everything that doesn't add meaning. Get rid of long words, empty phrases, flabby language, and excess adjectives and phrases. Use active voice and present tense.

- Become a word master, and use words with respect and precision. Get specific. Mean what you say and say what you mean.

- Create a rhythm by using consistency and parallelism. Your document will have a flow that's easy to follow, comfortable, and fast.

- Be correct in grammar and usage. Consider your audience as you make wording choices. And pay special attention to procedures, where the need for clarity is extremely high.

# Tools and Resources
# for Chapter 4

## 4-1: Wording Tip Sheet

### The Main Goal

☐ To create a message that's fast and clear

### The Main Problem

☐ Getting rid of old habits that cause us to use complicated language and vocabulary

### The Main Issues

☐ Recognizing that simple is good
☐ Being a ruthless, accurate word miser
☐ Being a precise word master
☐ Developing an easy rhythm
☐ Being correct
☐ Being both brief and clear

### The Key Techniques

☐ Active voice, present tense
☐ Common words
☐ Consistency
☐ Parallelism
☐ Saying what you mean and meaning what you say
☐ Short sentences and paragraphs
☐ Standard word order
☐ Writing as you would speak

### How to Word the Document

1. *Use active voice, present tense:*

   The shortest, clearest, most powerful message you can send in the English language is in active voice, present tense. Compare the following:

   > *The operator reports any accidents.*
   > *Any accidents will be reported by the operator.*

   *(continues)*

## 4-1: Wording Tip Sheet (*continued*)

In the second sentence, passive voice lengthens and makes it harder to figure out who's responsible for the action. The "who" now comes at the end of the sentence instead of the beginning. And when you switch to a verb tense other than present (the most common is future tense), you also add length.

The most significant problem with future tense is that it implies the action must be taken *sometime,* where present tense implies an immediacy. Stay with active voice and present tense most of the time.

*Note:* There are some exceptions. Certain procedures, such as software instructions, use passive voice to avoid endless repetition of "you" or "the operator."

2. *Use standard word order:*

Standard word order is active voice: subject-verb-object. It's standard precisely because it's the shortest, clearest way to convey a direct message. In policies and procedures, it's often best to make the subject an "implied" subject (leave it out and start with the verb). Both of the following sentences use standard word order, but the second sentence shortens by using an implied subject and starting with an action verb.

*Employees submit their timecards weekly.*
*Submit timecards weekly.*

The minute you deviate from standard word order, you begin to lengthen and generally add padding. Some variation in word order is desirable to prevent monotony. The problem is that we tend to get carried away with it and add too many fancy phrases and clauses, too much passive voice and future tense. The bulk of your writing should use standard word order.

3. *Use parallelism:*

Parallelism is a form of consistency that creates a rhythm in the document. It simply means using the same grammar construct for like items. Consider this nonparallel example:

*Read the document, be sure to sign it, and then it must be returned to Personnel.*

Nonparallel writing sounds awkward and stops the reader. It breaks the rhythm. Find the key concepts and put them into the same format. Use the same parts of speech (verb with verb, noun with noun). Use words or phrases of approximately the same length. The rhythm returns and the sentence is shorter:

*Read the document, sign it, and return it to Personnel.*

Use parallelism in sentences, paragraphs, lists, and headings. It applies everywhere and is one of the most important elements in making a document easy to read.

4. *Be consistent:*

Pick a few good verbs and nouns, then use them consistently. It may violate your vocabulary training, but it helps readers feel comfortable. They hate seeing a new word every time. It's just one more thing to cope with unnecessarily. Repetition of familiar, useful words increases both comprehension and speed.

5. *Use short words:*

The Gunning Fog Index defines a difficult word as any word of three syllables or more. Translation: Stick with words of one or two syllables. Short means fast and easy for the reader.

6. *Use common words:*

Don't get fancy. We really don't *utilize* a hammer, we *use* it. Common words are common for a reason: They work. Everyone understands them. They're fast and easy. And they're usually short.

7. *Use short sentences:*

The absolute maximum is twenty words, but even that's pretty long for this type of writing. Aim for a maximum of fifteen words

*(continues)*

## 4-1: WORDING TIP SHEET (*continued*)

per sentence; then, even if you occasionally run over, you're still OK. Short sentences help make sure that you're using standard word order and that you're not using too many extra clauses.

8. *Use short paragraphs:*

Use a maximum of one hundred words. Long paragraphs create a heavy, gray look that turns the reader off. If it looks long and complicated, readers assume it is.

In procedures, average paragraph length should be much shorter—forty words or fewer.

9. *Use lots of lists:*

Lists are a policy and procedure writer's bread and butter, a staple. They shorten, they force you into good habits such as active voice, and they encourage parallelism. They're also easy on the reader's eye because they indicate a flow and create lots of blank space on the page. Readers love lists. Writers should love lists. The whole world loves a good list.

10. *Write as you speak:*

This is probably the best way to avoid pompous language and windy phrases. But old habits keep telling you that it's not good enough to go on paper. In most cases, it's exactly what you do want on paper: simple, clear, to the point, and understood by everyone. Pretend a user has stopped by to ask you how to do something, then answer (yes, it's OK to talk to yourself). Write it down just as you would say it. Then edit out the words or phrases that seem too informal or trendy.

It's a lot easier to edit up from the spoken word than it is to edit down from the pompous language.

11. *Get rid of wordy phrases:*

We use them out of habit:
        *In an effort to . . . .*
        *In the event that . . . .*
        *In the eventuality of . . . .*

A lot of this comes from the increasing use of legalisms in our society. A lot of it also comes from that old habit of trying to please the teacher with more words. Ditch these phrases. See the List of Wordy Phrases (4-2) at the end of this chapter.

12. *Get rid of pompous language:*

Quit trying to impress. It does exactly the opposite. It sounds stuffy and overbearing and turns people off. No one really talks about "commercially hired rental vehicles." We talk about "rental cars." Come down to earth.

13. *Get rid of flabby language:*

Flabby language is just too much of a good thing. Where one adjective would do, we use three: "Use the proper, designated, authorized form." It's as if someone found the word trough and couldn't stop gorging. There are so many adjectives that the main idea gets lost. Remember to think in ones: One is better than two, and two is better than three. Avoid excess.

14. *Watch the adjectives:*

This is where a lot of the flab sneaks up on you. Adjectives are fun. They let you get creative and expressive. Unfortunately, that's not what your readers are interested in. Speed and clarity, not creativity and flowery description, are the goal. Keep an eagle eye on the number of adjectives.

15. *Get specific:*

One way to avoid flabby language is to be specific. Replace general descriptors with specific references:
**Use Form R-317b,**
*not*
**Use the appropriate request form.**

16. *Get rid of empty phrases:*

Empty phrases are usually found at the beginning of sentences or clauses:
*There are . . . .*
*It is . . . .*

It's OK to use them occasionally, but they often serve no purpose.

(*continues*)

## 4-1: WORDING TIP SHEET (*continued*)

17. *Watch out for weasel words:*

Weasel words are words that sound as if you're trying to wiggle out of a commitment: *Part A ought to fit into part B.*

Not likely to inspire much confidence in the reader, is it? Weasel words tend to destroy credibility. Most common are words like:

| | |
|---|---|
| could | probably |
| may | should |
| might | try |
| most of the time | usually |
| ought to | would |

18. *Use weasel words for flexibility where appropriate:*

Weasel words aren't always bad. They can make your statement elastic. Many policy statements in particular need to retain flexibility. Such statements are intended to cover normal operating conditions, not every conceivable circumstance that may arise. Rather than try to spell out everything, which is impossible, summarize those other circumstances:

*In extreme conditions, management may take alternative action. Operators should try every standard remedy to correct the situation. If these fail and danger appears eminent, operators may take evasive action. An operator must believe that the danger is real and unavoidable. He or she should also exercise the best possible professional judgment in light of the circumstances.*

19. *Avoid "turnoffs":*

Some words and phrases just make people mad. They include:

| | |
|---|---|
| absolutely | of course |
| always | persist |
| delinquent | terminate |
| fail | tolerate |
| never | unfortunately |
| obviously | |

Any word or phase that's rigid or sounds like a parent disciplining a child will turn readers off. If you use harsh words and phrases, have a good reason. Then be prepared for the reaction. See the List of Words That Turn People Off (4-9) at the end of this chapter.

| | | |
|---|---|---|
| 20. | *Avoid redundancies:* | We're in the habit of using so many words that we don't realize we're repeating ourselves unnecessarily. "Advance planning," for instance. How can you plan for the past? "Almost perfect." Really? "Reread again." Hmmm . . . . Remember your new status as a word miser and get rid of these nonsensical phrases. See the List of Redundancies (4-3) at the end of this chapter. |
| 21. | *Conquer problem words:* | Everybody has some word pair that's always been a puzzler. Is it *affect* or *effect? Lie* or *lay? Ensure, insure,* or *assure?* Make a list of your personal puzzlers and work with them every day until you conquer them. At the very least, review your list before you start to write. See the List of Problem Words (4-5) at the end of this chapter. |
| 22. | *Watch out for jargon:* | Jargon is simply language that's specialized for an organization or field. It saves time and space for people who are in the know. The danger is that some readers may be left out. So simplify. If there's any way to write it in plain language, do. Remember that even if jargon doesn't confuse, it usually lengthens.<br>    *Note:* This depends, too, on your audience. If the policy or procedure is for chemists in a laboratory, they're expecting the jargon. They want and need it, so use it. |
| 23. | *Use transitional words and phrases at the start of sentences and paragraphs:* | These words give readers an instant clue about what's coming. They serve two functions: speed and preparation. When readers see the word "and," they know the paragraph is a continuation. If they see "but," they know an exception is coming. If they see "finally," they know the discussion is winding up. In a split second, you've given them the |

*(continues)*

## 4-1: WORDING TIP SHEET (*continued*)

chance to prepare themselves mentally for the content ahead.

Ignore the old rule that said you should never start with a transitional word like "and." Remember, that's the rule for narrative writing. Ditch it in favor of speed and clarity. See the List of Transitional Words and Phrases (4-4) at the end of this chapter.

24. *Use one-sentence paragraphs:*

We all know the old rule said never to do this. Forget that rule. One-sentence paragraphs draw instant attention and help you isolate the most important statements in the policy and procedure:

*Any violation of safety rules is grounds for immediate dismissal.*

It's hard to miss the message.

25. *Limit the number of clauses and phrases:*

Clauses and phrases are dangerous. Used in moderation, they provide needed variety. But they're a little like rabbits: Turn your back and they seem to multiply in seconds. One phrase turns into three or four. Too many clauses and phrases are a dead giveaway that your sentences are too long and complicated. One, maybe two are OK. Anything more than that is highly suspect.

26. *Keep clauses and phrases short:*

You may occasionally need a lengthier clause of ten words or so. But the general rule is five words or fewer.

27. *Start with a verb:*

Readers want to know what they're supposed to do or know, so tell them with the very first word. This also helps eliminate long sentences, excess clauses, passive voice, inverted word order, and wordy phrases:

*A written request for a leave of absence, stating the specific reason, the duration of the leave, and the expected beginning and ending dates of the leave, should be submitted to your manager for approval.*

Whew! Readers who make their way through that deserve a medal. *Look for the verb.* Here it's "submit." Restructure the procedure around that and look what happens:

> *Submit a written request for leave to your manager. Include the following information:*
> - *The reason for the leave.*
> - *The length of the leave.*
> - *The beginning and ending dates of the leave.*

See the Verb Bank (4-11) at the end of this chapter.

28. *Avoid negative wording:*

Grammatical negatives make the message harder to understand:

> *Users should not be concerned if they are unable to meet these requirements without assistance.*

Is there an interpreter in the house? Grammatical negatives are opposites. They twirl readers around and point them in the other direction. Do it too often and users get dizzy. Focus on what you want them to do instead of what you want them not to do. See the Guidelines for Avoiding Negativity (4-10) at the end of this chapter.

*Note:* Negatives are perfectly legitimate words when used sparingly and properly. They convey important information clearly:

> *Do not add oil.*
> *Do not wait to submit your claim.*

The goal is to avoid misuse and overuse.

29. *Avoid misplacement:*

Misplaced words, phrases, or sentences change the meaning. They can be merely frustrating, but they can also be harmful. What does "it" refer to here?

> *When adjusting the valve in the engine, be sure it is shut off.*

See the Guidelines on Misplacement (4-6) at the end of this chapter.

(continues)

## 4-1: WORDING TIP SHEET (*continued*)

| | |
|---|---|
| 30. *Use gender-neutral language:* | The great sexism debate still rages. Some readers are highly offended by the use of "he" and "she." Others think it's all a tempest in a teapot. Still, it's a sensitive issue that reduces the document's credibility and increases reader resistance. It can also become one more point in a legal debate. Err on the conservative side. See the Guidelines for Avoiding Sexist Language (4-7) at the end of this chapter for alternative wordings. |
| 31. *Use an appropriate level of detail:* | How much do you really have to tell the reader? It depends solely on the audience and the purpose of the policy or procedure. If you have varied experience levels, you need more detail. If everyone is a Ph.D. in chemistry, you may need less detail. Analyze your audience carefully. |
| 32. *Use an appropriate reading level:* | A good range for policies and procedures is sixth- to eighth-year reading level. This is roughly the same range used by most newspapers, and your purpose is much the same as theirs: speed and clarity.<br><br>Reading level is basically a matter of simplicity. The shorter the words and sentences, the lower the reading level and the faster users can read. If you use all the techniques in this chapter, you'll automatically reduce the reading level. See the Formula for Calculating Reading Level (4-8) at the end of this chapter. |
| 33. *Analyze the audience:* | You have users and readers. You have experience and inexperience in both groups. Education, background, and expectation level may vary widely. Who your audience is, and what they're used to, helps you decide questions such as reading level, level of detail, and jargon. |
| 34. *Remain impartial:* | This may sound odd, but what happens if you have to write a policy or procedure you strongly disagree with? Your writing tends to reflect your disagreement. The tone becomes |

harsh and judgmental, short and choppy, or perhaps long and flowery in an attempt to cover up the disagreement. It's perfectly OK to disagree. Work to change the policy or procedure if you want. If you can't, try venting in writing. Draft a memo with all the reasons the policy or procedure is stupid or trite. Then throw the memo away. Just don't let your feelings affect your judgment as a good writer.

35. *Read out loud:*  When you've finished writing a section, read it out loud. If it sounds pompous or stilted, it probably is. The ear catches rough spots the eye misses. Better yet, have someone else read it. A fresh eye and ear are the ultimate test.

36. *In procedures, use one action per step:*  Procedures require special clarity. A misunderstanding can turn deadly. Limiting each step to one action ensures that the reader gets the message clearly. Look for the action verbs, then list one per step.

37. *In procedures, start with the verb:*  Procedure users want to know only two things: steps and sequence. Tell me what to do and in what order. Action verbs get to the heart of the matter and eliminate excess wording—no more searching. Use the more than one hundred common verbs in the Verb Bank (4-11) at the end of this chapter.

38. *In procedures, assign the action:*  Don't assume that people know who's responsible at each step. Clarify by adding titles. Avoid pronouns. (Who is that ubiquitous "they," anyway?) If your audience analysis shows that a single actor will complete the entire process, you only need to identify the responsible party once. But many policies and procedures require at least some interdepartmental activity. When responsibility shifts, make it clear. See the various procedure formats in Chapter 5.

39. *In procedures, pack a sentence:*  This is a good technique for warnings and cautions. Put the punch where people will remember it most: at the beginning and end of the sentence. Example 2, next page,

*(continues)*

## 4-1: WORDING TIP SHEET (*continued*)

is much stronger because the sentence was packed:

> *During repairs, there is a danger of electric shock if the power is not turned off.*

> *Turn off the power during repairs, or you may receive an electric shock.*

## 4-2:  LIST OF WORDY PHRASES

Wordy phrases merely clutter up your documents. Short phrases are much clearer. Use the clear phrases in the right-hand column rather than the dressed-up versions in the left-hand column.

| *Wordy* | *Succinct and Clear* |
|---|---|
| a large number of | many |
| ahead of schedule | early |
| at all times | always |
| at an early date | soon |
| at the present time | now |
| due to the fact that | because |
| during the time that | while |
| for the purpose of | for |
| in accordance with | by |
| in as much as | since |
| in light of | because |
| in many cases | often |
| in order to | to |
| in regard to | regarding |
| in the event of | if |
| in this day and age | today |
| in view of the fact that | because, since |
| it is clear that | clearly |
| made a statement saying | said, stated |
| prior to | before |
| take appropriate measures | act |
| take into consideration | consider |
| until such time as | until |
| with reference to | about |
| with regard to | regarding |
| with respect to | about |

## 4-3: LIST OF REDUNDANCIES

Redundancies are just unnecessary repetitions that take up space and serve no purpose. Stick to the simpler words in the right-hand column below.

| *Redundant and Repetitious* | *Simple and Precise* |
| --- | --- |
| absolutely essential | essential |
| advance planning | planning |
| any and all | all |
| appear to be | appear |
| appointed to the post of | appointed |
| as to whether | whether |
| attach together | attach |
| close proximity | near, close |
| continue on | continue |
| definite decision | decision |
| desirable benefits | benefits |
| each and every | each, all |
| end product, end result | product, result |
| filled to capacity | filled, full |
| final outcome | outcome |
| first priority | priority |
| full satisfaction | satisfaction |
| general public | public |
| invited guest | guest |
| joint cooperation | cooperation |
| major breakthrough | breakthrough |
| merged together | merged |
| month of September | September |
| more superior | superior |
| mutual cooperation | cooperation |
| on a daily basis | daily |
| one and only | only |
| one and the same | same |
| past history | history |
| period of time | period, time |
| plan ahead | plan |
| repeat again | repeat |
| root cause | cause |
| single unit | unit |
| surrounding circumstances | circumstances |
| throughout the entire | throughout, during |
| usual customs | customs |

## 4-4: LIST OF TRANSITION WORDS AND PHRASES

Transition words and phrases literally change the reader's thinking from one subject or purpose to the next. Use them at the beginnings of sentences and paragraphs to give a clear and immediate clue to what's coming next.

When going on to a new paragraph, always decide what you're trying to do: add, continue, contrast, end, illustrate, paraphrase, or something similar. Know where you're taking your reader.

Develop your own list of favorite transitions, using these as a start.

| | | |
|---|---|---|
| ☐ | *To add:* | also, and, in addition |
| ☐ | *To continue:* | also, and, in addition, next, then |
| ☐ | *To draw a conclusion:* | because, consequently, since, so, therefore |
| ☐ | *To end:* | finally, so, since, consequently |
| ☐ | *To explain:* | because, since, due to |
| ☐ | *To illustrate:* | for example, for instance |
| ☐ | *To paraphrase:* | or, so, in other words |
| ☐ | *To reverse or contrast:* | but, yet, still; although, however, nevertheless |
| ☐ | *To show direction or sequence:* | first, second, third (etc.); next, then |
| ☐ | *To show similarity:* | as, like |

## 4-5: LIST OF PROBLEM WORDS

Certain word pairs are commonly abused, misused, and confused. Every writer struggles with something different. Learn the proper usage, develop memory tricks, or look up your problem words each time. Know and conquer your personal puzzlers.

| Word | Meaning |
|------|---------|
| accept | to admit or agree; to regard as normal or usual, true, or right; to take in stride [*a verb*] |
| except | to exclude; an exception to [*a preposition*] |
| affect | to influence, to pretend (*a verb*) |
| effect | a result (*a noun*), to accomplish or bring about (*a verb*) |
| all ready | all is ready; in a state of readiness |
| already | existing, completed |
| all right | [*correct form*] |
| alright | [*incorrect form*] |
| advise | to offer suggestions |
| inform | to provide information |
| between | for two things [*as a general rule*], for three or more items if each item is considered individually |
| among | for more than two things [*as a general rule*] |
| biweekly | once every two weeks |
| semiweekly | twice each week |
| can | is able to, is capable of |
| may | has permission to |
| compliment | to praise; to say something favorable, kind, or flattering |
| complement | something making up a whole; work in accord with; suit well |
| continual | repeated frequently, lasts but with breaks or pauses |
| continuous | without interruption |
| discreet | prudent, knowing when to be silent |
| discrete | separate, disunited, discontinued |

| | |
|---|---|
| further | more, additional |
| farther | distance |
| fewer | a number |
| less | a quantity or volume |
| imply | to suggest or hint [*done by the speaker*] |
| infer | to surmise or conclude [*done by the listener*] |
| insure | to protect [*used with finances*] |
| ensure | to guarantee |
| assure | to pledge or make safe [*used with people*] |
| lie | to recline in a prone position [*used with people*] |
| lay | to put or place [*used with objects*] |
| like | similar to [*a literal comparison*] |
| as | in the same degree or amount |
| precedents | [*plural of* precedent, *meaning* a standard or norm, *or* a significant event that is a turning point] |
| precedence | precedes or comes first; takes priority over; comes before |
| principle | a fundamental law, doctrine, or assumption [*a noun*] |
| principal | most important or influential [*an adjective*] |
| regardless | in spite of, without concern |
| irregardless | [*no such beast—please don't use it!*] |
| stationary | solid, unmoving |
| stationery | a piece of paper |
| that | [*preposition used with a dependent clause that contains essential information—hint, no commas*] |
| which | [*prepositions used with an independent clause that contains nonessential information—hint, commas*] |
| will | to promise, to require to |
| shall | to make an absolute promise (a stronger form of *will*)— [*Note: These two words can be dangerous legally. See Chapter 3 for an explanation of how promises can become implied contracts. Use these two words with great care in policies and procedures.*] |

## 4-6: Guidelines on Misplacement

### The Problem

Misplaced words and phrases are a word master's worst nightmare. Words in the wrong place alter the meaning, often significantly.

It can be funny. There was the organization that announced a new child-care policy:

*For those of you who are parents and don't know it, nursery care is now available.*

Or the happy mother who notified an official agency of the recent birth of twins:

*In accordance with your instructions, I have given birth to twins in the enclosed envelope.*

All of this is very funny—until it pops up in a procedure. Consider what might happen:

*When adjusting the valve in the engine, be sure it is shut off.*

What will the user shut off—the valve or the engine? Chances are good that you'll have readers attempt some of both. And the sole reason is a misplaced pronoun: the little word "it." It's not clear what "it" refers to here.

Grammatically, "it" refers to the noun "valve." (It may seem like it should be engine, but it's not. Although engine is the closest noun, it's just part of a prepositional phrase that modifies the word *valve.*) So what the writer has really said is this:

*When adjusting the valve in the engine, be sure the valve is shut off.*

Can't you picture someone reaching into a running machine engine to shut off the valve? If the procedure isn't clear, you can bet there will be someone out there who thinks that's what it really means. And when that person files a lawsuit for damages, who do you think will win?

Misplacement is a serious, even dangerous, problem. Be constantly alert for it. It's easy to overlook one little sentence in the middle of a huge project, but one little sentence with poorly placed words is all it takes to cause real trouble.

**The Solution**

The best solution to misplacement is:

- ☐ To use standard word order of subject-verb-object
- ☐ To break sentences down into short, simple, direct statements starting with action verbs

Look what happens to our confusing and possibly dangerous procedure now:
*Shut off the engine. Adjust the valve.*

A word miser's joy. A word master's delight.

Sometimes, though, such ruthless elimination isn't possible. What do you do then? Ask yourself:

- ☐ Is every noun and every pronoun immediately and immaculately clear in its reference?
- ☐ Could there be any possible alternate interpretation based on this wording?

It's a good idea to avoid pronouns whenever you can, since they're often the biggest culprits.

**The Special Case of the Word *Only***

The word *only* warrants special attention solely because it shows up in so many policies and procedures. Its placement must be exact or readers will, without question, misinterpret it. Pay special attention each time you use it to make sure the meaning is precise:

**The engineer only operates the equipment,**
  *not*
**Only the engineer operates the equipment.**

The first says that all the engineer does is operate equipment. The second says that the engineer is the sole person who operates the equipment.

## 4-7:  GUIDELINES FOR AVOIDING SEXIST LANGUAGE

This is the great pronoun debate: "he" versus "she." Some readers don't care at all. Others are offended by any appearance of sexism in a document. It's best, for both practical and legal reasons, to avoid that appearance. Stay with gender-neutral language as much as possible.

None of the options are ideal, but any combination of them may work effectively. Experiment with them. The best option is to eliminate gender reference whenever possible.

1. *Use plurals:* This is one of the better options you have. *Not*
   **The manager submits his request,**
      *but*
   **Managers submit their requests.**

2. *Eliminate the pronoun altogether:* This can be done by substituting articles ("a," "the") or eliminating the pronoun or article completely. This is also one of your better options. *Not*
   **When the employee requests her leave,**
      *but*
   **When the employee requests leave . . .**

3. *Substitute another noun for the pronoun:* You can substitute another noun ("one") or repeat the proper noun. It works in some cases, but it usually sounds awkward. *Not*
   **An associate may submit a claim at any time. He may also submit a secondary claim as needed,**
      *but*
   **An associate may submit a claim at any time. One may also submit a secondary claim as needed,**
      *or*
   **An associate may submit a claim any time. An associate may also submit a secondary claim as needed.**

4. *Use disclaimers:* This can be very effective in a handbook or manual because it eliminates the need for lengthy, cumbersome wording over hundreds of pages. Unfortunately, it doesn't eliminate the sensitivity, and some users still react strongly to the continued use of gender-related pronouns.

*We have used the words "he," "his," and "him" when the meaning includes "she," "her," and "hers." This wording is used solely for ease of reading and should not be interpreted as gender bias.*

5. *Use some form of "he/she":*

This should be a last resort. A slash in the middle of a word isn't normal English and is disruptive. It draws the reader's attention to the pronoun when it should be elsewhere: on the verb (action) or noun (result). All of the following options draw undue attention to the pronoun, and all lengthen the document when used repeatedly:

*It is the employee's responsibility. He/she should . . .*

*It is the employee's responsibility. S/he should . . .*

*It is the employee's responsibility. (S)he should . . .*

*It is the employee's responsibility. He or she should . . .*

It's also possible to alternate "he" and "she" throughout the document. Use this technique with great caution, though. Readers, largely due to their own sensitivities, often perceive that one form is used more frequently than the other. In addition, consider the case of the woman who skipped a section of her handbook because the pronoun used was "he"—and she thought it didn't apply to her!

## 4-8: FORMULA FOR CALCULATING READING LEVEL

Have you ever looked at a policy or procedure and realized that only a Ph.D. in advanced robotics could understand it? It's written for a reading level somewhere out in the stratosphere.

What's appropriate for your document depends on your audience (background, experience, expertise) and the nature of the material itself (length, complexity). In general, a good reading level for policies and procedures is between the sixth and eighth grades.

Use the Gunning Fog Index to determine reading level.

### *The Gunning Fog Index*

1. Select a sample paragraph of approximately one hundred words.
2. Calculate the average sentence length in the paragraph.
   - Count the number of sentences.
   - Count the number of words.
   - Divide the number of words by the number of sentences.
3. Count the number of difficult words in the paragraph (defined as words of three syllables or more).
4. Add the results of steps 2 and 3 together.
5. Multiply by a factor of .4.
6. The resulting number is the reading level of the paragraph.

### Example

*If the bad sector table cannot be read, a backup table (B) is checked. If Bad Sector Table B cannot be read, or if the results of the second checksum of Bad Sector Table B differ from the results of the original checksum, no bad sector table information will be available in the reserved hard disk area. If you run FORMAT on a partition of this disk, the command will assume that the disk has no bad sectors and will format the disk without avoiding the bad sectors. If you use DETECT on the disk, it will find no bad sector table to which it can append new bad sectors. Therefore, DETECT will search the disk for all bad sectors and create a new bad sector table.*

| | |
|---|---:|
| Number of words in paragraph: | *127* |
| Number of sentences in paragraph: | *÷5* |
| Average sentence length: | *25.4* |
| Number of difficult words: | *+5* |
| Total: | *30.4* |
| | *×.4* |
| Paragraph reading level: | *12.16* |

## Comment

☐ A reader would have to have a twelfth-grade reading level—almost a college reading level—to understand this paragraph. That's very high for most purposes. Looking at the Gunning Fog Index results tells us that the problem isn't long words, it's long sentences. Break them down and the reading level will come down significantly.

## 4-9: LIST OF WORDS THAT TURN PEOPLE OFF

It's impossible to avoid unpleasantness altogether. Some policies and procedures will simply be unpopular. But your choice of wording can influence for good or ill, can antagonize or smooth. Certain words and phrases have been proved to turn people off. Here are some of them.

☐ Absolutes:      Absolutes are words that brook no exceptions for any reason. The very rigidity is what alienates readers. They're words like:

       *Absolutely*
       *Always*
       *Never*
       *Without exception*

An even bigger problem is that you usually don't really mean them. They turn out to be exaggerations, as in the following:
*We never give refunds. We always give credit vouchers.*

Are you sure? Are you positive that absolutely no one in any location has ever given anyone a refund for any reason? Even a 50¢ refund? You'd better be. Because all it takes is one exception, and the whole policy is out the window. If I can show that you gave a 50¢ refund to someone three years ago, I win. It's usually better to hedge your bet and err on the conservative side. It's possible to be firm and definitive without being absolute:
*It is our store policy to give credit vouchers. We do not give refunds.*

Use absolutes with great caution. The most appropriate use is when mistakes have serious consequences:
*Never smoke near the oxygen tanks.*

Absolutes are frequently and appropriately used in policies and procedures related to production, health, safety, heavy equipment operation, and medical matters.

☐ The word *obviously:*      This is tantamount to writing, "Dear Stupid . . . ." Readers take offense at being considered dense. If it were obvious, why would you have to say it? There is no substitute phrasing. Get rid of this word. *Not*

> **The operator should obviously report any such incidents,**
> > *but*
> **The operator should report any such incidents.**

☐ The words *easy* or *simple:*

This is a lot like saying "trust me." The minute people hear it, they assume the opposite. It smacks of insincerity, and it's only the writer's opinion anyway. If you have to say it's easy, it isn't. Eliminate these words completely. *Not*

> **Follow these five easy steps,**
> > *but*
> **Follow these five steps.**

☐ Harsh phrases, such as "If you persist in. . . ." or "We won't tolerate. . . .":

Feels as if you've just been called on the carpet in the principal's office. Don't treat adults like children or they'll start behaving that way.

In some cases you may mean to send a harsh message, as in this example:

> *We will not tolerate sexual harassment. It is grounds for immediate dismissal.*

But at other times you should search long and hard for alternative wording. *Not*

> **Employees who persist in taking extended breaks . . . .**
> > *but*
> **Employees who take extended breaks . . . .**

☐ Loaded words:

Certain words are like pointing a loaded gun at readers. They draw a strong negative reaction from most people, so use them only when you can't find an alternative word or phrase.

Add your own loaded words or instant turnoffs to this list. Each organization has its own sensitivities. Know what they are for your readers and avoid them.

*(continues)*

## 4-9: LIST OF WORDS THAT TURN PEOPLE OFF (*continued*)

- Delinquent
- Fail
- Inflexible
- Neglect

- Of course
- Problem
- Terminate
- Unfortunately

_____     _____

_____     _____

_____     _____

_____     _____

## 4-10: GUIDELINES FOR AVOIDING NEGATIVITY

No, this isn't to make readers feel good. Avoiding negative words and phrases does two things:

1. *It makes the material easier to understand:*

Grammatical negatives confuse the eye. They're all the *not* and *un-* words: *none, never, not, can't, won't, don't, unable, unwilling.* They're perfectly valid words but should be used sparingly because of their very strong impact. Some studies indicate that it's almost 50 percent harder to get the meaning when the writer uses negatives. Consider the following:

> *If you have a valid reason for not obtaining the proper signatures, your inability to meet the deadline won't prevent you from filing the claim.*

There are only three negatives in this statement, but who can figure out what it really means? By changing the wording to positive action, you get a much clearer picture:

> *You may still file the claim so long as you have a valid reason for the lack of proper signatures. This is true even if you miss the deadline.*

2. *It reduces resistance and bad feelings:*

Nobody likes to constantly be told not to do this and not to do that. We would all much rather be told what *to* do than what *not* to do.

Yet policies and procedures are often written because something has gone wrong, and you're supposed to tell people to stop doing it. You're given a mandate to write a "don't" policy or procedure instead of a "do" policy or procedure.

This gives the document a negative tone. Readers will resist that tone more than they do the actual content. Which of

## 4-10:  Guidelines for Avoiding Negativity (*continued*)

the following would you accept more readily?

> *For privacy reasons, employees should not attempt to gain access to another employee's e-mail messages without the latter's express written permission,*
> or
> *An employee may access another employee's e-mail messages. For privacy reasons, anyone doing so must have prior written permission from that person.*

> *Purchase orders over $500 cannot be approved by departmental supervisors,*
> or
> *Purchase orders up to $500 can be approved by departmental supervisors,*
> or
> *Purchase orders over $500 are approved by the Purchasing Agent.*

### Avoiding a Negative Tone

There are no formulas for eliminating negative wording. The best trick is this: Once you know what you want people to stop doing, ask yourself what you want them *to* do or what they *can* do.

There's almost always something, even if it seems minor. For instance, you may want them to stop spending too much time on breaks. So what is it you want them *to* do? Spend the designated time only. Say it that way. *Not*

**Employees may not exceed the allotted break times. Violators will be disciplined,**
   *but*
**Employees must observe scheduled break times under all conditions. Violations will be grounds for disciplinary action.**

You can be firm and communicate a clear message without being unnecessarily negative. But you must focus on what you want people *to* do instead of what you *don't* want them to do.

## 4-11: VERB BANK

Never stare at a blank page again, wondering where to start. Use this list of action verbs that are common in policies and procedures. They're all good, simple, honest verbs. They're also a word miser's delight, since most are only one or two syllables long.

Remember not to get carried away and try to use them all. Pick a few good ones for each application and stick with them. Consistency is just as important as simplicity.

| | | | |
|---|---|---|---|
| accept | distribute | maintain | restrict |
| aid | e-mail | make | review |
| approve | encourage | measure | rotate |
| ask | enforce | notify | schedule |
| assist | enter | obtain | select |
| attach | evaluate | open | send |
| buy | examine | operate | separate |
| charge | explain | participate | serve |
| check | fax | pay | show |
| claim | file | place | sign |
| close | fill out | plan | sort |
| compile | find | prepare | start |
| complete | finish | protect | submit |
| connect | follow up | prove | test |
| conserve | forward | provide | tighten |
| contact | gather | pull | total |
| contract | give | purchase | transfer |
| control | help | push | turn |
| correct | hold | read | use |
| decide | inspect | receive | validate |
| delete | issue | record | verify |
| deliver | install | reject | wait |
| describe | interview | release | weigh |
| detach | jog | remove | withdraw |
| determine | keep | repeat | write |
| develop | list | report | |
| discuss | mail | request | |

## 4-12: FORMULA FOR CALCULATING READABILITY IN PROCEDURES

The Gunning Fog Index helps determine the approximate reading level of your document, but in procedures you need more than that. You also need to minimize the number of actions per step. The following formula can help you determine whether you're in reasonable shape. Remember the basic rule: one action per step.

1. Count the number of steps in the procedure.
2. Count the number of action verbs in the procedure.
3. Divide the number of action verbs by the number of steps.
4. If the number in step 3 is higher than 1.5, check the steps to see if they can be broken down further.

**Example**

1. *After locating parts A and B, insert B into A.*
2. *While turning the handle to the left, tighten the screw.*

> Number of steps:             2
> Number of action verbs:      4
> 4 (action verbs) ÷ 2 (steps) = 2.0

This shows two full actions per step, indicating that the procedure needs to be broken down. It should come as no surprise when readers are slow or get confused.

Now see what happens when the procedure is rewritten:

1. *Locate parts A and B.*
2. *Insert B into A.*
3. *Turn the handle to the left.*
4. *Tighten the screw.*

> Number of steps:             4
> Number of action verbs:      4
> 4 (action verbs) ÷ 4 (steps) = 1

This shows only one action per step, which is what you're looking for.

# 5

# Is There a Certain Format I Should Use?

Writers often ask for the best format for policies and procedures. Unfortunately, that's like asking, "What's the best policy to have?"

There is no answer to either of these questions. In both cases you have a number of options, and in both cases your decision depends on what you're trying to achieve.

## Beginning to Determine Format

The best format for you depends entirely on whom you're writing for, what kind of material you're dealing with, and whether management accepts the format. What's good for one definitely isn't good for all.

### Format and Audience

Always ask yourself who your audience is. Who will read the document, scanning for general knowledge? Who will have to use or implement the contents? Then consider whether your audience has any preferences.

Certain formats seem to work better with particular audiences. Flowcharts, for instance, are often favored by engineers, scientists, and others with a technical background. Since they use this format often, they're accustomed to it and like it. Many of them prefer it even for very simple procedures.

On the other hand, readers without a technical background are often overwhelmed by all the symbols and arrows of a flowchart. They merely see a lot of confusing clutter and tend to prefer a standard narrative format.

The simple fact is that readers respond better to formats they're used to and are comfortable with. New or unfamiliar formats throw the reader off at first and require an adjustment period.

However, the mere fact that a format is new to readers doesn't make it a bad choice. Never use an ineffective format just because it's familiar or traditional. Switching to a new one may be both helpful and necessary, but be sure you consider readers' preferences and expectations when you do.

Consider their reactions as well. If you do opt for an unfamiliar format, make time to introduce it and explain it to the readers. You'll also have to field questions—and the inevitable complaint or two.

One final note of caution: If you're writing policies and procedures that must be approved by an outside licensing, accreditation, or regulatory body, you may not have a format choice. Certain certifications, for instance, such as those in the medical field or for ISO 9000, may require you to develop very precise information or even use prescribed formats.

Organizations that find themselves in that situation have occasionally been known to create parallel documents, one in the required format and another in a more user-friendly format for common reference. While this is considerably more work, it may be worth the time and effort if it increases clarity and reduces frustration for the readers.

---

### A BALANCING ACT

Choosing a format isn't a matter of personal preference. It's a question of what best suits your application. Balance the nature of the material against the needs of the audience, including management.

---

## Format and Material

The nature of your information narrows your format options. For instance, safety procedures require absolute clarity, total comprehension, and immediate compliance. Errors can be deadly. You therefore want a format that's visually distinct, clear at first glance, and makes the material look easy to comprehend.

In such cases, a standard narrative format, with regular sentence and paragraph structure, won't help the reader much. It will appear to be just a lot of words without any visible priority or structure. An outline or flowchart format would make the information both clearer and easier to access.

On the other hand, if you're explaining the organization's overall commitment to safety in a general policy statement, a standard narrative format is the better choice.

Procedures are typically very detailed and precise and lend themselves better to formats like flowcharts and playscripts. The standard narrative format works better with general information and policy statements. Some formats, such as the outline, can serve either purpose and work well in combination with other formats.

Examine the nature of the material closely before you settle on a format. Is the material lengthy and complicated or short and relatively simple? Is it full of statistical, quantifiable, precise data? Or is it more general in nature? Will it be used step by step or for quick reference? Choosing the best format is easier when you know what makes sense for the material.

The Format Options Chart (5-1) at the end of this chapter gives general guidelines on which formats to use with which types of material.

## Format and Management

Since upper management authorizes the policies and procedures, it must also understand and support the document and its contents. If you want to adopt a format that management is not comfortable with, explain it to the managers, present your reasons for choosing it, and get approval. You must ensure their comfort level, which is just as important as that of other readers.

---

PAGE LAYOUT AND THE READER

A good page layout standardizes basic information that's important for the reader to know. The same information is in the same place all the time. This standardization makes readers feel more comfortable: a quick glance and they can identify the type of document and the nature of the material immediately.

---

## Deciding on Page Layout

This is a good time to stop and consider another important issue: the overall design of your page. No matter which format(s) you choose for the body of the text, there are certain fundamentals that need to be standardized in the page layout.

The page layout gives the reader certain basic information about the policy or procedure, such as title, number, or effective date. The purpose is quite simply to tell readers what they're looking at and to tell them fast. The page layout can also identify information that's critical to proper use, such as revision status or who's covered.

A substantial amount of this information is usually at the top of the page in what are known as headers. The full header typically appears on the first page of the policy or procedure, and a shortened version appears on subsequent pages. See the sample header in Example 5-1.

Other page layouts include both headers and footers (standardized information at the bottom of a page). This is usually done when the information you're standardizing is substantial and placing it all in a header would make the page look top-heavy. See the sample footer in Example 5-2.

In yet other page layouts, certain parts of the text itself are standardized. These typically include short sections such as purpose, scope, background, or required equipment. They're placed at the beginning of the text, immediately preceding the policy or procedure itself but out-

**Example 5-1.** A sample header.

| Subject: | | No.: Page ___ of ___ |
| Applies to: | Effective date: | Supersedes: |
| | | |

**Example 5-2.** A sample footer.

| | | |
| Review No.: | Review date: | Page    of |

side the header. They're brief and are usually written in standard narrative format.

The amount and types of information you standardize are up to you. The simplest layout is just a title at the top of the page, consistently placed. Or you might choose to include title, date, page number, and policy or procedure name or number.

Many organizations also standardize a great deal of other information as well: the responsible party or department, issuer, authority, issue date, effective date, revision information, distribution, and so on. Virtually anything you wish can go in the page layout.

However, the goal is to keep it simple so that the standardized information doesn't detract attention from the policy or procedure itself. A clean, clear look to the page layout avoids clutter and makes the page more inviting to the reader's eye.

Choose information that you consider important for the reader to know about the document. Restrict it to basics that identify the document (title and number), orient the reader ("supersedes"), and ensure proper use of the document ("page 3 of 8"). Once you decide what the readers need to know about the document, you simply decide where and how to place it on the page. Remember, the goal is to make it easy to see without distracting the reader. Users should be able to scan the page layout quickly, then focus immediately on the body of the text.

See the Page Layout Tip Sheet (5-2) at the end of this chapter for details and examples.

## Choosing Among Format Options

Once you've decided on a page layout, you're ready to choose a format for the main text. You have several primary options: narrative, outline, playscript, or flowchart. These are known as primary formats because they're the mainstay of the document. They are often used in combination with each other.

You also have several secondary format options: question and answer, troubleshooting, matrix table, and list. They're known as secondary formats because they can be inserted into the document's main format at any time to help explain or clarify the material. Occasionally a primary format such as a flowchart is also used as a secondary format.

Remember that once you choose a primary format, you must use it consistently throughout your document. Moving back and forth between formats confuses readers and gives the document a jumbled, disconnected look. Establish your primary format, then use secondary

---

THE FORMAT OPTIONS

| *Primary Formats* | *Secondary Formats* |
| --- | --- |
| ▪ Narrative | ▪ Question and answer |
| ▪ Outline | ▪ Troubleshooting |
| ▪ Playscript | ▪ Matrix table |
| ▪ Flowchart | ▪ List |

---

formats only when they help to clarify the information or to speed readers on their way.

## Using the Primary Formats

Most of the primary formats are well known. Some, such as narrative and outline, are so familiar that we use them without even recognizing them as official formats. Others, such as playscript, are not as well known but are extremely effective.

The following descriptions are brief introductions to each primary format. The Tools and Resources at the end of this chapter give details and examples for each one.

### Narrative

This is the standard sentence-and-paragraph style that we all learned in school. Standard narrative format is usually a single column of unbroken print running from left to right on the page. See Example 5-3 for a sample narrative.

Two-column narrative formats are also common and are used to break up solid horizontal lines of print so that the material is easier to read. Depending on the nature of the material involved, some organizations successfully use a three-column arrangement.

Narrative format is more often used for policies than for procedures. Procedures, especially those that are highly detailed, require the clarity between steps that is created by greater visual separation. It's best to use narrative when the material is general in nature or is simple or short.

Narrative is not effective with complex, difficult, or lengthy mate-

**Example 5-3.**  A sample narrative.

> ### STORE CLOSING POLICY
>
>    Closing the store is an important responsibility. We take great pride in the appearance of our stores, and evening closing activities play a large part in that appearance. We also expect all closing activities to be conducted with the same professionalism and decorum as if a customer were in the store.
>
>    When the store closes for the evening, all employees are to direct their activities toward closing out the register and/or cleaning the store. Register closing duties will be rotated, with assignments made by the manager at the start of the shift. Those who are not responsible for register closing are expected to vacuum, straighten shelves and racks, replace merchandise, and generally clean the store in preparation for opening the following day.

rial. Line after line of unbroken print makes it hard to focus on the key information and discourages the reader from continuing.

See the Narrative Tip Sheet (5-3) at the end of this chapter for details on this format.

## Outline

The outline format is really just a variation on the standard narrative format. The text is simply separated into distinctly shorter sections and subsections, all clearly labeled. Example 5-4 shows a sample outline.

Sections are typically identified with numbers, letters, or an alphanumeric combination. Alphanumeric combinations are the most common because they show more levels more clearly. Some outlines also use side headings or margin captions to distinguish further between sections.

This format can actually vary widely. Some outlines use lengthy narrative in each section, while others use extremely short narrative that almost verges on being a list. The type of material you're working with determines which is more appropriate. Just bear in mind that for the reader, short is always faster and easier than long.

Outline format is used in both policies and procedures. It's logical and easy to follow. It identifies basic steps or groupings at a glance. It also gives the reader a quick, clear guide and a sense of the relative importance of each item by indicating which information is subordinate

**Example 5-4.** A sample outline.

---

LOG-ON PROCEDURE

1. Turn on the computer.

2. Enter your assigned security code and press any key.

    a. If you've misplaced or can't remember your code, call the Data Processing Manager.

    b. If entry is refused, try your code again.

        b-1. If entry is still refused after three tries, contact your manager.

3. Enter the file name and press the return key.

    a. A complete list of files is available in hard copy in the file room, or by calling up the directory on the disk.

---

and which is primary. And it allows readers to reference the document later by section or paragraph number.

See the Outline Tip Sheet (5-4) at the end of this chapter for details on this format.

---

WHY READERS LIKE OUTLINES

The value of the outline format is in the immediate sense of order and logic it conveys. At first glance, readers can tell the basic grouping and flow of the information. Where narrative format can seem to be merely a mass of words, the outline format breaks the material down into visually distinct units.

---

## Playscript

The playscript format is excellent for procedures that involve more than one person or department. The concept is remarkably simple: Like the script of a play, it's formatted by actor. The first thing the user sees is the name or title of the person who is supposed to take the action.

In its simplest form, a playscript has two columns. The first column tells who's responsible (the actor), and the second column describes

**Example 5-5.** A sample playscript.

| DRAFTING DEPARTMENTAL PROCEDURES | |
|---|---|
| *Responsibility* | *Action* |
| Writer | 1. Draft the procedure.<br>2. Review and correct the draft.<br>3. Circulate the draft to others for review:<br>   a. Supervisor<br>   b. Department head<br>   c. Designated users |
| Supervisor, department head, users | 4. Review draft for errors in content.<br>5. Mark corrections to content on the pages.<br>6. List major problem areas, if any, on a separate sheet of paper.<br>7. Return to writer within one week. |
| Writer | 8. Make final corrections. |
| Department head | 9. Approve final version. |

what's required (the action). The steps in the second column are in sequence, just as they would be in any other format. Example 5-5 shows a typical playscript.

This, however, is only the simplest form of a playscript. This format can be adapted for very complicated procedures involving many different actors, whether they're individuals, departments, or entire organizations. It can also be used as a secondary "if . . . then" format and is sometimes called the action format.

Playscripting's visual clarity makes it remarkably fast and easy to find information. Those who have used it like it because of its speed and clarity. Steps remain clear and sequential, but readers have an instant visual clue that takes them directly to the information that's most relevant to them.

When you use playscript for the first time, explain it briefly to the readers. It's foreign to most of them, but it takes only a few minutes for them to understand it. After one or two uses, most readers are enthusiastic advocates. When asked to choose between a narrative format and a playscript format for an export procedure, users at one food company unanimously voted for the playscript.

Playscript is highly recommended for virtually any procedure with more than one actor or responsible party. It is not appropriate for policies or simple, one-actor procedures. (For procedures with only one actor, stick with outlining.)

See the Playscript Tip Sheet (5-5) at the end of the chapter for details on this format.

---

### WHY USERS LOVE PLAYSCRIPTS

The real value of playscripting is that it quickly and clearly answers that most fundamental of reader questions: What am *I* supposed to do? Readers can spot their name or title in seconds. At the same time, it gives the reader a sense of the overall procedure and where he or she fits into it.

---

## Flowchart

A flowchart is a diagram of a process. It uses symbols and arrows to indicate flow and action. There are a number of standard symbols that are commonly used. A box or rectangle, for instance, usually represents an action; a diamond or triangle typically represents a decision or "if" point. Many organizations develop their own symbols with specific interpretations. Example 5-6 shows a sample flowchart.

Flowcharts are more commonly used in procedures than in policies, but they may be used in either. An organization chart is, in fact, a type of flowchart. Some flowcharts that contain significantly more narrative than others are referred to as narrative flowcharts.

The danger in flowcharts is that they can easily become cluttered and hard to read, with too many different symbols, too much text, or crisscrossing arrows. It requires great care to construct a good flowchart. It's often better to break one large flowchart into several smaller ones.

See the Flowchart Tip Sheet (5-6) at the end of this chapter for details on this format.

## Using the Secondary Formats

Secondary formats are those that are usually used as inserts inside the primary format. They can stand on their own as primary formats in some highly specialized documents, but this usage is relatively infre-

**Example 5-6.** A sample flowchart.

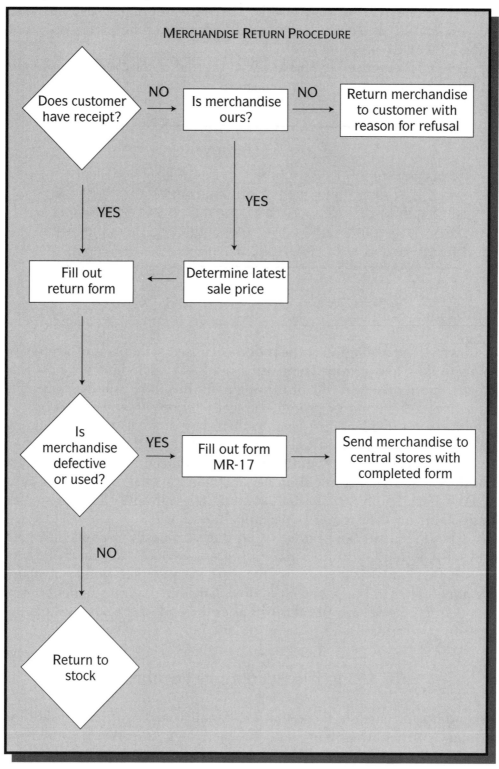

---

WHO LIKES A FLOWCHART?

Audiences with a technical background tend to favor flowcharts simply because they use them frequently. Nontechnical readers tend to ignore them or skim over them.

---

quent. There are four secondary formats: question and answer, troubleshooting (or help), matrix table, and list.

These formats summarize, clarify, or expand on the information in the body of the text. Their main purpose is to deal with:

- Other possibilities that may arise ("what if . . ." situations).
- Special conditions that may exist ("if . . . then" situations).

In addition, the secondary formats create fast, easy, permanent reference tools. They're easy to find because they stand out from the body of the text on the page or are separate sections altogether.

The descriptions that follow are, again, brief introductions. Details and examples of each of the secondary formats are in the Tools and Resources at the end of this chapter.

## Question and Answer

Question and answer sections are used in both policies and procedures and may be in either a narrative or table format. They're used to address items that are of particular concern to readers, and they usually contain questions that would be commonly asked by the majority of users. See Example 5-7 for a sample question and answer section.

Question and answer sections simulate a personal conversation and are generally well received. They're usually worded very informally to help readers feel more comfortable with both the content and the writing.

Question and answer sections are a good place to address the concerns you know many readers have about the policies and procedures you've written. Think about the most skeptical users, the naysayers. What doubts are they likely to raise? What questions are they likely to have? List those concerns with a short response in this section. This action addresses important issues and helps establish the document's credibility.

**Example 5-7.** A sample question and answer section.

CUSTOMER SERVICE

Q: *What if the customers get belligerent?*

A: First make every reasonable attempt to calm the customer down. It's important to listen to every customer, even an irate one. In fact, it's especially important to listen to unhappy customers, since they're the ones who make us better at what we do. Hear the customer out. Sometimes it's just a matter of their needing to vent. Remember, it's not personal. If that doesn't work, or if the customer is out of control, interrupt the exchange. There are three methods you can try:
   1. Ask the customer to come with you to another location nearby that's private. Move in that direction as you speak.
   2. Offer to get another representative or a manager.
   3. Tell them that you'll be happy to talk with them when they've calmed down, then move away.

Q: *What if a customer seems suspicious or even dangerous?*

A: Call security immediately, then contact the manager on duty. Keep an eye on the customer until help arrives, but don't confront the person or endanger yourself or anyone else.

See the Question and Answer Tip Sheet (5-7) at the end of this chapter for details on this format.

## Troubleshooting

Troubleshooting sections are also called help sections and sometimes reference sections. They're used primarily in procedures so that users aren't forced to reread the entire document to get on-the-spot help when

BEING REALISTIC

There is one condition that's essential if question and answer sections are to be effective: They must address questions readers really have, not those that management thinks they should have. If these sections aren't realistic, readers will ignore them.

**Example 5-8.** A sample troubleshooting section.

| ENGINE NOISE | | |
|---|---|---|
| *Symptom* | *Possible Causes* | *Solutions* |
| 1. Grinding noise | a. Loose belt | a-1. Tighten the belt and check for damage |
| | b. Worn belt | b-1. Replace the belt |
| | c. Torn belt | c-1. Replace the belt |
| | d. Oversize belt | d-1. Replace the belt |
| 2. Whirring noise | a. Broken fan blade | a-1. Replace the blade |
| | | a-2. Replace the whole fan |
| | b. Missing filter | b-1. Install new filter |

there's trouble. These sections don't deal with standard operating procedures. They deal with breakdowns or exceptions. Example 5-8 shows a sample troubleshooting section.

One of the biggest concerns of a user who's troubleshooting is speed. How do I stop the leak *now*? How do I answer the client's question *now*? For that reason, troubleshooting sections are often presented in a chart format, where each problem is listed individually along with the corresponding solution. However, narrative and list formats are also common.

Question and answer sections can also be used as troubleshooting sections, but they're generally not as effective. Users don't want to play "twenty questions" when they're in trouble. They want to skim down a page, locate their problem, and find an answer that will fix it. Their need is specific, unusual, and immediate.

See the Troubleshooting Tip Sheet (5-8) at the end of this chapter for details on this format.

## Matrix Table

Matrix tables connect one variable ("if *x* happens . . .") to a second variable ("then do *y*"). One variable is placed at the top of the chart, called the box head. The second variable is placed on the left side, called the stub.

The body of the table is ruled off and divided into boxes or squares

**Example 5-9.** A sample matrix table.

| FORMS FOR REPORTING MATERIAL PROBLEMS | | | | |
|---|---|---|---|---|
| | *Form* | | | |
| *Problem* | *P-12* | *A-131* | *R-6* | *F-32* |
| Critical materials shortage | | X | | |
| Major materials overage | | | X | |
| Defective materials | | | | X |
| Incorrect materials | | | | X |
| Late delivery of materials | X | | | |

known as data cells. Then the appropriate data cells are marked or Xed out to indicate what action should be taken. Readers scan the top and side of the table for the pertinent variables, then look to see what cells are marked. Example 5-9 shows a sample matrix table.

Matrix tables are an excellent format to use when readers need to refer repeatedly to the information *periodically* over time. At a glance, readers can tell what to do, how to do it, and when or under what conditions to do it. The matrix eliminates the need for constant rereading and searching.

Matrix tables also have a wide application. They can be used to help readers make a decision, use the proper forms, know which step of a process they're involved in, understand a schedule, follow simple instructions, or comprehend work distribution.

See the Matrix Table Tip Sheet (5-9) at the end of this chapter for details on this format.

## List

Use the list format often, then use it even more often. To a policy and procedure writer, it's like manna from heaven.

The reason is that the eye loves a list. Lists have wider margins and indentations. Line length is shorter, and excess wording is eliminated. Long paragraphs are broken up, and serial information is highlighted.

**Example 5-10.** A sample list.

USING THE WORD-PROCESSING PROGRAM

1. Boot the disk.
2. Enter your code.
3. Click on the word-processing symbol.

In short, lists break the denseness of the printed page and let the eye skim quickly. The reader gets the impression that the information is relatively easy to grasp and use. Example 5-10 shows a sample list.

Most of us think of a list as merely an indented group of related items. That's a standard list, called a displayed or vertical list, but there are other types. There are paragraph lists, nested lists, and parenthetical lists. One of them will fit almost any need.

Lists also permit you to become a word miser. They can be short or long, containing one word per item or a half-page per item, but they're still shorter than a narrative. You can take shortcuts that would sound odd in a regular sentence. Leave out the subject and start with the verb. Leave out articles ("a," "an," "the"). Use partial sentences or only key words.

The main purpose of a list is to shorten, organize, and clarify. The list should therefore be only as long as it needs to be to contain the information, and as short as possible.

See the List Tip Sheet (5-10) at the end of this chapter for details on this format.

A CAUTIONARY NOTE ABOUT LISTS

It's easy to get carried away with lists. We all love a good list, but having twenty-five lists in the space of a three-page procedure is overdoing a good thing. It creates a choppy look and feel. To avoid this problem, use variations such as the paragraph list. Then look at the finished draft with a critical eye to make sure that use of that list isn't excessive.

## Combining Formats

As mentioned earlier, all the different formats are often combined. If carefully done, such combinations can be very effective.

Suppose you have a policy that's written in a narrative format but contains an occasional procedure within the text of the policy. Rather than continue the narrative format throughout the procedure portion, change to a playscript or an outline for that section.

The same is true of all the primary formats. You can switch among them as needed for clarification. Be especially cautious with flowcharts, however; they create such a dramatic visual break that they should be used with great care as a secondary format.

Some documents use the combination approach as a standard. You might decide, for instance, to place policies and procedures together in one page layout. The policy statement will almost always be in standard narrative format at the beginning, but the procedures that follow may be standardized in playscript or outline form.

---

### MINIMIZE THE CONFUSION

Confine your use of different formats only to those that are necessary for clarity. Random or excessive change in format creates a consistency problem: It breaks the rhythm and becomes overwhelming. Keep it as simple as possible. Avoid unnecessary format switches.

---

## Experiments and Hybrids

None of these formats is sacrosanct. Experiment with them, modify them, and adapt them to your needs. Invent new combinations. It's all a search for better ways to communicate important information with clarity and speed.

One writer had an audience with a large number of technical users and an equally large number of nontechnical users. The technical people loved flowcharts, but the nontechnical people hated them. Her solution? Playscripts in which each step in the right-hand column was a flowchart. (See Example 5-11.)

You can combine virtually any format option with any other option.

**Example 5-11.** An experiment in hybrids (a combination of a playscript and a flowchart).

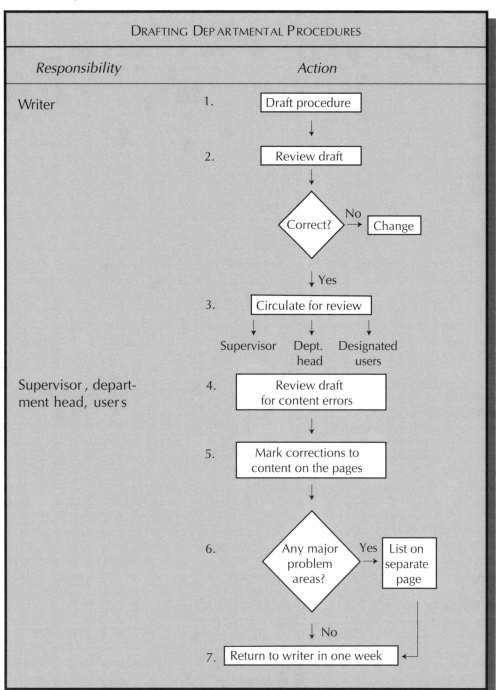

**Example 5-12.** A cross between a playscript and a matrix table.

| Limited Purchase Order (LPO) Procedure | | |
| --- | --- | --- |
| *$25 or less* | *$25.01 to $500* | *Over $500* |
| **Requester** 1. Get cash from petty cash. 2. Turn in receipt(s). | 1. Complete LPO form #267 (see p. 27). 2. Route LPO to supervisor. | 1. Purchase requisition is required. Contact Purchasing Agent. |
| **Requester's supervisor** | 3. Review LPO in accord with purchasing procedures. 4. Approve and sign LPO. 5. Route LPO to Purchasing Department. | |
| **Purchasing department** | 6. Date stamp LPO. 7. Log LPO. 8. Review for correct computation. 9. If incorrect, return to requester's supervisor. 10. Separate copies and forward per instructions on LPO. | 2. Get required information from requester on proposed purchase. 3. Review for appropriateness. 4. If approved, process according to standard Purchasing Department guidelines. 5. If not approved, return to requester with an explanation. |
| **Accounting department** | 11. Log LPO. 12. Assign payment code. 13. Return to requester. | |
| **Requester** | 14. Transmit LPO to vendor. | |

One group of writers revised a purchase order procedure and ended up with a cross between a playscript and a matrix table (shown in Example 5-12). Use your imagination and dabble with the possibilities.

## Chapter Summary

- The format is a key ingredient in readability, but there is no one "best" format. Consider the material, the audience, and management, then choose the best format for your application.

- Primary formats are the mainstay of the document. There are four of them: narrative, outline, playscript, and flowchart.

- Secondary formats are usually inserted into the primary format to clarify particular information. There are also four secondary formats: question and answer, troubleshooting, matrix table, and list.

- It's common to combine formats. However, be careful not to overdo it and end up with so many different visual formats that the document gets cluttered and the reader gets confused.

- None of the formats is sacrosanct, so experiment with any combination or hybrid that works for you.

# Tools and Resources
# for Chapter 5

## 5-1: Format Options Chart

Certain formats are better suited than others to certain types of policies and procedures. This table helps you choose the format option(s) that are most appropriate to your material. Remember, though, to consider all relevant factors before you decide on a format (the nature of the material, reader preferences and expectations, and management support).

| | Format | Policy | | Procedure | |
|---|---|---|---|---|---|
| | | *Short or Simple* | *Lengthy or Complex* | *Short or Simple* | *Lengthy or Complex* |
| | Single-column narrative | X | | X | |
| *Primary* | Multicolumn narrative | | X | X | |
| *Primary* | Outline | X | X | X | X |
| *Primary* | Playscript | | | X | X |
| *Primary* | Flowchart | X | | X | X |
| *Secondary* | Question and answer | X | X | X | X |
| *Secondary* | Troubleshooting | | X | | X |
| *Secondary* | Matrix table | | X | | X |
| *Secondary* | List | X | X | X | X |

## 5-2:  PAGE LAYOUT TIP SHEET

### Reader Preferences

☐ This depends on what readers are used to. All they want is a clear, concise layout that gives relevant information fast and that is used consistently.

### Best Use

☐ In individual policies and procedures that are part of a grouping.
☐ In manuals and handbooks.
☐ Whenever you want to convey standardized information to the user.

### Other Uses

☐ All policies and procedures should have some form of intentional page layout. Even if it's only a title at the top, use it consistently.

### Format Variations

| | | |
|---|---|---|
| ☐ *Header:* | Short, standard pieces of information placed at the top of the page, usually in blocks. |
| ☐ *Header-footer:* | Short, standard information placed in blocks at both the top and the bottom of the page. Used to prevent a top-heavy look when there's too much information to fit well in only a header. |
| ☐ *Text:* | Lengthier blocks of standardized information (e.g., purpose, scope, equipment) that are located outside the header, usually at the beginning of the document's text. Commonly used when policies and procedures are combined in one format. Sections are usually brief paragraphs, but they can be lists. |

### Rules for Use

| | | |
|---|---|---|
| 1. *Select the information to be standardized:* | Decide what information is necessary or helpful to the users. Headers and footers may include: |

☐ Subject or title     ☐ Revision vs.
☐ Effective date         new issue
☐ Page no.               ☐ Document no.
☐ Responsible unit    ☐ Issue date
☐ Superseded by      ☐ Forms used
☐ Revision             ☐ Issuer
   information        ☐ Distribution

Information in the text may include:

☐ Purpose      ☐ Policy or procedure
☐ Scope         ☐ Background
☐ Authority     ☐ Content/overview
☐ Definitions    ☐ Applicability

2. *Decide what should go in the header:*

Information in the header is primary and is the first thing the reader sees. Identifiers such as title, number, and effective date always go in the header.

3. *Decide whether to use a footer:*

Footers usually include reference items that are less critical (e.g., revision date, revision number). Use footers when there's too much information to fit in a header. Just be careful: Footers can constrict the page and make it look cluttered.

4. *Decide whether any information belongs in the text:*

Standardized sections of any length belong outside the header. They're placed at the beginning of the document, immediately before the body of the policy or procedure. These sections can be further distinguished by visual means such as indenting the text blocks.

5. *Keep it simple:*

The layout shouldn't call attention to itself. It's there just to give basic information and move readers quickly to the gist of the policy or procedure. Resist the temptation to include too much.

6. *Consider whether to box in the entire page:*

Some love this format, others hate it. The advantage: It creates a structured look. The disadvantages: It can look heavy, and less information fits on the page. If you use a box, the rules (lines) should be light so as not to draw emphasis away from the text.

*(continues)*

## 5-2:  PAGE LAYOUT TIP SHEET (*continued*)

| | |
|---|---|
| 7. *Create a shorter version of the header for subsequent pages:* | Multiple pages still need identification. Abbreviate the information from the main header on the first page. |
| 8. *Don't put the approver's signature in the layout:* | Although lots of layouts have one, a signature can make the document appear out of date or suspect. Individuals come and go, but policies and procedures remain. (Suzanne Lambert may have approved the policy, but she left three years ago—therefore, readers may assume that it's old and should be ignored.) The approver's signature is an administrative formality. Keep it in the file for reference only, not in the layout. |

### Comments

☐ Page layout is the first thing readers see. A clean layout encourages reading, a cluttered one discourages it. Experiment with different combinations of header, footer, and text. Keep the lines simple and the information minimal. Page layouts are a tool for visual clarity, but the real focus of the document is the policy or procedure itself.

### Examples

Main Headers

| Subject: | | No.: | |
|---|---|---|---|
| | | Page ___ of ___ | |
| Applies to: | Effective date: | Supersedes: | |
| | | | |

| Section: | | SOP No.: | |
|---|---|---|---|
| Subject: | | Effective:<br>Page: | |
| Applies to: | | ___ New Issue<br>___ Partial Revision<br>___ Complete Revision | |

| Manual: | Regulation No.: |
|---|---|
| Subject: | |

Headers for Subsequent Pages

| Subject *(continued)*: | Effective Date: | No.: |
|---|---|---|
| | Page ___ of ___ | |

| Subject: *cont.* | Page ___ of ___ |
|---|---|

*(continues)*

## 5-2: Page Layout Tip Sheet (*continued*)

Footers

| Revision No.: | Supersedes: | Date: |
|---|---|---|

| Revision No.: |
|---|
| Revision Date: |

Page Layout With Header, Footer, and Standardized Text

| Subject:<br><br>Covers: | Policy No.:<br>Page No.:<br>Effective: |
|---|---|

| Purpose: | The purpose of this policy is to xxxxxxxxxxxxxxxxxxxxxx xxxxxxxxxxxxxxxxxxxxxxxxxxxxxxxxxxxxxxxxxxxxxxxxxxxxx xxxxxxxxxxxxxxxxxxxxxxxxxxxxxxxxxxxxxxxxxxxxxxxxxxx. |
|---|---|
| Scope: | This policy applies to all situations where xxxxxxxxxxx xxxxxxxxxxxxxxxxxxxxxxxxxxxxxxxxxxxxxxxxxxxxxxxxxxx. |
| Background: | This policy has been established because xxxxxxxxxxx xxxxxxxxxxxxxxxxxxxxxxxxxxxxxxxxxxxxxxxxxxxxxxxxxxxx xxxxxxxxxxxxxxxxxxxxxxxxxxxxxxxxxxxxxxxxxxxxxxxxxxxx xxxxxxxxxxxxxxxxxxxxxxxxxxxxxxxxxxxxxxxxxxxxxxxxxx. |
| Policy: | 1. All members of the ABC organization are responsible for<br>xxxxxxxxxxxxxxxxxxxxxxxxxxxxxxxxxxxxxxxxxxxxxxxx<br>xxxxxxxxxxxxxxxxxxxxxxxxxxxxxxxxxxxxxxxxxxxxxxxx<br>xxxxxxxxxxxxxxxxxxxxxxxxxxxxxxxxxxxxxxxxxxxxxxxx<br>xxxxxxxxxxxxxxxxxxxxxxxxxxxxxxxxxxxxxxxxxxxxxxxxx. |

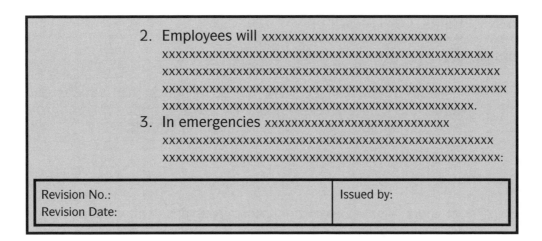

## Page Layout With Sample Boxes and Page Measurements

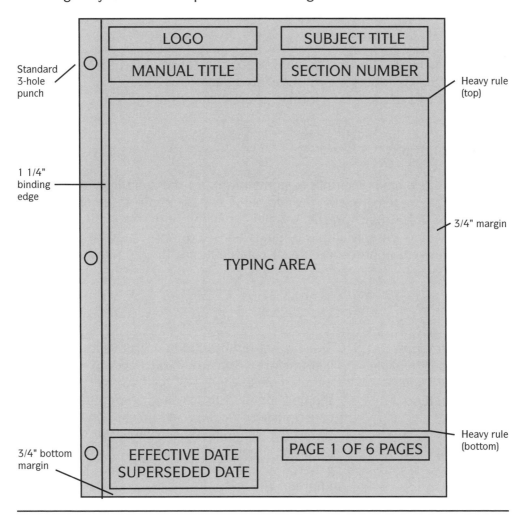

## 5-3: NARRATIVE TIP SHEET

### Reader Preferences

- [ ] Generalists and managers like narrative better than experts and technicians do. However, everyone is basically comfortable with narrative format because it's the style taught in schools.

### Best Use

- [ ] For short, simple information; short groupings of information.
- [ ] For general policies.
- [ ] For short blocks of standard information in the page layout (purpose, revision dates, and so on).

### Other Uses

- [ ] In narrative flowcharts (abbreviated narrative).
- [ ] In matrix tables (very abbreviated narrative).
- [ ] As part of an outline format (short blocks of narrative).

### Format Variations

- [ ] *Multicolumn:* Multiple columns break up the solid line of print and make reading easier. Two columns are common, three slightly less so. More than three is usually confusing and should be used with extreme care. Multiple columns are used more frequently in procedures, or in procedure-policy combinations, than in policies.

### Rules for Use

1. *Structure your thinking and your material:* The biggest temptation in narrative format is just to start writing, but you'll end up with a jumbled mess. Ideas will be disconnected and the flow lumpy. This is called stream-of-consciousness writing, and unless you plan to be the next William Faulkner, don't try it. Organize, organize, organize. Plan and prewrite the same way you would with any other format (see Chapter 2).

2. *Keep it short and simple:*  Be a word miser. Use short sentences, short paragraphs, and short words. See Chapter 4 for the rules on clear, concise wording and grammar. Observe every one of them, from sentence length to parallelism.

3. *Design it well:*  Make it look fast and easy. Break up the text whenever possible. See Chapter 6 for guidelines on making the page easy to read. Observe all of these guidelines, from the use of white space to color.

## Comments

☐ Be careful not to fall into the lengthy prose style we all used to get good grades in school. You may be using a narrative format, but you're engaging in technical writing. The members of your audience want information, not Shakespeare, and they want it without lengthy prose.

Study and use all the preparation techniques in Chapter 2, the wording techniques in Chapter 4, and the design elements in Chapter 6. Skillfully mixed together, they relieve the drudgery of page after page of unbroken text.

Pay special attention to the tightness with which you construct each paragraph and sentence. It's tempting to include everything, but leave it out unless it adds meaning or clarity for the reader. Ask yourself what readers need to know and what they want to know, then eliminate excess detail and language.

Multicolumn formats help avoid these problems. They force your sentences and paragraphs to be shorter and your wording more concise.

*(continues)*

## 5-3: Narrative Tip Sheet (*continued*)

**Examples**

Standard Single-Column Narrative

> STANDARD VEHICLE MAINTENANCE
>
> NEUTRAL START SWITCH ADJUSTMENT
> IN AUTOMATIC TRANSMISSIONS
>
> Be sure the manual linkage is properly adjusted first, then check the starter engagement circuit in all positions. The circuit must be open in all drive positions and closed only in park and neutral.
>
> Remove the screws and plates that hold the selector lever handle to the lever. Remove the handle and detent control (Figure 3). Then remove the screws from the rear of the console top panel. Pull the panel back to unhook it from the front of the console and remove the panel.
>
> Loosen the combination starter neutral and backup light switch screws (Figure 7). Then move the selector lever back and forth until the gauge pin (#33 drill) can be fully inserted into the gauge pin holes (Figure 10).
>
> Place the transmission selector lever firmly against the stop of the neutral detent position.

Two-Column Narrative

> STANDARD VEHICLE MAINTENANCE
>
> NEUTRAL START SWITCH ADJUSTMENT IN
> AUTOMATIC TRANSMISSIONS
>
> Be sure the manual linkage is properly adjusted first, then check the starter engagement circuit in all positions. The circuit must be open in all drive positions and closed only in park and neutral.
>
> Remove the screws and plates that hold the selector lever handle to the lever. Remove the handle and detent control (Figure 3). Then remove the screws from the rear of the console top panel.
>
> Pull the panel back to unhook it from the front of the console and remove the panel.
>
> Loosen the combination starter neutral and backup light switch screws (Figure 7). Then move the selector lever back and forth until the gauge pin (#33 drill) can be fully inserted into the gauge pin holes (Figure 10).
>
> Place the transmission selector lever firmly against the stop of the neutral detent position.

## Three-Column Narrative

### AMC STAFF TRAINING MANUAL

environment, so that all customers can enjoy the movie undisturbed by small children. If there is another feature available, to which children are allowed to attend, offer this as an alternative. If the customer becomes uncooperative or abusive, refer the situation to a manager.

The remainder of the Cashier Training Manual is divided into two sections that contain specific information on each type of ticket selling system. If your theatre has an automated box office, turn to page 95 for detailed instructions on that system. If your theatre has a manual box office, continue reading below.

## MANUAL BOX OFFICE INSTRUCTIONS

### Opening Procedures

The cashier must perform the following opening procedures, to prepare the box office for business, before the theatre can open to serve the customers.

Cashiers should be in the proper uniform, ready to begin opening procedures at the scheduled time. The following duties are to be performed:

1. Pick up box office keys, gift certificates, re-admit tickets, yesterday's Box Office Report Summary Page, service charge tickets, and a copy of yesterday's Box Office Reports.
2. Open cabinets. Put out typewriter, calculator, and telephone. Turn on box office microphones.
3. Open ticket machines and check for sufficient supply of tickets. Thread the ticket machines. Check the actual opening ticket numbers against the closing ticket numbers on yesterday's Box Office Reports. If there are any discrepancies, call a manager.
4. Compare the opening numbers on gift certificates, re-admit, and service charge tickets against yesterday's Box Office Report Summary Page. If there is any discrepancy, tell a manager. In addition, check the opening numbers on gift certificates and all types of tickets with the numbers on today's prepared Daily Attendance Worksheet.
5. Count the money in the box office bank. This should total a fixed amount. If not, notify a manager immediately.
6. Prepare the Daily Pass Log by recording the opening numbers for re-admit and service charge tickets and filling in the theatre name, day and date.
7. Check the box office menu boards for correct show times and information with today's performance schedule. Change if incorrect.
8. Check newspaper listings for correct show times and information. Notify a manager if incorrect.
9. Call the theatre code-a-phone to check for correct information. If incorrect, notify a manager.
10. Read any box office memo updates. These may include new procedures regarding coupons and passes. In addition, look for information on new movies so that you will be able to answer questions that our customers might ask.
11. After completing all opening procedures, check for any burned out lights in the box office and lobby. Lock the cash drawer and assist the opening concessionist if necessary.

If your theatre participates in the MovieWatcher Program, complete these additional opening procedures:

12. Make sure the box office computer has been updated for the day (check with the manager).
13. Turn on the computer, monitor, and printer.
14. From the Main Menu, select Ticket Sales, and press <Enter>.
15. Enter your password when prompted.
16. Check the sales screen against the performance schedule for accuracy.
17. Lock in the first performance by typing <N> <1> <L>.

### Walk-In Procedures

The following walk-in procedures are intended to aid the Cashier in performing the various operational and administrative duties when the theatre is open for business.

### Selling Tickets

1. When a customer approaches the box

87

With thanks to AMC Theatres, Inc., and Jack Lew & Associates. Used by permission.

## 5-4: OUTLINE TIP SHEET

### Reader Preferences

☐ All readers like outlines as long as they're kept relatively simple. Readers with a technical background, however, are used to complex hierarchies and follow highly complex, multilevel outlines with more ease than nontechnical readers do.

### Best Use

☐ In procedures of all types, whether simple or complex.
☐ In policies where at least some of the information is lengthy.
☐ In any policy or procedure with numerous groups or levels of information.
☐ As part of a consistently used layout in a manual or handbook.

### Other Uses

☐ As a secondary format inserted into other formats. (A narrative flowchart might contain some steps that are individually outlined.)

### Format Variations

☐ *Type of outline:*     There are key word outlines, sentence outlines, paragraph outlines, or section outlines. Entire manuals can be outlined, or individual documents and sections can be outlined.

☐ *Number of levels:*     May be two, but can go as high as needed.

☐ *Numbering system:*     May use numbers, letters, or alphanumeric combination. Complexity depends on the number of subsections.

☐ *Labeling:*     May use regular, side, run-on headings, or even margin captions.

## Rules for Use

1. *Write down all relevant topics or items:*

   If you did a mind-map (see Chapter 2), you're ready for this. If not, create a list now of all relevant information using key words or phrases. Then put each item on a separate notecard or sticky note.

2. *Identify the main categories:*

   Lay out the cards or notes and pick out the primary groups of information. Grouping is sometimes determined by the material itself and sometimes by the way in which readers will use it.

3. *Identify subordinate groupings:*

   Study the main categories. Then group supporting detail underneath the appropriate category. Material can often be related to two or three main categories, so decide which grouping is the best fit.

4. *Experiment with different groupings:*

   With the cards or notes, you can quickly rearrange the levels and sublevels. Shuffle them around, shifting the groups and the order until you have what you believe are the most logical groupings—not from your standpoint, but from the audience's standpoint (you want reality, not theory).

5. *Determine how many levels are necessary:*

   Use as many levels as necessary and as few as possible. Levels indicate a subordinate relationship, so be sure that each item in the same level carries the same weight and that each level is a division of the prior one. You can vary the number of levels from section to section as required. One section may have three levels of information, another may require six.

6. *Decide what type of outline to use:*

   You can use a sentence outline, a paragraph outline, a section outline, or a key word or phrase outline. Sentence outlines are used for brief information. Paragraph outlines are the most common as a main format. Section outlines are often used in manuals, where each section of the book is also a main category in the outline. Key word and phrase outlines are used for the initial outlining

(*continues*)

## 5-4: Outline Tip Sheet (*continued*)

|  |  |
|---|---|
|  | process or for simple or brief policies and procedures. |
| 7. *Examine for flow:* | Look at the order in which topics appear. Is it logical to readers? Are items in the order in which readers need to use or reference them? Do this for all levels and sublevels. |
| 8. *Examine for sequence:* | In some outlines, sequence must be absolute. If you're outlining a maintenance procedure, a single step that's too early or too late can cause serious damage or injury. |
| 9. *Examine for weight and value:* | Make sure corresponding levels contain items of equal value. If section 1 is Orders and section 2 is Cash Orders, things get confusing. Cash orders are really a subgroup of the orders category. Each topic or item in a level must carry approximately the same weight as other items in that level. |
| 10. *Decide on a numbering system:* | You can use numbers or letters. The most common is an alphanumeric combination, such as "7.1a." However, many technical organizations use a straight numbering system no matter how many levels exist. Use numbers instead of letters in a procedure, since they're the clearest indicator of sequence. Also, keep the numbering system as simple as possible. "Section 4.1.1.14" gets confusing. |
| 11. *Indent each successive subsection:* | Anywhere from two to five spaces is appropriate, but use five whenever possible for clear visual separation. Experiment with a sample to see what looks best. |
| 12. *Note responsible party where necessary:* | Outline format usually doesn't identify the actor separately. Responsibility, if directly assigned, is in the body of the text. If it's important to clarify, identify the actor separately (in the margin, a separate column, italics, and so on). |

## Comments

☐ Outlines occupy the middle ground between straight narrative and more detailed graphic formats such as flowcharts. They display material in a visually organized way and are familiar to all readers. Their value lies in the fact that they give an instant snapshot of the relationships between groups of information and are easy to reference later by section number.

Beware the temptation to create lots of levels. It's easy to fall into the kitchen sink syndrome—including every bit of available information just because it fits neatly into the outline. The fact that it fits doesn't mean the reader needs it. Stick with the appropriate level of detail for your purposes.

Always adapt outlines to the audience. The complicated outline that a high-tech firm would use might drive other readers over a cliff.

## Examples

A Sentence Outline

---

CLIENT SERVICES

Client Assessment

Base Assessment
The caseworker performs a base assessment for all clients except those who, in the caseworker's best professional judgment, require a complete psychological assessment due to the nature of the service provided or the client's individual situation.

CS 4-100  Do a preliminary evaluation of need.

CS 4-101  Gather information on client's past use of agency services, if any.
a. Check historical files and current files.
b. Consider any possible name changes.

CS 4-102  Consider any determinant factors such as cultural background.

CS 4-103  Determine whether services are likely to be short term or long term.

---

*(continues)*

## 5-4:  Outline Tip Sheet (*continued*)

A Combination Key Word and Sentence Outline

Note that key words are used at the first level, sentences at the second level, and a combination of the two at the third level.

| **Subject:**  Contracts With Outside Consultants | **No.:**  A-43 |
|---|---|
| | **Revised:**  5-9-97 |
| | **Page:**  1 |

1.0 Purpose
This regulation tells you when you may use outside consultants, how to follow proper bidding procedures (if required), and how to get approvals.

2.0 Scope
It applies to all departments and all outside contracts over $500.00.

3.0 Definitions
An *outside consultant* is any outside individual or organization that provides advice or assistance for a fee. *Outside* means that the individual or organization is not employed by the company or any of its subsidiary business operations.

4.0 Policy
Contracts for specialized services of a technical nature may be awarded without bids. All other contracts must be bid.

5.0 Selecting the Consultant
   5.1 Selection
      A. Prepare a memo that identifies the need for the service. Send two copies to Purchasing. Include:
         1. Cost estimates
         2. Alternatives
         3. How you located or knew about the consultant
   5.2 The contract
      A. The contract will be reviewed by Purchasing for compliance with all necessary guidelines.
      B. It will also be reviewed by the Legal Department.
      C. If approved, the final contract will be issued by Purchasing and returned to the originating department.
         1. Originating department sends the contract to the consultant.

## 5-5: PLAYSCRIPT TIP SHEET

### Reader Preferences

☐ Almost everyone who's seen and used a playscript prefers it.

### Best Use

☐ In procedures involving two or more parties (individuals, departments, or entire organizations). Especially effective with complex procedures or those requiring lots of interaction among parties. Not for use with policies.

### Other Uses

☐ In relatively short or simple procedures.
☐ As a secondary format for a procedure within the body of a policy.
☐ As an "if . . . then" table for a single actor.

### Format Variations

☐ *Numerous variations:* Options depend on (1) how many parties are involved, and (2) how complex the procedure is. All use some form of table, chart, or list. For a large numbers of actors, construct a table and put the actors at the top of the table. Then list the steps in the body of the table in sequence.

### Rules for Use

| | |
|---|---|
| 1. *Create a two-column table:* | This is the simplest form of a playscript. Simply divide the page in two, with headings for each column. |
| 2. *Label the left column "Responsibility":* | This column contains the name of the actor or responsible party. |
| 3. *Label the right column "Action":* | This column contains the steps in the sequence they should be performed. |
| 4. *Start in the Action column and list the steps in the order they were performed:* | Start with what needs to be done and in what order. Define each step in the procedure and place them in perfect order. |

*(continues)*

## 5-5: Playscript Tip Sheet (*continued*)

| | |
|---|---|
| 5. *Number all steps sequentially regardless of actor:* | Don't begin all over again every time you come to a new actor. If the mechanic and the service representative both have a step 1 to perform, things will get confusing. But if the mechanic is responsible for steps 1 and 2 while the service representative is responsible for steps 3 and 4, it's easy to reference the proper step every time. |
| 6. *Start each step with an action verb:* | Readers want to know what to *do,* so tell them. This format allows you to eliminate a lot of extra words. Start with a command or directive, such as "take," "complete," "stop," or "check." |
| 7. *Move to the Responsibility column and identify the actors:* | Identify who's responsible for each step. If the actor remains the same for several steps, do not list the title each time. List it only once; then when the actor changes, identify the new one. Actors should be listed only when they change. Two or more actors can be listed for one step. |
| 8. *Use titles, not names:* | Any procedure that uses names becomes obsolete as individuals come and go in the organization. Responsibility should be assigned to a position or department. |
| 9. *Box in the playscript for a finished look:* | Box the playscript if it will stand alone. If it's part of a page layout that's in another format, such as narrative, skip the boxing. It's too distracting. |
| 10. *Consider inserting a playscript into another format:* | Even if you're using an outline or narrative format, a playscript is a good secondary format for a procedure that's contained within the material. |

## Comments

☐ This format dramatically reduces the possibility of misunderstandings because it's hard *not* to tell who's responsible for what. The visual clarity instantly tells readers what their part is and how it fits into the overall procedure. It also minimizes the sheer volume of words necessary to get the message across.

## Examples

Standard Playscript

| GUIDELINES FOR REQUESTING EXPORT DOCUMENTS | |
| --- | --- |
| *Responsibility* | *Action* |
| Export coordinator | 1. Prepare export applications forty-eight hours prior to ship date.<br>2. Take applications to inspector-in-charge. |
| Inspector-in-charge | 3. Issue certificate numbers for each application.<br>4. Return applications to export coordinator. |
| Export coordinator | 5. Put certificate numbers in order detail of each export order. |
| Shipping supervisor | 6. Print load sheets.<br>7. Contact inspector-in-charge to advise of export and pick up export stamp.<br>8. Match certificate number to load sheet.<br>9. Have product stamped and prepared for shipment.<br>10. Call inspector to advise export is ready to check for release. |
| Inspector-in-charge | 11. Check export and advise "can go" or "rejected." |
| Shipping supervisor | 12. If released by inspector, print bill of lading.<br>13. Write following on bill of lading:<br>   a. Certificate number<br>   b. Pack dates<br>   c. Separate weights for each plant<br>   Example:<br>   P-300 275 cases 8662.50<br>   P-67 225 cases 7087.50<br>   Total 500 cases of Maple Leaf 003-0100-50<br>14. Make copy of bill of lading.<br>15. Attach copy of tally sheet to bill of lading and give to export coordinator. |

With thanks to Maple Leaf Farms of Milford, Indiana. Used with permission.

*(continues)*

## 5-5:  PLAYSCRIPT TIP SHEET (*continued*)

Playscript With Multiple Actors in One Step

| RESOLVING CUSTOMER DELIVERY DISPUTES ON-SITE | |
| --- | --- |
| *Responsibility* | *Action* |
| Driver | 1. Compare customer information with the delivery order. |
| | 2. Identify areas of dispute. |
| | 3. Call the appropriate traffic department contact from the site. |
| Traffic department, driver | 4. Compare information on the delivery order against original routing request.<br>  a. If incorrect, traffic department corrects and issues new order with priority delivery code. Driver communicates new date to customer.<br>  b. If correct, contact the account representative. |
| Account representative, traffic department, account representative | 5. Compare original sales order to original routing request. |
| | 6. If incorrect, issue immediate correction with priority code. |
| | 7. Call driver back with explanation and new delivery date. |
| Account representative | 8. If correct, call customer and discuss acceptable solutions. |

## 5-5: PLAYSCRIPT TIP SHEET (*continued*)

Multiple Department Playscript

| LIMITED PURCHASE ORDER (LPO) PROCEDURE<br>PURCHASE ORDERS UNDER $500 | | |
|---|---|---|
| *Requesting Department* | *Purchasing Department* | *Accounting Department* |
| 1. Complete LPO (form 27-67). | | |
| | 2. Date stamp and log the LPO. | |
| | 3. Review for completeness. | |
| | 4. File pink copy. | |
| | 5. Forward LPO to Accounting. | |
| | | 6. Log LPO. |
| | | 7. Assign payment code. |
| | | 8. File blue copy. |
| | | 9. Return white and yellow copies to requesting department. |
| 10. Place order. | | |
| 11. Mail vendor's confirmation copy (white). | | |
| 12. File yellow copy. | | |
| 13. When order arrives, mark yellow copy "received" and send to Accounting. | | |
| | | 14. File yellow copy with blue copy pending receipt of bill. |

(*continues*)

## 5-5:  PLAYSCRIPT TIP SHEET (*continued*)

Playscript as an "If . . . Then" Format for a Single Actor

| Condition | Action |
|---|---|
| IF the alarm bell rings . . . . | 1. Stop the line.<br>2. Check the monitor to find the location of the problem.<br>3. Check the equipment to confirm the reported location.<br>4. Call maintenance. |
| IF the red light flashes . . . . | 1. Check the warning system for a message.<br>2. If no message appears, run a system check.<br>3. If the system check is negative for a problem, turn off the light and file a false indicator report. |
| IF the indicator moves outside the normal range . . . . | 1. Double-check the reading.<br>2. Run a system check.<br>3. If no malfunction appears, call shift supervisor immediately. |

Playscript Inside an Extensive Page Layout

| Subject: Payroll Processing | Category: Accounting | No.: P-35 Page: 1 |
|---|---|---|

Purpose: To process payroll quickly and efficiently and to get paychecks out on time.

Policy: The company will process payroll in a timely and accurate manner that is consistent with all legal requirements.

Conditions: All time sheets must be returned to Accounting by Monday at 10:00 a.m.

Procedure:

| *Responsibility* | *Action* |
|---|---|
| All departments | 1. Collect and review all time cards and time sheets first thing Monday morning. 2. Department heads approve and sign. 3. Send to Accounting for processing. Must be received in Accounting by 10:00 a.m. on Monday. |
| Payroll Department | 4. Review time cards and time sheets. 5. Process time cards and time sheets. 6. Enter data into payroll system. 7. Prepare paychecks. 8. Send checks to department heads. |
| Department heads | 9. Review and sign checks. |
| Supervisors | 10. Distribute checks on Friday morning. |

| Effective Date: 1–1–99 | Revision Date: 12–31–00 | Revision No.: 1 |
|---|---|---|

## 5-6: FLOWCHART TIP SHEET

### Reader Preferences

☐ Flowcharts are favored by people with a technical background. Often disliked or ignored by nontechnical readers.

### Best Use

☐ In complex procedures or processes. Often used for detailed technical material.

### Other Uses

☐ In simple procedures, but can make them look more complicated.
☐ In policies. Simple versions (i.e., organization charts) are often used.

### Format Variations

☐ *Narrative flowcharts:*  Symbols are enlarged to contain more information, or else additional information is listed outside the symbols.

☐ *Information other than processes:*  May also show actor, workflow, services, schedules, decisions, forms or documents, and physical layout.

### Rules for Use

1. *Use as few different symbols as possible:*  Avoid overwhelming the reader's eye. The simpler, the better. See below for some standard symbols.

2. *Use a key:*  Don't assume all readers know the symbols. Insert a key on the flowchart.

3. *Be consistent:*  Changing symbols from chart to chart just confuses the reader.

4. *Be aware of specialized symbols:*  Know what, if any, specialized symbols are normally used in your field or organization.

5. *Use footnotes where appropriate:* Explain special conditions that exist or the chart's connection to other materials or flowcharts. Use footnotes sparingly—they only add to the visual clutter.

6. *Use some narrative with it:* Stand-alone flowcharts may generate as many questions as they answer. Narrative text outside the flowchart orients the reader to what's in it.

7. *Place the flowchart after the narrative:* The narrative is an entree into the details and reinforces the message.

8. *Make sure symbols are large enough to be seen clearly:* One of the reasons many readers don't like flowcharts is that they have to squint to see them. Tiny detail is hard to see, much less concentrate on.

9. *Label the responsible party (actor) as needed for clarity:* Remember that flowcharts don't automatically indicate who is involved or responsible at any given step. You must consciously add this information where needed. Be sure names or titles are close enough to the appropriate symbol to be clear.

10. *Break long flowcharts down into several shorter ones:* It takes more space but is more readable. Indicate where the related charts are to be found. The exception to this rule is with technical users who are used to complex graphics.

11. *Use arrows to indicate flow:* Some versions may just need connecting lines. Use arrows only when indicating direction or flow.

*(continues)*

## 5-6: FLOWCHART TIP SHEET (*continued*)

### Standard Symbols

You can also customize your own.

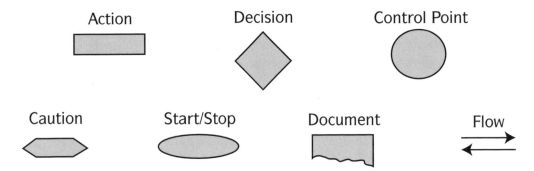

### Comments

☐ The major drawback in flowcharts is visual clutter. Too many symbols and arrows can hit the eye at once and cause confusion. Be careful when arrows cross each other. If the scale is too small, the reader's eye may follow the wrong arrow. Break up long flowcharts.

Remember that many flowcharts assume a single actor: Whoever starts the process will also finish it. If there are multiple actors or parties involved, or if identifying the responsible party is a critical factor, consider using a playscript instead.

**Examples**

Simple Flowchart

*Note:* Steps are shown in sequence, but the responsible parties aren't identified. This assumes one person performs the entire procedure.

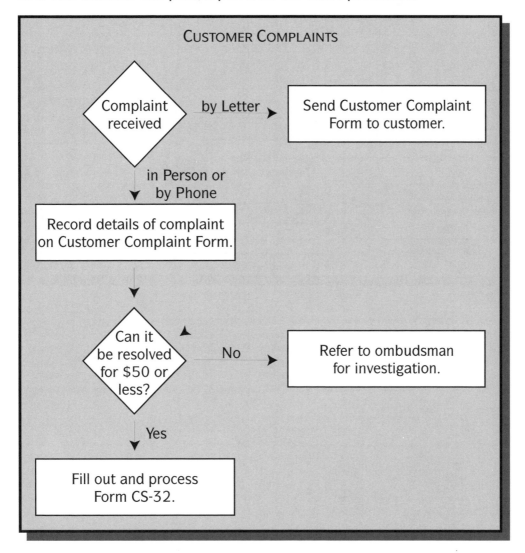

(*continues*)

## 5-6:  FLOWCHART TIP SHEET (*continued*)

Process Flowchart

*Note:* Some actors are identified.

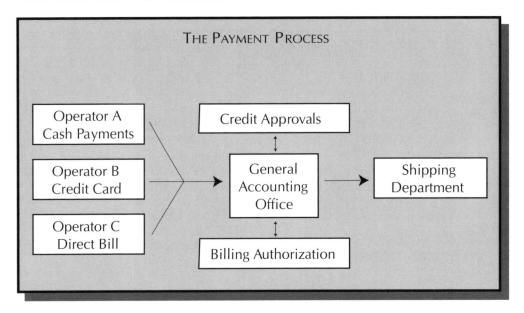

Procedure Flowchart

Note that there is no movement back and forth between departments; otherwise, this type of chart will not work. This is actually a hybrid—a cross between a flowchart and a playscript.

ORDER PROCESSING

| *Order Department* | *Shipping Department* | *Billing Office* |
|---|---|---|
| 1. Receive customer request.<br>2. Check to see if item is current.<br>  a. If not, search back stock.<br>    1. If available, go to step 3.<br>    2. If not, notify customer.<br>3. Fill out form OR-363 and forward to Shipping Department. | 4. Pick order per form OR-363.<br>5. Pack order.<br>6. Complete shipping portion of form OR-363.<br>7. Forward white copy to Billing Office and file the pink copy. | 8. Enter customer information into computer system.<br>9. Verify data as entered.<br>10. Issue a bill or receipt to the customer.<br>  a. If prepaid (check, credit card), issue a receipt. |

*(continues)*

## 5-6:  FLOWCHART TIP SHEET (*continued*)

### Narrative Flowchart

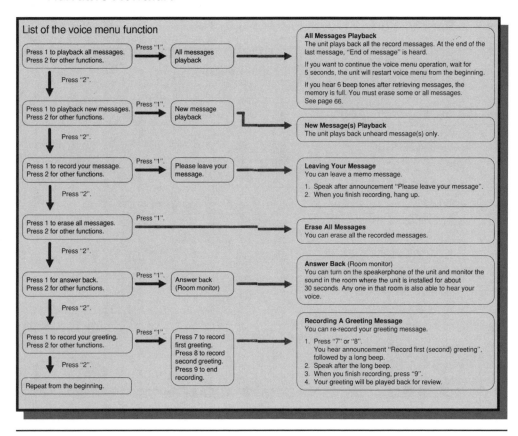

With thanks to the Panasonic Division of the Matsushita Electric Corporation of America. Used by permission.

Organizational Flowchart

Note that the chart shows both relationships and information exchanges.

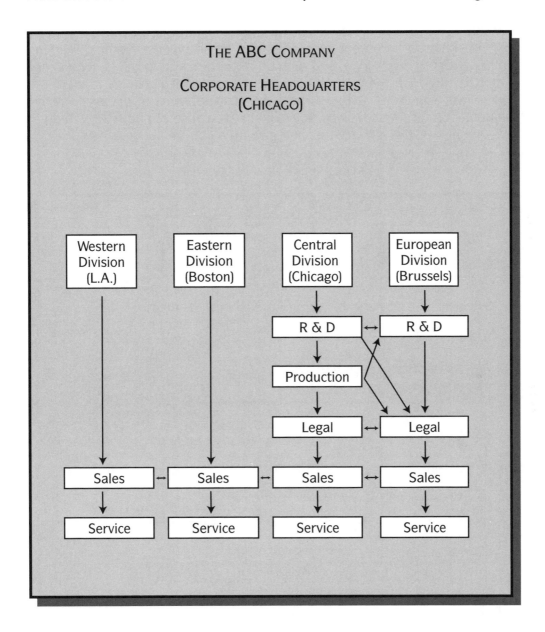

(*continues*)

## 5-6: Flowchart Tip Sheet (*continued*)

### An Uncontrolled Flowchart

Flowcharts can startle readers at first glance. Symbols that aren't defined may be confusing, different type sizes can create visual overload, varying symbol sizes are distracting, and directional arrows add to the general sense of clutter. Although the content isn't particularly difficult, many readers will wonder why you didn't just give them the information in a regular narrative or outline format. Readers who don't like or aren't used to flowcharts tend to take one glance, get a headache, and give up.

### PROBLEM-SOLVING FLOWSHEET

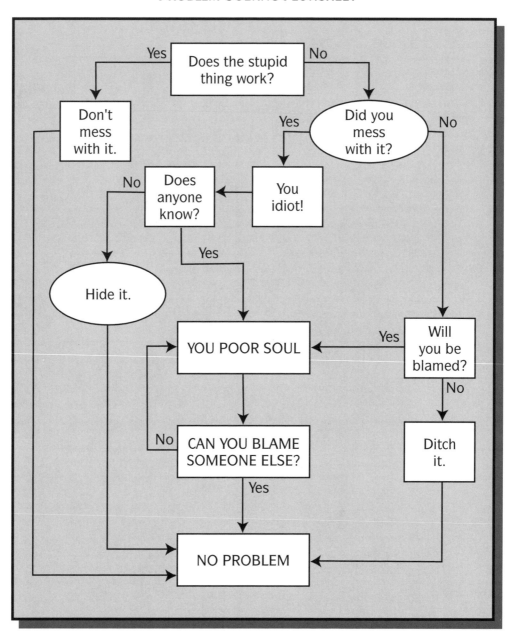

## 5-7: QUESTION AND ANSWER TIP SHEET

### Reader Preferences

☐ Most readers like question and answer sections because they simulate a personal conversation.

### Best Use

☐ In confusing policies or procedures.
☐ In policies or procedures with lots of variations or twists.
☐ In newly implemented policies or procedures.
☐ For areas of special concern to readers.
☐ For "what if . . . " situations that arise frequently or are unusual.

### Other Uses

☐ To explain policies and procedures that have encountered strong resistance or backlash from users.
☐ To summarize basic information (not good for detailed or lengthy information).
☐ To reinforce key issues through repetition ("Why is this procedure really so important?").

### Format Variations

☐ *Placement:* Question and answer sections are commonly placed at the back of a manual to address main concerns, but they can be placed at the end of a section when dealing with only one subject area.

☐ *Length:* A typical answer is one or two paragraphs long and gives a brief response in narrative format. Others are a page long. And some act almost like a table of contents. ("Q: What if the valve sticks? A: See the procedure on page 276"). If they're very brief, they can be put into a table and inserted anywhere in the document that's appropriate.

*(continues)*

## 5-7:  QUESTION AND ANSWER TIP SHEET (*continued*)

### Rules for Use

1. *Decide what questions users will have:* — Question and answer sections have to deal with reality or users ignore them. There's a tendency to guess what readers will ask or to put in things management thinks users should be asking. Analyze users' real concerns.

2. *Put them in a separate section:* — Inserting questions and answers into the body of the policy or procedure is usually distracting. Do it only when the questions and answers are short and directly relevant, and then use only one or two questions at a time.

3. *Use a narrative format:* — It's usually single column, but you can use double columns if the questions and answers are very short. Short tables or charts can be inserted into the answer for statistical information.

4. *Experiment with multiple columns:* — See number 3 above.

5. *Highlight the questions:* — Treat them as you would headings. Distinguish them visually from the answers with boldface, italics, or some other device.

6. *Keep questions and answers as short as possible:* — If answers begin to get lengthy, refer the reader back to the policy or procedure itself. This section is for a quick reference only.

7. *Word it simply and clearly:* — Since question and answer sections use some form of narrative approach, it's tempting to be wordy. Write the questions as readers would ask them, then write the answers as if you were giving them in person.

### Comments

☐ Question and answer sections send a message: Management understands what readers really deal with out there every day. If kept concise, they're a valuable reference tool.

## Examples

Standard Question and Answer

---

### SITUATIONS YOU MAY ENCOUNTER

Q: *What if a customer is still in the store after closing?*

A: Don't rush the customer despite the late hour. Be gracious and pleasant, and continue to wait on him or her. But do be efficient, and don't engage in small talk that might encourage the person to linger. Remember you're there to serve the customer, even when it's occasionally inconvenient to do so.

Fortunately, with proper warnings at five-minute intervals prior to closing, this won't happen very often.

---

Abbreviated Question and Answer in Double-Column Format

---

### FREQUENTLY ASKED EQUIPMENT QUESTIONS

Q: What if the lever's stuck?

A: See the procedure on page 37.

Q: How do I start the machine?

A: See the explanation and figures on page 40.

Q: What if the warning light comes on?

A: Stop the machine immediately and refer to the emergency procedure on page 221.

Q: What if it shuts down by itself?

A: Call maintenance immediately.

---

## 5-8: Troubleshooting Tip Sheet

### Reader Preferences

☐ Technicians, maintenance people, and anyone who's called on when things go wrong like troubleshooting sections.

### Best Use

☐ As a separate section. The whole point is to make discussion of the special situations fast and easy to find.
☐ In procedures that deal with more complex processes or equipment.
☐ For emergency instructions.

### Other Uses

☐ Any policy or procedure that needs to point out certain conditions or possibilities. A good "if . . . then" tool.

### Format Variations

☐ *Questions and answers.*
☐ *Matrix tables* (usually the best and clearest format).
☐ *Lists.*
☐ *Narrative* (usually the least desirable format).

### Rules for Use

| | | |
|---|---|---|
| 1. | *Create a separate section:* | If it's in a manual or handbook, this section is usually put at the back with a tab divider. It can also be placed at the end of a section or even an individual document. Just be sure the placement is obvious so readers can get to it fast. |
| 2. | *Choose a format:* | Decide what best suits the type of information and the way the audience will use it. You can use any format that's fast and clear, just put it in a separate section of some kind. |

3. *Divide the material into major and minor categories:* Categorize it however it makes sense in your situation (life-threatening versus nonlife-threatening, common versus uncommon, critical versus noncritical, and so on).

4. *Get to the point fast:* The whole point of a troubleshooting section is to get specific answers fast. Don't mince words or worry about refined language.

5. *Keep wording to a minimum:* This is one way to get to the point fast. It's also a good reason to avoid narrative in troubleshooting sections when possible.

6. *Be deadly clear:* There's already trouble or users wouldn't be looking in this section. Another mistake will just cost time, money, or even lives.

7. *Include all pertinent information:* Be brief and to the point, but don't skip important information just for the sake of brevity.

8. *Consider a separate set of troubleshooting procedures:* On occasion it may help to create an entire manual or handbook that contains only troubleshooting information. Many large organizations with on-call technicians do this so the technicians can carry it as an on-the-spot reference. Even a short book, spiral-bound but separate from the main manual, can help.

9. *For short, quick troubleshooting information, consider a sidebar or table in the text:* This is only good for very brief, simple material. Or it can be used in both the text and the troubleshooting section to reinforce the importance of the information.

## Comments

☐ Troubleshooting sections are the opposite of standard operating procedures. Users sometimes find a manual or handbook useless in immediate situations, but this section gives quick guidance.

*(continues)*

## 5-8:   TROUBLESHOOTING TIP SHEET (*continued*)

**Examples**

| RECORDS MANAGEMENT PROBLEMS | | |
|---|---|---|
| *Symptom* | *Possible Causes* | *Solutions* |
| 1. Missing files | a. Poorly defined check-out policy | a-1. Review and revise the policy. |
| | b. Failure to enforce existing check-out policy | b-1. Develop an enforcement procedure and designate the authority to use it. |
| | c. Careless users | c-1. Counsel users. |
| | | c-2. Train users. |
| | | c-3. Restrict access to the files (for worst offenders only). |
| 2. Excessive retrieval time | a. Misfiles | a-1. Review the classification system for logic and ease. |
| | b. No system index or cross-reference | b-1. Create a system index immediately. |
| | c. Users can't remember the file names | c-1. Shorten and simplify file names. |
| | | c-2. Use common names. |
| | | c-3. Use acronyms or abbreviations. |
| | | c-4. Use a numerical system with cross-references. |

Also see the Question and Answer (5-7), Matrix Table (5-9), and List (5-10) Tip Sheets for examples of other formats that can be used in a troubleshooting section.

## 5-9: Matrix Table Tip Sheet

### Reader Preferences

☐ All readers tend to like matrices because they permit fast, permanent reference and eliminate the need for constant searching.

### Best Use

☐ As a summary of important information readers need to refer to frequently.

☐ In policies or procedures in which actions are conditional ("if . . . then") or have several alternatives ("what if . . .").

### Other Uses

☐ Can be used to clarify numerous types of material, including schedules, decisions, simple instructions, responsibility, work distribution, and forms or document distribution.

### Format Variations

☐ *Narrative matrices*: Text is placed in the cells, instead of an X or a checkmark. Useful when there are two separate variables that affect the action rather than just one.

### Rules for Use

1. *Place one factor on the left side, or stub:* The primary factor, the one that readers look for first, usually goes in the stub. In most cases the eye looks to the left column first because that's how we read.

2. *Place the second factor at the top, or box head:* The secondary factor is usually placed in the box head. However, sometimes it's a matter of length. If one factor is long and the other short, the short one usually goes at the top.

*(continues)*

## 5-9:  MATRIX TABLE TIP SHEET (*continued*)

| | |
|---|---|
| 3. *Label the stub and box head:* | Label horizontally from left to right. Box head labels can be angled up and away from the table, but they're hard to read that way. It's usually done only when the box head factors are lengthy, so try switching the box head and stub. If that's not possible, abbreviate. |
| 4. *Rule off the body of the table into data cells:* | Data cells are the squares (cells) created where the lines cross vertically and horizontally. If you're using a narrative matrix, be sure the cells are large enough to accommodate the text without being crowded. |
| 5. *Mark out or X the relevant cells:* | Checkmarks or Xs are the common mark, but any simple symbol will do. |
| 6. *Box in the entire table:* | Keep the lines (rules) dark enough to be distinct but light enough not to be overwhelming. |
| 7. *Use the motto, "Shorter is better":* | Keep labels and factors as short and simple as possible. Matrices can handle a fair amount of information, but if you use too much, the lines and text interfere with each other. |
| 8. *Use plenty of white space:* | Don't crowd rows and columns together. Visual separation is the key to speed for reading a matrix. Cramming factors together is usually the result of an attempt to put too much material into one table. |

**Comments**

☐ A matrix table doesn't substitute for an explanation or description in the text. It's a secondary format. Use a matrix as a way of focusing and summarizing important information, especially when users will have to refer back to that information frequently. The table should be clear enough that it requires little or no explanation.

## Examples

Decision or Action Matrix

### HANDLING GUEST REQUESTS

An (X) indicates that the designated department has secondary or backup responsibility.

| Request | Department | | | | | |
| --- | --- | --- | --- | --- | --- | --- |
| | *Front Desk* | *House-keeping* | *Mainte-nance* | *Bell Stand* | *Catering* | *Restau-rant* |
| Billing questions | X | | | | | |
| Cleanliness | | X | | | | |
| Food service | | | | | X | X |
| Iron/board | | X | | | | |
| Laundry | (x) | X | | | | |
| Luggage questions | | | | X | | |
| Meeting or convention assistance | | | | | X | X |
| Noise | X | | X | X | | |
| Parking | | | | X | | |
| Room changes | X | | | (x) | | |
| Room service | | | | | (x) | X |
| Room temperature | X | | X | | | |
| Towels/linens | (x) | X | | | | |

*(continues)*

## 5-9: Matrix Table Tip Sheet (*continued*)

Usage Matrix

| APPROPRIATE USE OF INGREDIENTS | | | | | | |
|---|---|---|---|---|---|---|
| | *Type of Spice* | | | | | |
| *Dish* | *Mustard* | *Vegetable Flakes* | *Dill* | *Paprika* | *Nutmeg* | *Ginger* |
| Fish | | | | ✓ | | |
| Baked goods | | ✓ | ✓ | | ✓ | ✓ |
| Soups | | | | | | |
| Meat | ✓ | | | ✓ | | ✓ |
| Gravies | ✓ | | | ✓ | | |
| Vegetables | | | | ✓ | ✓ | ✓ |
| Sauces | ✓ | ✓ | ✓ | | | |
| Pickling | | | ✓ | | | |

Activity Matrix

| ACTIVITY SCHEDULE | | | | |
|---|---|---|---|---|
| | *Period* | | | |
| *Activity* | *1st Quarter* | *2nd Quarter* | *3rd Quarter* | *4th Quarter* |
| Budget Analysis | X | X | X | X |
| Budget request | | | X | |
| P & L | X | X | X | X |
| Sales forecast | | X | | X |
| Staffing analysis | | | X | |

Procedure Responsibility Matrix

Note that the box head labels have been angled vertically, which makes them harder to read.

| THE RESEARCH AND DEVELOPMENT PROCESS | | | | | | |
|---|---|---|---|---|---|---|
| *Steps* | Researcher | R&D Manager | Invention Review Committee | Legal Department | Marketing | Production |
| 1. Develop idea or product. | ✓ | | | | | |
| 2. Review for applicability and appropriateness. | | ✓ | ✓ | ✓ | | |
| 3. Study cost and marketability. | | | ✓ | ✓ | ✓ | |
| 4. Conduct brief customer survey. | | | | | ✓ | |
| 5. Develop a prototype. | ✓ | | | | | ✓ |
| 6. Conduct focus groups and other market tests. | | | ✓ | | ✓ | |

*(continues)*

## 5-9: MATRIX TABLE TIP SHEET (*continued*)

Narrative Matrix

| ENGINE MAINTENANCE | | | | |
|---|---|---|---|---|
| | *Mileage* | | | |
| *Model* | *5,000* | *7,000* | *10,000* | *15,000* |
| EKC-400 | Replace filters. Check hydraulic fluid. Check spark plugs. | N/A | Perform level 1 maintenance check (see page 73). | Perform level 2 maintenance check (see page 103). |
| EKC-600 | Perform level 1 maintenance check (see page 67). | N/A | Inspect fuel lines for wetness, or washed or stained areas. | N/A |
| EKC-650 | Drain and replace coolant. | Inspect the cooling system. | Flush the cooling system. | Perform level 1 maintenance check (see page 84). |
| EKC-800 | Drain and replace oil. Check air filter. | N/A | Inspect the exhaust system. Lubricate steering linkage. | Perform level 1 maintenance check (see page 78). |

## 5-10: List Tip Sheet

### Reader Preferences

☐ All readers love a list.

### Best Use

☐ In procedures where speed and clarity are critical.

### Other Uses

☐ Virtually any time you have three or more related items.

### Format Variations

| | |
|---|---|
| ☐ *Displayed list:* | Also called a vertical list. It's the standard indented list that most us are referring to when we talk about lists. |
| ☐ *Paragraph list:* | Written in regular sentence format as part of the regular text of the paragraph. Often set off by lowercase letters or numbers in parentheses, although very short items don't require it. |
| ☐ *Nested list:* | A list within a list. |
| ☐ *Parenthetical list:* | A list set off from the sentence with parentheses. Used only for extremely short lists or when the information is not central or critical. Often used as a reminder of prior information. |

### Rules for Use

| | |
|---|---|
| 1. *Mark each item with a number, letter, or symbol:* | Choose the identification marks carefully. We typically see numbers (1, 2, 3) or letters (a, b, c), but these also indicate sequence or importance to many readers. Use them only when you intend to indicate the order. When you have a group of related items that are nonsequential, use neutral symbols (called dingbats) such as bullet points, checkmarks, or other computer symbols. |

*(continues)*

## 5-10:  LIST TIP SHEET (*continued*)

2. *Indent generously:* The whole key to a list is that it's easy to read because it has more white space around it than a standard sentence or paragraph. If you skimp on the margins, you defeat the purpose of the list.

3. *Separate the list from the surrounding text:* The space above and below lines (called leading) is just like indenting: It adds the white space that the eye loves. Use enough space above and below the list. If each individual item in the list is long (two to three lines or more), put a blank line between each item. If the items are short, you may only need blank lines before and after the list. Experiment with the right amount.

4. *Keep it short:* Eliminate the articles ("a," "an," "the"). Start with the verb. Use phrases or key words only. Use short, choppy sentences. You can do things in a list that you can't do in normal writing, so do them.

5. *Make the items in the list parallel:* Parallelism was emphasized back in Chapter 4, but it bears repeating. The content of each item is different, but the form should be the same. If you start one item with a verb, start them all with a verb. Parallelism creates a rhythm that's essential to smooth reading, and it makes the items in the list all sound connected. It applies to grammar, length, and style. Match each item as closely as possible.

**Comments**

☐ The eye loves a list. Readers love a list. And writers should love a list. Lists can be used with material that's general or specific, short or long, narrative or outlined. There are very few limits on lists. They shorten, summarize, and clarify virtually any material. They're so good that other formats are based on them (playscript and outline are really just dressed-up lists). Think lists, lists, lists.

## Examples

Displayed List

> ### USING LISTS
>
> Use a displayed list when:
> - The list is long
> - Each item on the list is long
> - You want to emphasize the list
> - Items are in descending order of importance
> - Readers will have to reference items on the list

Paragraph List

> ### SAFETY POLICIES
>
> Safety policies are based on (a) published OSHA standards, (b) industry standards, and (c) internal requirements.

Nested Lists

> ### REPORT GUIDELINES
>
> 1. The standard length should be no more than twenty-five pages.
> 2. The standard setup is:
>    a. Times Roman
>    b. 12-point text
>    c. 16-point headings
>    d. Italics or boldface for emphasis

(*continues*)

## 5-10:  LIST TIP SHEET (*continued*)

---

### REPORT GUIDELINES

1.  The standard length should be no more than twenty-five pages.
2.  The standard setup is (a) Times Roman, (b) 12-point text, (c) 16-point headings, (d) italics or boldface for emphasis.

Parenthetical List

### DESIGN GUIDELINES

The main design elements (white space, chunking, and emphasis) should be observed at all times.

---

# 6

# How Do I Get Them to Read This?

All right, so you have a document that's clear, concise, and well formatted. Now the problem is how to convince readers of that. In fact, how do you even convince them to look at it in the first place?

Past experience might lead a lot of readers to think that all policies and procedures are incomprehensible or, at best, boring. Your challenge may be just getting them to look these over, much less read them.

The solution to this has nothing to do with the policies or procedures themselves. The solution is good design. If the first thing the readers see looks crowded, fussy, or confusing, you've lost them.

Let's face it. First impressions count.

## Setting the Stage

Before you can use good design effectively, though, you have to set the stage. Your first step is to think about your own internal communications.

Are they good? Will people believe you when you say that it's important for them to read the policy or procedure, or are they more likely to roll their eyes and think, "Oh, sure"? If they're more likely to roll their eyes, you have a credibility problem.

Resolving this problem requires a lot of patience and a lot of honesty on your part. There are no quick fixes. When you distribute your concisely written, easy-to-read document, you have to acknowledge that there have been problems with past documents—and you must explain how you've changed that.

Be prepared for skeptical looks and comments. If readers' past experience with policies and procedures has been bad, it's normal for them to expect the same again—until new experience with your new document changes their perspective.

# Hooking Them

And what if your credibility is already pretty good? Then readers may believe you when you tell them that they need to read the document. But they may also come up with lots of wonderfully creative reasons why they can't do it: no time, doesn't apply to me, done it for years, know how to do it already, can figure it out faster than I can read it. The list is a long one.

There is a way around this. It's to remember the old rule: Appearances count.

There's an old saying that 70 percent of what you know about people (and things) is based on their appearance. Appearances do count.

It's true. It's always been true. And nowhere is it truer than in policy and procedure writing. Appearances count. (If you've ever felt someone give you the sixty-second once-over, or you've done it to someone else, you know it's true.)

Your readers eye the document in exactly the same way they would a person, and for exactly the same reasons. They're sizing it up, assessing it so they know what to expect. Will it be easy to read? Clear? Confusing? Mind-numbing? Fast? Or is it depressing just to look at?

At a single glance, readers assess simplicity, form, clarity, shape, color, highlights, density, sharpness, and contrast.

What they really want to know is this: Will it be worth my time and effort to read this? Could I get the same information faster and easier by guessing, by asking someone, or by just using good sense?

If the appearance of the document is fussy, crowded, or confusing, readers ignore it and find another source of information. They hate chaotic, crowded, noisy documents.

So remember that appearances count. First impressions count. Design your document to be appealing at first glance. Use the hidden power of document design, and you'll find that it (1) gets readers in the door and (2) encourages them to stay and read.

---

## No More Excuses

Users have lots of wonderfully creative reasons for not reading policies and procedures. But as a writer you can overcome that by making the document easy to read and use. Make a good first impression, make the document look good, and you've hooked the reader's attention. Appearance counts!

---

# Creating Visual Appeal

The hidden power of document design is in what it does for the appearance of your document. You have to use design to invite readers into the document. Draw them to you. Entice them. Seduce them. Learn the lesson of Madison Avenue: If it *looks* organized, uncrowded, and easy, it must really be. Then you've got them through the door, reading the policy, procedure, or manual.

You're using something known as visual appeal. Make the document look easy to read, and readers assume that it is. Make it look easy to understand, and they assume it is. Make it look fast, and they assume it is.

In fact, saying that something is easy to read really means that the document is visually appealing. It looks good. It looks clear. It looks easy to understand. And above all, it looks like relatively fast reading.

Conversely, saying that something is hard to read means the document lacks visual appeal. It looks crowded, fussy, or complicated. And most readers who come to that conclusion don't actually read the document. They merely glance at it and decide that if the policies and procedures look complicated, they must be.

How, then, do you create visual appeal? Is it possible to make the document so appealing that it will be hard for readers not to use it? Yes. Just make it easy to look at and easy to read.

---

ADVERTISE YOUR DOCUMENT

Writers can take a lesson from Madison Avenue: Make it look good and easy, and readers assume it is. When people say something is easy to read, they really mean it has visual appeal.

---

# Avoiding Visual Clutter

Making it easy to look at and read requires two things: simplicity and visual clarity. A document that doesn't look simple and clear will stop readers cold. It's like slamming a door in their faces.

At all costs, you must avoid visual clutter. That's the term used when a document looks overwhelming (see Example 6-1). There's no

**Example 6-1.** Visual clutter.

---

Narrow margins, poor paragraph spacing, and overuse of devices such as capitals and underlining make this document crowded and unreadable.

| Classification | Subject | Number PR-61 |
|---|---|---|
| | | Date |
| Payroll | Travel Time | Page 1 of 2 |

**COMPENSABLE TRAVEL TIME**

Travel time is normally not compensable because it is considered part of an employee's obligation to arrive at the plant on time via transportation of his or her own choosing. However, IF THE EMPLOYEE IS ASSIGNED A COMPANY VEHICLE, the following types of travel time ARE compensable:

1. If the employee begins the day receiving instructions at home from the dispatcher. In this case, worked time begins with the receipt of the assignment.

2. If the employee begins the day traveling from home to a job site. In this case, worked time begins with the travel to the job site.

3. If the employee ends the day by returning from a job site to the plant. In this case, worked time stops when the employee leaves the plant.

4. If the employee ends the day by traveling directly from a job site to home, securing the company vehicle overnight. In this case, worked time stops when the employee arrives home.

The employee will be paid the lesser of (1) the time spent driving from home to the first work site or (2) the time spent driving from the plant to the first work site.

If the employee voluntarily drives the company vehicle to and from home each day, or does so at his or her own request, the employee will be paid the lesser of (1) the time spent driving between home and the first/last work site or (2) the time needed to drive between the plant and the first/last worksite. This is in addition to trips between work sites.

**NONCOMPENSABLE TRAVEL TIME**

Travel time between the employee's home and the plant at the beginning and end of the workday is not compensable. This is considered normal travel to the job and is the employee's responsibility.

**RECORD KEEPING**

Payroll must maintain records of all the time employees spend traveling if employees use company vehicles to travel between their homes and service calls.

**Example 6-1.** (*continued*)

| Classification | Subject | Number PR-61 |
|---|---|---|
| | | Date |
| Payroll | Travel Time | Page 2 of 2 |

It is the company's responsibility to document all required time in case of audit by the Wage and Hour Division. It is especially important to maintain accurate records as relates to the beginning and the end of the workday. If start and end times are unclear or poorly documented, Wage and Hour will take the position that <u>ALL THE TIME SPENT TRAVELING IS COMPENSABLE.</u>

**OTHER TRAVEL**

The "day trip": Travel time is also compensable when it is part of the principal activities of the employee's day or when it is required during a shift. This is true even if the employee is using his or her own vehicle (commuting time from/to the employee's home to the first/last work site are still non-compensable).

The "overnight stay": Travel time as part of an overnight stay is compensable to the extent that the employee travels during his or her normal work hours. In addition, travel on a regularly scheduled day off is compensable for all travel time during the employee's normal working hours.

Emergencies: Travel time for emergencies and callbacks after the end of a shift is compensable.

mystery about it, either. In fact, it's just like the clutter most of us accumulate in the attic or garage.

We often refer to it as "that stuff in the garage." If you have a minimal amount of stuff, you can keep things pretty orderly and find them when you need them. When the amount of stuff grows, you get confused and lose track of things. And once it goes beyond a reasonable point, you just close the door and ignore it.

The eye reacts in much the same way to the printed page. If it's simple in design and format, the reader feels comfortable and in control. That's because the page looks fairly straightforward, clear, and easy to read.

But as the sheer clutter of design and format elements grows, readers get confused and lose track. There's too much stuff here for comfort, so they give up. They shut the door and walk away.

# Designing for Visual Appeal

The question, then, is how to keep the stuff under control. The answer is proper use of the elements of document design (see Example 6-2).

There are twenty basic design elements. That may seem like a long list, but don't panic. Each one is easy to understand once you get into the swing of it. Each also has the same basic logic behind it: Make the document look easy, fast, and clear. In other words, create visual appeal.

What's more, almost all of the design elements are familiar to you—things like sentence and paragraph length (short), adequate spacing between lines and sections (called leading), and sparing use of emphasis (boldface, italics, capitals). There are also typeface and typesize, color and contrast, margins, indentations, and justification.

The list goes on, but none of the design elements are complicated. And all are easy to apply once you become more conscious of them. Each element is listed and described individually in the Design Tip Sheet (6-1) at the end of this chapter. Keep this tip sheet handy whenever you begin the actual design of any policy or procedure document.

Master all of the design elements and your reader's first impression will be, "Hey, this looks OK." (Don't expect ecstasy over a policy or procedure.) That statement means you've got what you want: their attention.

# Why the Elements Work

As effective as these design elements are, they aren't magical. They must be used properly.

The bottom line is that there's a limit on what, and how much, you can do with them before you lose the reader. By staying within the limit, you create visual appeal. Stray outside it, and you create clutter.

And it's all because of two things: (1) the human brain and (2) eye movement.

## The Human Brain

Psychological studies show that the human brain can deal with as many as seven different items at one time. That's the good news.

The bad news is that the brain can clearly distinguish among only three of the seven at one time.

What this means for writers is very simple. You can give readers seven different chunks of information at once, but they'll be confused. By giving them only three at once, they'll be more likely to get it straight.

**Example 6-2.** Visual appeal.

Note that increased white space in margins and between paragraphs, greater list indentation, and sparing use of emphasis in headings improve the look considerably. Even more could be done to shorten and refine the wording.

| **Classification:** | **Subject:** | **Number:** PR-61 |
|---|---|---|
| | | **Date:** |
| Payroll | Travel Time | **Page:** 1 of 2 |

**COMPENSABLE TRAVEL TIME**

Travel time is normally not compensable because it is considered part of an employee's obligation to arrive at the plant on time via transportation of his or her own choosing. However, if the employee is assigned a company vehicle, the following types of travel time ARE compensable:

1. *If the employee begins the day receiving instructions at home from the dispatcher.* In this case, worked time begins with the receipt of the assignment.

2. *If the employee begins the day traveling from home to a job site.* In this case, worked time begins with the travel to the job site.

3. *If the employee ends the day by returning from a job site to the plant.* In this case, worked time stops when the employee leaves the plant.

4. *If the employee ends the day by traveling directly from a job site to home, securing the company vehicle overnight.* In this case, worked time stops when the employee arrives home.

The employee will be paid the lesser of (1) the time spent driving from home to the first work site or (2) the time spent driving from the plant to the first work site.

If the employee voluntarily drives the company vehicle to and from home each day, or does so at his or her own request, the employee will be paid the lesser of (1) the time spent driving between home and the first/last work site or (2) the time needed to drive between the plant and the first/last worksite. This is in addition to trips between work sites.

*(continues)*

**Example 6-2.**  (*continued*)

| Subject:<br><br>Travel Time | Number: PR-61 | Page: 2 of 2 |
|---|---|---|

## NON-COMPENSABLE TRAVEL TIME

Travel time between the employee's home and the plant at the beginning and end of the workday is not compensable. This is considered normal travel to the job and is the employee's responsibility.

## RECORD KEEPING

Payroll must maintain records of all time employees spend traveling if employees use company vehicles to travel between their homes and service calls.

It is the company's responsibility to document all required time in case of audit by the Wage and Hour Division.

It is especially important to maintain accurate records as relates to the beginning and the end of the workday. If start and end times are unclear or poorly documented, Wage and Hour will take the position that all the time spent traveling will be compensable.

## OTHER TRAVEL

*The "day trip":* Travel time is also compensable when it is part of the principal activities of the employee's day or when it is required during a shift. This is true even if the employee is using his or her own vehicle (commuting time from/to the employee's home to the first/last work site are still noncompensable).

*The "overnight stay":* Travel time as part of an overnight stay is compensable to the extent that the employee travels during his or her normal work hours. In addition, travel on a regularly scheduled day off is compensable for all travel time during the employee's normal working hours.

*Emergencies:* Travel time for emergencies and callbacks after the end of a shift is compensable.

## THE DESIGN ELEMENTS

These are the twenty elements of good document design, and they're what give your document visual appeal. You entice the reader into your document when you use them properly:

- Sentence length
- Paragraph length
- Line spacing
- Typestyle
- Typeface
- Emphasis
- Paragraph spacing

- Justification
- Indentation
- Margins
- Headings
- Graphics
- Visual weight
- Contrast

- Color
- Symbols
- Columns
- Lists
- Forms
- White space

I call this the Rule of Three. If you use one, two, or three different design variations, you can be virtually assured of creating visual clarity. But the further away from the Rule of Three you get, the more clutter you create.

Whatever you do, don't go over seven. Anything over that guarantees confusion for the reader. In fact, even seven is highly suspect since it's at the outer limits of visual clarity.

Can you picture a page with seven different typestyles on it? Seven different colors of ink? Seven different sizes of type? It sounds confusing and it is—visual clutter. Anytime you use more than three variations of a design element, you risk confusing—and losing—the reader.

However, some material just doesn't fit well into seven levels or subdivisions. Highly complex technological procedures, for instance, may require ten or more separate levels of material.

If you absolutely must use more than seven levels because of the nature of the material, use other design elements to counteract the clut-

## PART WRITER, PART PSYCHOLOGIST?

A good writer understands the reader's limits. Know how much the brain can deal with and how eye movement affects comprehension. Stick with the Rule of Three, and use the design elements appropriately. You're after the ideal balance for your document.

ter. You might use even shorter sentence or paragraph lengths or add more white space. It's a difficult balancing act.

Just remember that you really can have too much of a good thing. All the design elements are effective. Each one encourages readers to use the document and understand the message. Just don't get carried away and use all of them, in all their variations, at all times. Exercise moderation and stick with the Rule of Three.

## Eye Movement

The eye, like the brain, is a remarkable instrument. But it has its peculiarities and limits. It does four things that dramatically affect your reader's comprehension. It:

1. Takes in approximately forty characters at once
2. Takes in three or more words per second
3. Reads two or more words at one time
4. Moves from top to bottom and left to right, in a zigzag or Z pattern

The overall effect of these processes is that readers tend to read what they *think* they see. That works against the writer's goal of clarity and precision.

1. Think about line length. If the line is forty characters long, your reader can absorb it at one glance. But if it's more than forty characters long, the reader has to use twice the number of glances, and almost twice the time, to read each line.

The standard preset on most word-processing programs is between sixty and seventy characters per line, which is fine for business letters and many memos. But don't fall into the trap of using it unthinkingly for your policies or procedures. Consider breaking your page into columns, or perhaps a one-third/two-third layout. Both capitalize on how much the eye takes in at one time.

In fact, this little secret is actually the reason that formats such as outlines, playscripts, and lists are so effective: They break the information down into smaller chunks that are easier on the eye and can be read faster.

2. The eye takes in three or more words per second. It's only trying to keep up with the brain, but the sheer speed at which it is moving tells us that readers are apt to miss or transpose something.

So use every tool you have, such as headings, sections, or concise wording, to make the message obvious. And don't use unfamiliar words or strange spellings. The eye refuses to accept them.

3. The eye reads two or more words at once. When you see the word "push," do you see the letters *p, u, s, h?* Not likely. You probably visualize yourself in the act of pushing something. That's because we were all taught to read for ideas. As a result, we see groups of words.

What's potentially dangerous about this is that the eye tends to ignore the small words in any group. It may skip "unimportant" little words such as "when," "if," "no," or "until." Yet these words carry critical meaning.

Reinforce these words. The military does it by repetition: "Do not, REPEAT NOT, turn the handle." They understand that the reader can easily overlook the short word *not.* How you emphasize doesn't matter, whether with repetition, boldface type, indentation, or some other design element. Just be sure these words are seen.

Also, keep your word groupings succinct. Avoid using lots of adjectives, descriptors, fancy phrases, and complicated clauses. Pare the information down to bare facts as much as possible.

4. The eye moves in a Z pattern from top to bottom and left to right. That's because in English we read by starting at the top left of the page and move to the bottom right. The eye instinctively follows the Z pattern unless it's drawn elsewhere by some special emphasis or break.

Think about what happens, for instance, when text in the middle of the page is emphasized. The eye is drawn there first, but then it instinctively resumes its normal downward Z pattern. The reader has to make a genuine effort to stop, go back to the top, and start over. This is a good reason to use emphasis carefully and sparingly.

And the Z factor affects more than just the use of emphasis. It can also affect a number of other design decisions, from labeling to the positioning of graphics on the page.

## The Importance of Chunking

These combined quirks of the brain and eye have a number of implications for writers, some of which were addressed above. But probably the single most important implication is this: You must "chunk" the material in your document.

Chunking is a visual technique. It simply refers to breaking the printed matter down into chunks the reader can deal with easily.

Think about it. Would you rather try to read a new software manual all at once or a little at a time? Would you rather be handed twenty-eight instructions at once or given three at a time until you finish? If you'd rather have it in smaller bits and pieces, you prefer your information in chunks.

The longer the printed matter continues without a visual break, the bigger the bite you're forcing readers to swallow. If you give them information in reasonable chunks, they can digest it before going on to the next chunk. They can reread it, think it over, identify questions, and generally be sure they understand it.

On the other hand, if you make them swallow huge chunks of information all at once, they can't digest it at all. They'll end up with verbal indigestion: confused, frustrated, or even hostile.

All of us have been the victims of verbal indigestion when reading policies and procedures. You glance at one and it looks long, complicated, and tedious. Your stomach churns just thinking about having to read it. Then you decide it simply isn't worth the time and effort.

Avoid giving readers verbal indigestion. Chunk information into pieces that are easy to swallow and understand. There are lots of ways to do it. Shorten sentence and paragraph lengths. Use short words. Indent. Bring the margins in. Use emphasis, headings, and color to create definite breaks. Use lists, columns, and graphics. Think about symbols.

How you do it doesn't really matter. Just do it.

---

### A Writer's Design Motto

All policy and procedure writers should remember this fact: *"The human brain can seemingly understand any amount of complex information so long as it is presented in small, simple chunks that are well organized."* —Anonymous

---

## White Space

One of the most important chunking techniques merits special attention. It's called white space, and it's nothing more than the amount of unprinted space on any page.

It may not actually be white. If you're using blue paper, for instance, it will be blue space. But it's officially known as white space and is sometimes also called blank space.

Whatever you call it, it makes the document inviting to the eye because it makes the printed page look as if it can be read quickly and easily. In fact, a good writer should think of white space as silence on a page.

Imagine asking a colleague to explain a procedure and having him tell you everything in one long continuous speech, without stopping for breath. Now imagine that the same colleague pauses regularly and gives you time to think about what's been said.

Which would you prefer? There's not much contest. Yet the nonstop talker is the equivalent of a page with nonstop printed matter. The frequent pauser is the equivalent of a page with plenty of white space.

Your readers notice the lack of white space immediately, but very few say, "There's not enough white space on this page." Most simply say, "It's hard to read."

What's more, many policies and procedures are necessarily quite lengthy. The longer the document, the more important white space becomes as a visual break. What slows all of us down is the density of the printed matter. (How many of us actually read everything that's in a contract or guarantee?) The more white space there is, the faster we can get through the document.

Print experts refer to high-density pages as gray pages. Continuous, unbroken blocks of printed matter create a gray look to a page that's uninteresting, uninviting, and tedious. By adding frequent open spaces to the same page, you can break up that grayness and draw the reader in.

You only have to look at the documents you receive every day to understand how important white space is in enticing the reader. Which ones do you read right away, and which do you set aside in the to-be-done-later stack? Not many of us are in a hurry to plough into five pages of nonstop print.

## The Drawbacks to White Space

As important as white space is, it does have its limits. There are two main problems you have to tackle.

First, adding more white space can make the document considerably longer. Why take a 203-page manual and turn it into 247 pages?

It seems like a logical question on the surface, but don't be misled. You're usually better off adding the white space. The reason? Users are still more likely to read the pages, even though there are more of them, because of the visual ease and appeal. You're better off with a 247-page manual with lots of white space than with a 203-page manual that crams everything in by printing nonstop from side to side and top to bottom.

However, occasionally you may face a situation where you have so many policies and procedures that using the desired amount of white space would make the manual too massive. When sheer size alone makes it unusable, you have to consider the trade-offs.

You have only two choices: (1) Put it all in one manual with the pages densely packed, or (2) split it into two manuals with more white space on the pages. You must make this decision with your user firmly in mind. It's a matter of what's the most practical and convenient for the readers, considering how they'll use it.

The second potential problem with white space is overuse. Blank space that's too generous confuses the eye. The reader gets lost between chunks of information. Attention wanders and may not come back.

Avoid creating vast amounts of white space that make items appear unrelated. Such spaces distract the eye and make the document look disjointed.

Proper balance is the goal. It can be achieved by using a combination of design elements such as sentence and paragraph length, margins, indentation, and line spacing. When in doubt, print out a sample page and check its visual appeal.

---

### DESIGN DISCIPLINE

A word of caution to all writers: Good design requires not just knowledge but discipline. If you use everything at one time, your document will look like the Las Vegas Strip: overwhelming.

Choose well, then exercise restraint, discipline, and moderation. Your readers will feel more at home with the document—and be more likely to stay awhile.

---

## Being Consistent

There is one final guiding principle in document design: consistency.

Consistency is not, repeat not, the hobgoblin of small minds. In policy and procedure writing, it's a power tool to keep the reader with you and increase understanding.

It actually applies to everything you do in both the writing and the design of the document. Consistent use of certain words, formats, and design elements keeps the reader moving. They make the reader comfortable.

If you use seven different typestyles, nine levels of headings, and four different layouts, readers are never sure what's coming next. It's too much. They want some stability and predictability in the document.

The same is true if you use a technique consistently and then change for no noticeable reason. The change breaks the reader's rhythm.

Most writers don't pay much attention to rhythm, but they should. Readers concentrate better, and therefore retain more, when they're in a comfortable rhythm. Think how often we use phrases such as "getting in the swing of things" or "hitting my stride." It's all to do with rhythm. In fact, rhythm is the reason parallelism is so effective as a wording device (see Chapter 4).

Think how often athletes use the word "rhythm." Talk to the winner after a race and you'll hear comments such as, "I found my rhythm." Those who lose or don't place often say, "I just couldn't get into a rhythm."

Consider your readers as information athletes. Winning this race means understanding what's expected of them, and it's mandatory. Help them find a rhythm: Choose a few good design elements, formats, and wording techniques and use them consistently.

---

### THE ENVELOPE, PLEASE?

You design your document to meet the reader's needs. You create visual appeal and avoid clutter. You chunk information, use white space, and design the document effectively. You're consistent and establish a rhythm.

But don't wait around for an award. Not many readers are likely to say, "Thanks *so* much for that lovely policy!" What you're really after is the simple, "Hey, that looks OK." If you hear that, give yourself a pat on the back and take yourself to lunch. You've done a great job of document design.

---

## Chapter Summary

- Even with a well-worded, concise, clear document, you may have trouble convincing users to read it. Use the hidden power of document design to overcome this reluctance.

- First set the stage for good design by considering the state of your internal communications. If they're good, the design elements will draw the reader right away. If they're not good, you have to go to extra lengths to help readers understand why it's important for them to read the document.

- Then create a document that's visually appealing. Remember that appearances and first impressions count. Use the hidden power of document design to entice the reader into your document. Use any of the twenty basic elements of design.

- But avoid visual clutter. Use the design elements in proper balance and don't overuse any of them. There are limits to what, and how much, you can do because of the way in which the eye and the brain function. Observe those limits, especially the Rule of Three. And be consistent in your choice of techniques so that readers can get into a rhythm.

# Tools and Resources
# for Chapter 6

6-1:   Design Tip Sheet

## 6-1: Design Tip Sheet

### Guiding Principles of Document Design

☐ *Chunking:* Breaking information down into reasonably sized chunks.

☐ *Consistency:* Using a few basic techniques throughout the document to create stability and predictability. This allows the reader to get into a rhythm and creates a comfort level with the document.

☐ *Rhythm:* Setting up a consistent cadence in the design and wording of the document.

☐ *Rule of Three:* The ideal number of items or variations for the brain to deal with at one time. You can use as many as seven, but anything over three increases the risk of visual clutter and confusion. This applies to everything you do as a writer, not just design issues.

☐ *Visual appeal:* Making it look easy to read, uncluttered.

☐ *White space:* Unprinted space on the page.

### Twenty Design Elements to Use

☐ *White space:* This is the amount of unprinted space on a page. Use plenty of it so the eye can take in material faster and more easily. However, be careful not to overdo it and create so much blank space that items no longer look related or connected. Print out a sample page and look at it to be sure.

☐ *Sentence length:* Sentences should be approximately twenty words long, shorter when possible. Short sentences chunk information better. Note that policies usually have longer sentences than procedures.

☐ *Paragraph length:* Paragraphs should be approximately one hundred words long, shorter when possible. Short paragraphs chunk information and create more white space on the page. As an example, the average length of the paragraphs in this book is

*(continues)*

## 6-1: DESIGN TIP SHEET (*continued*)

about fifty-five words. Policies generally have longer paragraphs than procedures.

☐ *Paragraph spacing:* Paragraphs spaced too closely tend to run together, and paragraphs spaced too widely look disconnected. Paragraph spacing should be like a red light: just long enough to stop the user and make sure things are clear before proceeding. Consider triple-spacing, indenting the first line, or both.

*Note on desktop publishing programs:* Use the program's paragraph spacing command. If you use two carriage returns, the spacing will probably be too wide.

☐ *Line spacing:* Too much or too little space above and below the line of type creates a problem. This space is called leading, and it should generally be a larger point size than the text. (Like typesize, leading is measured in points.) Stay within a range of 20 percent to 50 percent larger than the typesize.

Also vary the leading with the length of the line. Shorter lines require less leading, longer lines require more. A three-column format requires less leading than standard narrative. Also consider typestyle. Sans-serif styles in the body of the text are usually more readable if they have additional leading.

☐ *Justification:* You have a choice between *ragged right,* which allows lines to end naturally and have varied lengths, and *justified,* which creates a right margin that's flush up and down the page. Some organizations have preferences or standards, but ragged right is generally easier on the eye. It's a more natural line for the eye to follow. In addition, right justified can create excess space between words that results in "rivers" of white running up and down the page, distracting the eye.

☐ *Indentation:* This is a way of adding white space to create a visual break from the preceding item. It's typically used to set off lists, cautions, special notations, and paragraphs.

Vary the degree of the break by varying the

number of spaces you indent. For paragraph breaks, two to five spaces are acceptable. Stay with five where possible, since two tends to be so subtle that it's hard to see.

Be especially careful about identation when using multicolumn formats. Make indents proportionate to the typesize and column width, and use them sparingly. Also check the preset tabs on your word-processing or desktop publishing program. They may be too wide for your use.

☐ *Margins:* Margins must create enough white space to attract the eye to the page. Good minimums are 1 1/4" for top and left margins, 1" for right and bottom margins. Experiment with larger margins as appropriate for your document.

And always consider your binding method. Readers hate it when they find a vital piece of information has been hole-punched out. Also remember that manuals that don't lie flat require a larger left margin. If there is printing on both sides of the page, it affects both right and left margins.

*Note of caution on word-processing and desktop publishing programs:* First, adjust the margin presets. Don't automatically assume the default settings will work for you. Second, be conscious of proportional spacing. You may have considerably more characters on a line with proportional spacing, but what matters is the margin width.

☐ *Lists:* Lists shorten line length, eliminate excess wording, and create more white space. Use them frequently. See Chapter 5 and the List Tip Sheet (5-10) for a detailed discussion of lists.

☐ *Columns:* Like lists, columns shorten line length, eliminate excess wording, and create more white space. They're also easier on the eye than standard narrative. Two- or three-column formats are common; more than that can be too busy (it violates the Rule of Three). Column width is usually dictated by the type of information you have. A one-third/two-third column layout is often very effective.

*(continues)*

## 6-1: DESIGN TIP SHEET (*continued*)

☐ *Symbols:* These are a means of drawing special attention to certain areas of text or statistical data. They're commonly used in procedures to identify warnings or cautions. They can also be used to identify items in a list, but do this cautiously. Symbols have strong visual impact and should be used both sparingly and consistently.

☐ *Forms:* When the policy or procedure contains forms, consider providing an example that's filled out. It can be in the body of the text or in a separate section. Fill it out in handwriting, and clearly label it as an example. You don't want perfectionists laboring for hours to get theirs looking exactly like yours (unless that's required, then say so). Pay special attention to form design.

Users have three common complaints about forms: There's not enough room to fill them out, there are too many unnecessary forms, and there are too many irrelevant items on forms. Eliminate absolutely everything that you don't need, and make the blanks long enough and large to hold the information.

☐ *Visual weight:* Visual weight refers to the relative importance of an item from the eye's perspective. At a glance, what looks more important on the page? Whatever is visually different or distinct carries more visual weight. Your eye and common sense tell you what creates visual weight.

Big weighs more than small. Dark weighs more than light. Color weighs more than black and white. Pictures weigh more than words.

If you give everything the same visual weight, you're talking to readers in a monotone. Use visual weight to give readers obvious clues to content and relative importance.

☐ *Contrast:* Documents with frequent areas of dark and light that are well defined are high-impact documents. Documents with insufficient contrast suffer from gray-page syndrome.

Major elements to manipulate are white space, typestyle, typesize, and typeweight. A quick test for contrast is to turn the page upside down.

The eye can't read the text and is immediately drawn to the areas of contrast instead.

☐ *Color:*  Color is an immediate visual clue that this material or item is different. It's very effective if used sparingly and consistently. Be cautious with color because of its power, which comes from its ability to affect mood and feelings ("seeing red," "feeling blue"). Follow these rules:

- Use appropriate colors (no lime green or orange neon).
- Avoid color combinations that have special connotations (red and green; red, white, and blue).
- Use colors that reinforce the message: blue for authority, red for warnings, green for background.
- Stick with dark, basic colors for text: black, dark blue, dark brown, or dark green against a white background.
- Mix and match colors carefully. Be sure they don't clash or look like faded versions of each other.
- Limit the number of colors to two or three. Two plus the dark print is a good rule.
- Change the typesize and weight as needed. Color print can look smaller than black.
- Recognize that some readers may be color-blind (roughly 10 percent of people can't distinguish green from red).
- Use color mostly for headings and graphics. It's often too strong for text.
- Be consistent. (If you use blue to label charts, use blue to label all graphics.)
- Keep backgrounds pale and foregrounds bright. The eye adjusts better.

☐ *Typestyle:*  Typestyle, font, and typeface (which are different to professional printers but the same for our purposes) affect readability. There are thousands to choose from, and more are being invented all the time.

It's best to stay with the more traditional and accepted fonts for policy and procedure documents. This isn't the time to dress up in Script or Old English. Times Roman is the most

*(continues)*

## 6-1: DESIGN TIP SHEET (*continued*)

popular typestyle in the English-speaking world. Other common fonts are Helvetica, Garamond, Avant Garde, and Century Schoolbook.

Experiment, but bear in mind that documents printed in an unfamiliar typeface are harder to read. Look for one that's (1) legible, (2) has proportional spacing, and (3) is a serif style (with small strokes added to the edges).

To test legibility, print out a sample. Proportional spacing is generally more legible, partly because it gives the document a typeset, polished look and partly because readers have come to expect it. Serif fonts are often more readable for text, although sans-serif styles (without the small strokes) may be just as readable with proportional spacing and extra leading. Also be careful not to use too many different typestyles in one document. Stay with the Rule of Three.

☐ *Typesize:*   Typesize is measured in points, with 72 points to the inch. Word processors usually vary in one-point increments, desktop publishing in $^1/_2$-point increments. Use 10- to 12-point type, 12 points if you want to be kind to the reader's eye. But make the typesize proportionate to the message and the format. The longer the line, the larger the type should be; the shorter the line, the smaller it can be. (When using larger type in multicolumn formats, also use more space between them. You may also need larger margins and more leading.)

Be aware that all 12-point types are not created equal. A 12-point Helvetica, for instance, looks and is bigger than a 12-point Garamond. The reason has to do with the size of old-fashioned print blocks, which varied considerably. What this means is that you must print out a sample to see what's best in terms of readability and legibility for your document.

☐ *Headings:*   These are a major chunking device and the reader's roadmap to the document. Stick with the Rule of Three whenever possible; having nine different sublevels gets confusing. Differentiate among levels with placement, typesize, typeweight, numbering, lettering, or emphasis.

With placement, the primary heading is usually in the center. The second level is flush right, and the third level is indented. After that, you can use appearance variations on these three (see below). You can also use run-on headings, which are part of the text, usually the first few words of the sentence, and are printed in boldface or a different font. Be careful when using multicolumn formats not to create visual clutter. Generally, headings in columns are either flush left or centered.

Appearance variations for headings include boldface, italics, color, capitals, underlining, or different fonts. Maximum typesize depends on the document, but a rule of thumb is somewhere around 18 points. (I've seen as much as 36 points, but it startles the reader and almost disconnects the heading from the text.) For each sublevel, move down several points in size.

The wording of headings is up to you, but keep them both short and parallel in structure. Single-word headings, however, sometimes get lost. Also be sure the heading is inclusive, telling the reader clearly what's in the section. Consider using questions as a heading. Last, if using two or more lines in a heading, adjust the leading (it should generally be tighter).

□ *Emphasis:* Emphasis is one of the most misused and misunderstood design elements. Readers can't retain everything on a page, so emphasis essentially says, "If you get nothing else, get this." Use it to:

- Accentuate or stress information of special importance
- Be sure information doesn't go unnoticed
- Draw attention to a particular point first
- Shock the reader

The main problem with emphasis is overuse. Too much emphasis on a printed page is like having someone shout at you throughout a conversation. It wears you out. If you underline half a page, you've just yelled at your reader.

*(continues)*

## 6-1: DESIGN TIP SHEET (*continued*)

The most common methods of emphasis are **boldface** (the most effective and least disruptive), *italics* (next best), CAPITALS (hard to read), and underlining (can draw attention to the line instead of the text). However, you can use a number of other ways to emphasize information: marginal notes, color, scoring/screening, varying typestyle and typesize, boxes, symbols, single-sentence paragraphs, graphics, headings, and different formats. Pick the ones that are most effective for your audience and material.

☐ *Graphics:*  Everybody loves a good graphic, but computer capability has led to overuse. Never throw in a chart or table just because it looks nice on the page. There are two rules for use. First, if it adds clarity or increases readability, use it. If not, don't. Second, if you want the reader to visualize what you're saying, use it. If not, don't

Graphics clarify if they help readers see unfamiliar objects, complex data, main ideas, or relationships. Consider reader preferences, if any, and be sure all graphics are clearly labeled and inporated into the text.

Use generous borders and white space around each graphic so it doesn't look crowded. Use high-quality images that won't fade when copied. Use the design elements of emphasis and contrast to isolate the important information in the graphic.

Different types of graphics commonly used in policies and procedures include illustrations, line drawings, photographs, tables, charts, decision matrices, and information graphics (charts or graphs with artwork added).

# 7

# What's the Secret to Creating Good Manuals and Handbooks?

Good news: There are no secrets to creating a good manual or handbook. You just need to answer two questions.

First, can readers find what they're looking for in a fast, logical way? And second, will the book physically be easy to handle and hold up to daily wear and tear?

## What to Put in a Manual or Handbook

As stated in Chapter 3, handbooks are sometimes distributed to a general audience, whereas manuals may be restricted in circulation to a select audience. For the purposes of this chapter, however, the terms are used interchangeably.

But what goes in the manual or handbook? Inclusion is a difficult question because there are no formulas for it. The type of policy or procedure, and the level of detail required, depends entirely on the purpose of the document and on the audience.

Are you creating the manual because it's a legal or regulatory necessity or a program requirement? In organizations attempting ISO or QS certification for quality standards, manuals must contain extremely detailed, precise procedures.

Are you attempting to outline emergency procedures? To create one central source for all general employment information? Is the manual meant to be an informal list of internal departmental procedures?

Ultimately, only you can judge what belongs in the manual, how much should be included, and how detailed it needs to be.

## What Users Want

Users are the ultimate pragmatists. They want easy access to information, physical convenience, and usability.

Hand a 350-page manual in a 3″ binder to even the bravest of users, and watch them wilt. The mere thought of having to plough through all that to find an answer is depressing. And any manual that needs to be carried with two hands is a candidate for the least-used manual of the year.

## How to Give It to Them

The trick, then, is to make sure that the handbook or manual is easy to use from both a physical and an information standpoint. Remember that most people reach for a handbook or manual when they need an answer. They're confused, or they've forgotten something. They don't understand, or they're doing something new. They need help immediately.

To give them that help, you merely use certain mechanical elements of design and production. You don't have to change the individual documents at all.

Design elements deal with the book's structure. That structure must send the message that users won't have to spend hours searching for the right policy, procedure, or subject. The content must be in a logical order, with a reference system that's quick and easy.

The production elements ensure physical usability. The book must be an appropriate size and shape. It must be durable enough to stand up to the level of use it will get. And it must accommodate revisions easily.

## The Design Elements

There are seven design elements for handbooks and manuals, and they're collectively referred to as *front matter* and *back matter*. Each in some way makes it easier and faster to locate information in the book.

All of them are familiar to most of us. In fact, they're so familiar that we usually don't give them a second thought.

The table of contents, for example, is a standard fixture in most manuals. There might also be a list of illustrations and a list of forms. Then there are the other old standards: introductions, indexes, and appendices. Add a glossary where appropriate to the subject.

Incorporating these elements into the manual does everything possible to speed users to the policy or procedure they're looking for. What follows in this section is a brief summary of each element. See the Tools and Resources at the end of this chapter for detailed guidelines on each design element.

---

DESIGN ELEMENTS: LOCATING INFORMATION FAST

- Table of contents      ▪ Introduction      ▪ Appendix
- List of illustrations   ▪ Glossary          ▪ Index
- List of forms

---

## Table of Contents

This part of the front matter is a list of what's in the book, how items are grouped together, and where to find them. A manual can have more than one table of contents. A separate one for each section is convenient if the sections are complex or lengthy.

Many writers create the table of contents before they begin drafting, but it should be done last. It's an overview of what's in the book, and even you don't have a complete overview of the contents until you've finished writing. You may discover then that you need to change the flow of topics or the subject groupings.

The table of contents is critical because it's the first impression readers have of the manual. A good first impression encourages users to read further. A negative one discourages them from reading at all. If the table of contents looks crowded, confusing, or hard to read, users assume that the rest of the document is the same—or worse.

See the Table of Contents Tip Sheet (7-1) at the end of this chapter for details on this element.

## List of Illustrations

This is a list much like the table of contents, but it's for illustrations and graphics rather than for text. It's usually placed immediately after the table of contents at the front of the book and so is also part of the front matter.

You can use one list that includes all illustrations, or you can break each component into its own separate list: list of figures, list of tables, list of photographs, and so on. The most frequently used titles are a list of illustrations or a list of figures.

These lists are helpful to the reader because they eliminate the need to scour the book looking for the right graphic. Readers can usually tell which one they want just by scanning the titles in the list.

See the List of Illustrations Tip Sheet (7-2) at the end of this chapter for details on this element.

## List of Forms

This part of the front matter is just like the list of illustrations except that it deals strictly with forms. If your policies and procedures contain numerous forms, it's helpful to separate them into their own table. (It's also possible to use a forms index.)

If there are very few forms, you may opt to list them with the other illustrations or in the main table of contents. But in most cases, it's best to create a separate list simply because most readers dislike forms and will seize any excuse not to deal with them. A list of forms helps eliminate that common excuse, "I couldn't find it."

See the List of Forms Tip Sheet (7-3) at the end of this chapter for details on this element.

## Introduction

The introduction conducts readers into the document. This part of the front matter sets the stage for what's coming and orients the reader to certain basics about the manual, such as the purpose and scope. The length depends on the type of manual and on the audience, but keep it as brief as possible. Some form of introduction is usually helpful in all manuals.

See the Introduction Tip Sheet (7-4) at the end of this chapter for details on this element.

---

### What the Introduction Tells Readers

- Purpose
- Scope
- Application
- Relationship to other policies and procedures
- Consequences of noncompliance
- Confidentiality
- Management support

---

## Glossary

This is a list of special words, acronyms, abbreviations, terminology, or jargon that readers need to understand. It can be placed at either the front or the back of the book.

The definitions are usually brief, unless you're dealing with a specialized scientific or technical area where complete definitions are necessary for accuracy. You can include both formal and informal definitions, and examples are often used for clarity.

Glossaries are useful in cases where the organization has a specialized language or has developed unique terminology. To a medical organization, "hospital" may refer to the physical structure where medical service is provided. But to a lending institution, "hospital" may refer to the status of an ailing loan.

Experienced users and frequent users know the jargon. Inexperienced users and new users don't. Occasional users may forget from one reading to the next. Audience analysis can help determine whether you should use a glossary, what type, and how in-depth it needs to be.

See the Glossary Tip Sheet (7-5) at the end of this chapter for details on this element.

## Appendix

An appendix should contain information that supplements the text. It rids the text of material that isn't essential to understanding or compliance and distracts readers from the main point. If the information *is* essential to either understanding or compliance, it belongs in the body of the text.

A common problem, though, is material that is essential to understanding but so long and complicated that it disrupts the flow and focus. Try a compromise: Place the appendix at the end of the section or at the end of the policy or procedure to which it applies. Traditionally, appendices go at the end of a book (and so are part of the back matter), but you can vary this if you wish.

The reason that appendices can cause problems is basically psychological: People hate to flip pages. It may sound trivial, but it's reality. Very few readers break off in the middle of a sentence or paragraph to flip back to an appendix. Most wait until they're finished, and then they may forget it or forgo it. Placement is thus an issue that requires some careful consideration.

See the Appendix Tip Sheet (7-6) at the end of this chapter for details on this element.

## Index

An index is probably the most valuable "speed tool" you can give your reader. It's merely an alphabetical list of the items in the manual, but there is no faster method of looking up a reference than to do it alphabetically.

When most of us think of indexes, we're thinking of the standard subject or key word indexes. They're the most common, but there are other types: specialized indexes, categorical indexes, and multimanual indexes.

| TYPES OF INDEXES | |
| --- | --- |
| *Type* | *Example* |
| ▪ Subject (may be key word, topical, or corporate): | The standard index |
| ▪ Specialized: | Forms Index, Title Index |
| ▪ Categorical: | Safety Policies Index |
| ▪ Multimanual: | Procedures Index |

Whatever type of index you develop, the single most important factor is this: Use the terminology the readers use. Stay with realistic language and avoid corporate-speak.

How will the reader look this concept up? If you list "compensation" when readers call it "salary" or "pay" in everyday use, they may never find it. Even cross-references won't help much.

It takes discipline and good judgment to prepare an index. It's easy to fall into officialese or to throw in everything under the sun.

Most indexes are part of the back matter, but placement can vary in some circumstances.

See the Index Tip Sheet (7-7) at the end of this chapter for details on this element.

## The Production Elements

There are six production elements for handbooks and manuals and, like the design elements, they're so familiar that we often pass over them without much thought. It may simply be assumed that the size will be standard 8 1/2" × 11", or that the paper color and weight will be the standard bond. Those binders in the storeroom may be used automatically. And who even thinks about things like the style of the dividers or the type of cover?

---

THE PRODUCTION ELEMENTS: MAKING IT DURABLE AND USABLE

- Size      - Color      - Cover
- Paper      - Binders      - Dividers

---

If you really want people to use these books, make sure they'll stand up to the physical demands of frequent use. Heavy daily use requires sturdy materials: paper that won't tear and tabs that won't break. Rings that break, paper that won't stay in, and books that look like a hundred others on the shelf discourage users from even picking them up.

The main items to consider when deciding on production elements are:

1. How readers will use the manual
2. Under what conditions they'll use it
3. How frequently they'll use it

See the Production Tip Sheet (7-8) at the end of this chapter for a summary of how to apply production elements.

## Size

Most manuals are standard dimensions (8 1/2" × 11"), but there may be occasions when a smaller or larger size works better. A short manual might be printed on 8 1/2" × 11" paper, folded in half, and stapled so that it's easy to carry.

Don't be bound only by the conventional standards, either. You might pull critical procedures out of the manual and reproduce them on small laminated cards. One organization did this for routine equipment maintenance procedures and attached the laminated cards to the equipment. Monthly maintenance improved considerably.

But be sure to consider all the ramifications if you use outsize or undersize manuals. A service organization produced its employee handbook in a 7" × 9" format, thinking it would take up less space and be easier to handle. In reality, it got lost on the shelves, hidden by larger full-size handbooks.

## Paper

Many writers use whatever standard copy paper is at hand. This is usually a 20- to 24-pound paper, which is more than adequate for most applications. But if you expect heavy use, the paper must be sturdy enough to resist wear.

Bent corners, torn edges, and ripped binder holes make a manual almost unusable. Pages get lost, and users waste a lot time. For heavy use, try a paper in the range of 24 to 32 pounds.

Also be aware of special conditions under which certain groups may use the manual. Production and maintenance areas are filled with chemicals and other substances that can spill or splash on the paper. Even water is enough to ruin a manual. In these cases, consider a paper stock that doesn't bleed, a plastic-coated paper, or a laminate.

There is obviously a budget issue here, but recognize that it's a trade-off in terms of practicality for the user. You may save money in the short run, but what if readers get tired of chasing loose pages and give up?

## Color

There are three color issues: (1) page color, (2) section color, and (3) binder color.

Standard paper color—what you probably choose for regular pages—is white for a good reason: It's the easiest on the eye. But don't be shy about printing sections of the book on different colored paper. (The Tools and Resources at the end of the chapter recommend doing just that with your index, table of contents, or glossary.) Or you might use colored paper for a few important pages.

Color is simply a device to draw immediate attention to the desired section, enabling the reader to bypass the need to look at the index or table of contents. If you're doubtful about how well this really works,

---

Color Is Good, But. . . .

Don't use extreme paper or binder colors. Wild and crazy colors may look appealing at first, but they're hard on the eye. The ink also often doesn't take well, and they're too nontraditional for some users. Print a sample page or two first if you're in doubt.

---

just look at the blue government pages in your phone book. Users get the numbers they need faster and call information less frequently.

The same is true with binder color. If users have a whole shelf of black binders, yours is just one of the group. But a red cover stands out and allows the user to pick it off the shelf instantly.

## Binders

Being budget-conscious, many of us use the least expensive binders we can find. But inexpensive binders can batter and tear away from the spine with minimal use. Rings separate or break, making it hard to turn pages or allowing them to spill out. If you anticipate heavy or frequent usage, consider the sturdiness factor before you buy.

Also look at the size you use. A 2″ binder that's full requires two hands to pick up and use. A 1/2″ binder that's full can be pulled off a shelf with only one hand. Will users be on the telephone or holding a tool while reaching for the manual? If so, stay with smaller binders even though you may need two of them: It's often better to separate a thick manual into two usably sized binders. And don't go beyond a 2 1/2″ binder.

---

HOW MUCH WILL FIT?

These are the general rules about ring size (which is a measure of the ring itself and not the binder):

| | |
|---|---|
| *1/4″*: | 50 pages |
| *1/2″*: | 100 pages |
| *1″*: | 200 pages |
| *2″*: | 400–500 pages |

---

Always use a three-ring binder if you anticipate many revisions to the manual over time. Options such as spiral binders allow readers to fold the manual flat, but they're best reserved for cases where the manual contents won't change much. Whatever binding system you use, be sure pages lie flat and are easy to turn.

## Cover

The cover and the binder may be one and the same. But a popular option is a ring binder with a clear plastic envelope on the front for the cover page. Be sure your cover page fits snugly into the plastic envelope without tearing. Make certain the envelope is sturdy enough, wide enough, and deep enough not to rip or pull away from the binding easily.

And be absolutely certain that your binder has an envelope on the spine for a title strip. A beautiful cover is a fine thing, but no one stores manuals with the front facing out. They stand on a shelf with only the spine showing, and an anonymous manual is likely to go unused and unloved.

If you use a printed cover or an imprint, check colors and durability. Will the logo rub off with use? Will frequent handling erase parts of the print?

## Dividers

If you've ever gone to a handbook and found the divider tabs broken off, you already know the problem here. Tabs physically divide sections from one another and are one of the main "speed tools." Again, if you anticipate heavy use, buy sturdy dividers that can take some abuse and survive.

## Distribution Issues

Haphazard distribution of handbooks and manuals can cause misunderstanding and resentment, so approach this issue just as carefully as you do the rest of the project.

Develop a distribution list and check it with several other people. Set it aside for a day or two, then come back to it. You may find an individual or department that simply slipped your mind. Those users may be upset that everyone has the manual except them. The last thing you want now is bad feelings that will increase resistance.

When you create the distribution list, consider who will have to implement the policies and procedures, who will enforce them, and who has a general interest in them. The first two groups must receive copies. The third group, which usually includes senior management and other departments, may not need copies. A summary, a file copy, or copies of only individual items or sections may do.

Your distribution list is also a control mechanism. Check off each recipient as you send out the manuals. If you require an acknowledgment signature (which you should for the legal reasons discussed in Chapter 3), use the distribution list to track who has acknowledged receipt and who hasn't. If your copies are numbered, or if you require users to return their copies at some point, you can also use the distribution list as a tracking mechanism.

See the Sample Distribution Form (7-9) and the Sample Log Form (7-10) at the end of this chapter for forms you can use.

## Chapter Summary

- Creating a good manual is no magic trick. It's a matter of using certain production and design elements that (1) make it easy to locate information quickly and (2) ensure physical durability and usability. All are "speed tools" of some type.

- There are seven design elements: table of contents, list of illustrations, list of forms, introduction, glossary, appendix, and index.

- There are six production elements: size, paper, color, binders, cover, and dividers.

- Also consider the mechanics of distribution. Be sure to include all appropriate parties and get signatures as needed. Use a distribution list to control the process.

# Tools and Resources
# for Chapter 7

## 7-1: TABLE OF CONTENTS TIP SHEET

### Reader Preferences

☐ All readers seem to use them.

### Best Use

☐ In any manual or handbook over ten pages in length.

### Other Uses

☐ Manuals less than ten pages long may also benefit from a table of contents, e.g., a short-but-intensive instruction manual brimming with detailed, complex bits of data. Can be formal or informal when used in shorter manuals.

### Design Variations

☐ Supplement it with a matrix or checksheet that groups items in a different order than in the table of contents. Serves as a cross-reference, depending on how readers will use the information.
☐ Use a different color of paper for instant access.

### Rules for Use

1. Do the table of contents last.
2. Indicate section and chapter titles and subtitles.
3. Indicate page numbers. If paging each procedure or policy separately, indicate section numbers.
4. Include both front and back matter.
5. Use leader dots from chapter and section titles to page numbers.
6. Use a numbering system for sections only if you also use it in the text (Section 1, Section 2, and so on).
7. Use blank lines and indentation for visual ease.
8. Use boldface, italics, or other emphasis for major divisions.
9. Be sure all sections and subsections that appear in the table of contents also appear in the text.
10. Indent subsections by five spaces each. Clearly indicate the subordinate relationships.
11. Update as material is added, deleted, or revised.

*(continues)*

## 7-1: Table of Contents Tip Sheet (*continued*)

12. Use the same numbering system in the table of contents as you do throughout the text.
13. Avoid alphabetizing. Revisions will skew the order.
14. Limit the number of divisions to a reasonable level. Major divisions and one subdivision are standard.
15. Use sequential page numbering if the manual won't change much.
16. If you anticipate much revision activity, number by section (e.g., Section 5.1).
17. Use separate tables of contents for each section in lengthy or complex manuals. The main table of contents then lists only major section divisions.
18. Choose the best location indicator for your audience and material. You can use any of these:
    - ☐ Starting page number:
        *Repair* ....................................................................... *37.*
    - ☐ Starting and ending page numbers:
        *Repair* ................................................................. *37–43.*
    - ☐ Section number:
        *Repair* ..................................................................... *5.1.*
    - ☐ Secton number and starting page number:
        *Repair* ................................................................. *5.1–37.*
    - ☐ Section number and starting and ending page numbers:
        *Repair* ................................................................. *5.1 (37–43).*

### Comments

☐ A table of contents must make a good first impression. If it looks organized, inviting, and easy to read, users assume the rest of the document is the same way, and vice versa. You can either pull readers in with an inviting table of contents or turn them away with a crowded, confusing one.

Pay special attention to spacing. Use indentation and blank lines between sections to create clear groupings. Readers should be able to tell where divisions and subdivisions occur simply by noting the space in between.

Consider your page numbering system. Some organizations number sequentially (page 178). Others number each policy or procedure separately (page 1 of 3). If you number separately, use section numbers instead of page numbers in the table. This is common in technical procedure manuals where there's a need to ensure that users don't accidentally skip information or stop reading too soon.

Think about the order in which divisions and subdivisions are placed. How it would strike you if you opened your employee handbook and the first item in the table of contents was "Firing"? Not a good start. A quick rule when organizing the table of contents—and the entire book—is to put good news first, then insert bad news, and end with neutral news.

## 7-2: List of Illustrations Tip Sheet

**Reader Preferences**

☐ Users find a list of illustrations very convenient, especially in highly technical manuals with numerous graphics that require frequent referencing.

**Best Use**

☐ In any document over ten pages long that has extensive graphics.

**Other Uses**

☐ Can be used as a table of contents for a separate section in the manual that contains only tables, illustrations, or other graphics.

**Design Variations**

☐ Create separate lists for categories of illustrations: a list of tables, a list of photographs, a list of drawings, a list of call-outs, and so on. It depends solely on your audience and their usage patterns.

**Rules for Use**

1. List illustration number, title, and page/section number.
2. List in numerical sequence.
3. Use a consistent numbering system (sequential, sequential by section).
4. List in the order in which illustrations appear in the text.
5. Use leader dots from title to page/section number if the list is lengthy.
6. Use a common nomenclature for all items on the list (example, exhibit, figure, and so on).
7. Use a single column, flush left. There are no subdivisions.
8. Double-space the list.

**Comments**

☐ Lists or tables of illustrations are important to users as a handy, quick reference device. It's frustrating to spend time looking for one simple table that the reader remembers seeing. A quick glance at titles usually steers the user to the right one the first time.

## 7-3: LIST OF FORMS TIP SHEET

### Reader Preferences

☐ Readers tend to like these lists. If there are numerous forms, they may even prefer an entirely separate manual of forms only.

### Best Use

☐ In any handbook or manual with more than a few forms. Since most readers dislike forms, they'll give up the search more quickly than usual. Make forms especially easy to find.

### Other Uses

☐ Can be used as a table of contents for a separate section that contains only forms. Can also serve as a table of contents in a forms manual.

### Design Variations

☐ Can be broken down by type, department, or any other category you wish, e.g., customer service, quality assurance, safety, acounts receivable, accounts payable, billing, and so on.

### Rules for Use

1. List each form by title and number.
2. Use leader dots from title to page/section number if the list is lengthy.
3. Use appropriate spacing between items for visual ease.
4. Use a single-column or double-column format.
5. Sequence in the manner most useful to your readers:
   - In the order they appear in the text
   - In numerical order
   - Subdivided by general subject matter

### Comments

☐ Forms are a point of contention with many readers. They don't like them and hate filling them out. Make it as easy as possible for them to find the proper forms for the task and to fill them out correctly.

(*continues*)

## 7-3:   LIST OF FORMS TIP SHEET (*continued*)

Also consider whether forms should be grouped together in one section or kept with the individual procedure. This depends entirely on how readers will actually use both form and procedure. A separate forms section is faster if readers will use the form independently of the procedure (i.e., read the procedure once, get it down, then only use the form from that point on). If readers will normally refer back to the procedure whenever using the form, keep them together.

## 7-4: Introduction Tip Sheet

### Reader Preferences

☐ Readers don't have any particular preferences. In lengthy manuals, many readers look for some sort of summary up front.

### Best Use

☐ In virtually any manual or handbook. Even a brief paragraph sets the stage for the reader.

### Other Uses

☐ Can also serve as a summary of the contents.

### Design Variations

☐ Can include many different sections:

- Author or originating department
- Compliance (and consequences of failure to comply)
- Confidentiality
- Content summary
- Disposition
- How to use (e.g., format, numbering system)
- Management statement
- Purpose
- Related documents (relationship to other manuals, cross-references)
- Revision method
- Scope
- Special conditions

### Rules for Use

1. Keep the introduction as brief as possible.
2. Include only those sections readers need, given the type of document.
3. Use a regular narrative format.
4. List it in the table of contents.
5. May either assign page numbers to the introduction or not.
6. Write it last, after the manual is finished.
7. If using a signed management statement, update it when there are personnel changes.

*(continues)*

## 7-4: INTRODUCTION TIP SHEET (*continued*)

**Comments**

☐ A brief introduction orients readers to basic information about the manual. Include at least a few paragraphs, even if you don't necessarily label it as an introduction. Readers should be informed of the thinking behind the manual and how the document affects them.

It's tempting to write the introduction early in the process, but avoid doing so. The introduction sets up information that appears in the rest of the manual, so don't write it until you know what the "rest" is.

## 7-5: GLOSSARY TIP SHEET

### Reader Preferences

☐ New users, inexperienced users, or occasional users who may forget between readings like glossaries.

### Best Use

☐ Any manual or handbook with unusual or specialized language, internal jargon, or unique applications. Also helpful with general terms, to distinguish among words that sound much the same (e.g., "mission," "goal," "objective").

### Other Uses

☐ Can be used as a general dictionary for daily use. Usually duplicated and placed in its own binder, so that it becomes an additional reference document separate from the manual.

### Design Variations

☐ Usually kept brief, but may contain extensive formal definitions in certain scientific or technical manuals. Include examples if they enhance understanding of critical items.

### Rules for Use

1. Develop a list of terms that should be included.
2. Decide how extensive the definitions should be (this depends on the audience and subject matter).
3. Decide whether to use formal or informal definitions, or a combination of the two.
4. Include examples if they clarify.
5. List terms in alphabetical order. Do not number the terms.
6. Choose the best format for your document:
   - *Standard narrative,* with terms in boldface or otherwise emphasized at the beginning and set in a single column
   - *Two-column,* like standard narrative but with two columns to the page (for very short definitions)
   - *Split page,* with terms in a narrow column on the left, and definitions and examples in a wider column on the right    *(continues)*

## 7-5: GLOSSARY TIP SHEET (*continued*)

7. Do it as you go, or after writing is finished.
8. If including forms, give information on title, number, where to find it, and when to use it.
9. Consider placing it in the middle or front of the book, on colored paper, for faster reference. (Traditionally, it's placed at the back of the book.)
10. Construct manually or by computer:

   - *Manually:* Use a separate note card for each term, finalize it, then place the cards in alphabetical order.
   - *By computer:* Check your word processor's glossary function. Most allow you to code terms as you enter them, then collate and alphabetize them.

**Comments**

☐ The glossary must reflect the real world of the readers. What terms do they need to know? Which create stumbling blocks for the majority of readers? Which areas require absolute clarity and understanding? What terms are frustrating to users? Who really uses these terms (management or frontline personnel)? What application do the terms have in your organization?

Using a word-processing program to generate your glossary is helpful, but don't rely on it entirely. It's like relying on the spelling program: It does the basics, but the tricky items are left for you. You still have to make decisions about what to include, how formal or informal to make the definitions, and whether to include examples.

## 7-6:  APPENDIX TIP SHEET

### Reader Preferences

☐ Readers with a technical background like appendices because they're used to them and use them well. But most readers hate to flip pages and so ignore them.

### Best Use

☐ For supplementary but nonessential material (e.g., the text of regulations, or statistical data that supplements information in the text).

### Other Uses

☐ For essential material when that material is so voluminous that putting it in the text of the policy or procedure would be distracting.
☐ In complicated procedures with large amounts of statistical data, such as mechanical, equipment, or medical procedures.
☐ If using it for essential information, consider placing the appendix at the end of the section or at the end of the pertinent policy or procedure for faster access.

### Design Variations

☐ Format can vary widely. Whenever possible, use a standard page layout for instant visual identification.

### Rules for Use

1. Develop a standard page layout for all appendices.
2. Introduce each one with a statement that clarifies the relevance of the material.
3. Decide on placement. The appendix should always be at the end of the policy or procedure, section, or manual.
4. Title each one.
5. Identify each by number or letter. Numbers should be in sequence, letters in alphabetical order.
6. List each appendix separately in the table of contents.
7. Place them in the order in which they appear in the text. *Note:* This may not work if you have many revisions over time.

*(continues)*

## 7-6: APPENDIX TIP SHEET (*continued*)

8. Cross-reference the policy or procedure to which the appendix applies.
9. Avoid using appendices as a dumping ground for nice but unnecessary information.

### Comments

☐ Just remember one thing: Most people hate to flip pages. Technical users are the exception, in that they're used to lengthy data such as tables and charts at the ends of documents. Consider your audience and the essential nature of the material.

## 7-7: INDEX TIP SHEET

### Reader Preferences

☐ All readers love a good index. The fastest way to get an answer is to look it up alphabetically.

### Best Use

☐ In all manuals and handbooks. Always use one in a manual that (1) has fifty pages or more, (2) has frequent users, or (3) has a large number of users. Only extremely short documents are good candidates for omitting the index.

### Other Uses

☐ The most common type of index is a subject index, but you can create indexes to cover special interest areas (e.g., Title Index, Forms Index, Graphics Index, Equipment Index). You can also develop indexes for groups of subjects (e.g., Policy Index, Procedure Index, Safety Rules Index, Personnel Index).

☐ Another, though less common, type is an index that covers several handbooks. If users have a large number of manuals to reference, it's easy to forget which one contains what information. This index is usually a stand-alone document because of its volume.

### Design Variations

☐ Can use single, double, or even triple columns, depending on the length of the terms.

☐ Is often helpful to use boldface, italics, or another emphatic method to set off the terms from page-section numbers.

### Rules for Use

1. Identify areas readers are most likely to be interested in, given the purpose of the manual. Write down terms associated with the areas.
2. Identify other terms that readers may use for the items and cross-reference them (CARS. See: Motor Vehicles).
3. Include all items that are in headings or titles.

*(continues)*

## 7-7: INDEX TIP SHEET (*continued*)

4.  Use a single subject index for smaller manuals.
5.  Consider separate or specialized indexes for larger manuals.
6.  Consider a subject title index for larger manuals, and place it immediately behind the table of contents.
7.  List items by word or phrase, with page/section number.
8.  Update the index as you add, delete, or revise the manual's content.
9.  Construct it as you go, not after you finish writing. Update final page numbers before printing.
10. Construct manually or by computer:
    - *Manually:* Use a separate note card for each item. As you write each one, note the page/section number on the appropriate card. Then place the cards in alphabetical order.
    - *By computer:* Use your word processor's indexing feature. Most allow you to code words or phrases as you enter them (the code doesn't appear in the printed text), then collate and alphabetize them. *Note:* If inserting into a desktop publisher, the page numbers may not be correct.
11. Use a two- or three-column format.
12. Use colored paper for instant access.
13. Consider placing it in the middle for quicker access and to avoid as much page-flipping as possible. (Traditionally, it's placed at the back of the book.)
14. Consider placing short indexes in the front of the manual.
15. Consult *The Chicago Manual of Style* or a similar guide for detailed discussions of spacing, subdivisions, alphabetical headers, and similar issues.

**Comments**

☐  If you want readers to use the manual as a permanent reference, a well-done index is critical. It speeds them to the information they need.

As simple as it sounds in concept, a good index is a challenge. Even if you generate yours by computer, you are responsible for judgments about what to include, what to cross-reference, and which terminologies to use.

Remember that it's essential to use the terminology readers use. Don't get bogged down in official corporate jargon. Use the language that readers will have in mind when they think about the issues.

Watch out for the temptation to cover everything in the index. An extremely detailed index is time-consuming and expensive to prepare. It's especially tempting if you're doing it by computer, since you could easily list a dozen or more key words on each page of text. Try for balance. Too much and you swamp the readers; too little and they can't find what they need.

## 7-8: PRODUCTION TIP SHEET

### Reader Preferences

☐ Readers like anything that helps them find the information fast. Since most of the production elements create clearer and more immediate distinctions among sections, they're all helpful. Readers don't usually notice these elements unless they're missing.

### Elements of Production

☐ Size (of paper or binder)
☐ Color (of pages, or binder, or tabs)
☐ Paper (weight, durability)
☐ Binder (durability, size, color)
☐ Dividers (durability, color)
☐ Cover (spine identification, durability)

### Design Variations

☐ Almost unlimited. You can use any combination of elements you wish. Design variations should be chosen with an understanding of how, when, where, how often, and under what conditions the handbook or manual will be used.

### Rules for Use

1. Use the standard approach for standard applications (e.g., $8^1/_2'' \times 11''$ white paper and so on).
2. Don't be afraid to experiment with nonstandard approaches.
3. Consider the sturdiness factor. If readers use the book quickly, frequently, and under difficult conditions, invest in more durable items. A 20- to 24-pound paper stock is fine in most cases, but use a 24- to 32-pound stock for books that will require heavy use.
4. Consider different colors of paper for special sections or frequently referenced sections or items. This is especially helpful in large books.
5. Consider different binder colors to categorize books by type of subject, or to make a book stand out on the shelf.
6. Keep the binder bulk reasonable. A $1^1/_2''$ binder is large, a 2" binder requires two hands to use, and a $2^1/_2''$ binder is almost unusable. Never use a ring size greater than $2^1/_2''$.

7. Choose a binding system that best accommodates both your revision needs and the reader's working needs. Spiral-bound books lie flat and are good for use during work conditions, but don't allow revisions. Ring binders allow revision, but can be awkward to use within confined spaces.

## 7-9: Sample Distribution Form

Here is a sample distribution form to use when handing out manuals and handbooks. Use it to keep track of who has received the book and acknowledged that receipt.

| Distribution List for: _____ | | | |
|---|---|---|---|
| Name and Department | Title | Date Sent | Acknowledgment Received |
| | | | |
| | | | |
| | | | |
| | | | |
| | | | |
| | | | |
| | | | |
| | | | |
| | | | |
| | | | |
| | | | |
| | | | |
| | | | |
| | | | |
| | | | |
| | | | |
| | | | |
| | | | |
| | | | |
| | | | |
| | | | |
| | | | |
| | | | |

## 7-10: Sample Log Form

Here is a sample log form to use when you want to track both distribution and return, or when you number and assign your books.

| Manual Log for: _____ | | | |
|---|---|---|---|
| *Manual Number* | *Assigned to (Name and Department)* | *Date Sent* | *Date Returned* |
| | | | |
| | | | |
| | | | |
| | | | |
| | | | |
| | | | |
| | | | |
| | | | |
| | | | |
| | | | |
| | | | |
| | | | |
| | | | |
| | | | |
| | | | |
| | | | |
| | | | |
| | | | |
| | | | |
| | | | |
| | | | |
| | | | |

# 8

# Did I Forget Anything?

Right now you should congratulate yourself, because the hardest part of the project really is over. But you've got one more task: the review process. You must revisit the document to be sure it's both workable and correct.

Writing policies and procedures is a major undertaking, and the person in charge (writer—that's you!) is ultimately responsible for mistakes and errors. Your goal, by definition, is to make both content and form as nearly perfect as possible.

## Creating a Perfect Document

Yes, you can create a perfect document. In fact, sometimes you have no choice. A near-perfect electrical procedure can leave someone dead.

But remember that you're already close. You have a clear, concise document that's well designed and easy to read. Now is the time to make sure that it does what you really want it to do. The review process fine-tunes your document, double-checking everything from accuracy to spelling. However, this can't all be done at once, so there are five different types of review:

1. Verification
2. Validation
3. Editing
4. Proofreading
5. Approval

These reviews all deal with different issues, starting with accuracy (verification reviews), and moving straight through to spelling and punctuation (proofreading) and finally getting clearance (approvals). It's important that they be done sequentially so that the most critical issues are addressed first.

The rest of this chapter describes key elements of each review level. Tools and Resources with detailed methods are at the end of this chapter.

---

### Do It Right

Conducting reviews in the proper order saves you time. Imagine having spent hours editing a section, only to discover that the procedure in it is unworkable and has to be rewritten. Validating first would have saved precious time spent on premature editing.

---

## Combining Reviews

Writers often say that they don't have time for all these reviews. Can you combine the different types and make one or two passes at the document?

You can, and it sometimes works very effectively. But it's a much more demanding task and requires greater skill on the reviewer's part.

When you compress many tasks into one, something usually suffers. It's tough to look for format, grammar, punctuation, accuracy, reading level, legality, and usability all at one time. The tasks are widely varied in nature, and there are just too many of them.

If you do combine several reviews into one, make a conscious decision about what you're really reading for. Limit yourself to a reasonable group of items. Don't fool yourself into thinking that you can make just one pass at that manual and achieve the same result as you would with several separate reviews.

One way to avoid this problem is to use multiple reviewers to speed the process. But the real key is to build adequate review time into the schedule up front. Include time for verification, for validation, for editing, for proofreading, and for approval. Failure to plan your review time is a guarantee that the document will go out with mistakes in it.

---

### "I Really Don't Have the Time. . . ."

None of us have it. Good policy and procedure writers *make* it. If you must, compress several types of review into one. It isn't ideal, but it can work if it's done with care.

---

## A Note About Verification and Validation

Many writers skip verification and validation and go right to the editing process. It's tempting, but it's also a mistake.

These first levels of review deal with accuracy and usability. Is the policy or procedure correct? Does it make sense? Does it work? These are the main concerns of both the reader and the organization.

They're also the foundation of the finished document. Readers may forgive a typographical error, poor word choice, poor layout, or even illogical flow. They're far less forgiving about inaccurate, impractical, or unusable content.

Verification and validation are usually discussed together because they're often conducted as one review. In policy and procedure writing, however, they may be independent processes and so are discussed separately here.

## Verification

When you verify, you're checking for accuracy. Is the information correct and up-to-date? Are the equipment dimensions accurate? Are the eligibility requirements correct? You're double-checking the information and data.

There are a number of different verification methods. You can compare the final draft to the original draft. You can check it against source documents. You can confirm numerical and statistical data. You can assign a content expert to do the review.

Some writers combine these methods and some use them separately. The more critical accuracy is in your situation, the more checks you want to perform.

Verification is especially important in procedures, where near-perfection may not be good enough. In mechanical or medical procedures, for instance, one small mistake can create a large crisis. Time spent verifying is time well spent.

One note of caution: You can sometimes combine verification with editing, but it's usually best if it's a separate review. Checking for accuracy while also thinking about flow, wording, or layout usually doesn't work. You're trying to do too much at once, and accuracy is too important to sacrifice. You may be able to combine verification with validation, but try to separate this review from the others—especially if the subject is complex, lengthy, or highly technical.

See the Verification Tip Sheet (8-1) at the end of this chapter for details on this review.

---

### User vs. Document Errors

Two types of errors surface in verification and validation: (1) possible user error and (2) possible policy or procedure error. The first is an error on the part of the user, the second is an error built in to the policy or procedure.

It's important to distinguish between them because the solutions are different. For user error, alter the wording or format to make the policy or procedure clearer, or give additional training and supervision. For policy or procedure error, change the content or sequence.

---

# Validation

When you validate, you're checking for usability. Is the policy or procedure understandable and well delivered? Does it work in the real world?

For policies, the main purpose of validation is to be sure the concept is understandable. For procedures, the main purpose is to be sure the steps are both understandable and doable.

## Validating Policies

Read the policy completely through to see if it makes sense or if anything is missing. Some writers do this themselves, but it's best to use at least one or two other reviewers. What is to you a simple, straightforward concept may be mind-boggling to someone else.

Policies can be difficult to validate. They're often ambiguous and hard to measure. The best way to test a policy is to give it to several people and watch their reactions as they read it. If they look puzzled or confused, something's wrong.

It may be poor wording, or it may be that something is missing. Make notes of their reactions and ask them about it. You need honest feedback.

## Validating Procedures

Validating procedures takes longer because you're actually testing the steps and the sequence. As with policies, you can do this yourself, but it's more effective to have others involved.

There are numerous techniques for validating procedures: walkthroughs, observation, focus groups, and surveys. You can use them together or separately, depending on how much testing you think the procedure warrants.

All of the methods require you to go through the basic steps of preparation, testing, debriefing, and documentation. First familiarize yourself with the procedure, then test it by the chosen method. After the test, analyze what happened and document it so that the appropriate changes can be made.

## What to Look For

When validating either policies or procedures, look for anything that indicates a problem on the user's part: hesitation, guesswork, rereading, page flipping, or improvisation. Is the user having trouble locating parts or equipment? Taking an excessive amount of time? Constantly flipping from one section to another?

See the Validation Tip Sheet (8-2) at the end of this chapter for details on this review.

# Editing

Editing is the next level of review and the one most of us are familiar with. Once you're sure the content is correct and understandable, you're

---

### THE EDITING CHALLENGE

An editor's greatest challenge in policies and procedures is to make sure that the editing doesn't alter the meaning. Even the simple act of substituting one word for another can lead to misunderstandings and unique interpretations. Tell a user to "hit the key," and you might see a different reaction from what it would be if you said "press the key." Good editors are constantly on guard to avoid accidental alterations of meaning.

---

ready to refine the document's style and tone. But editing presents a unique challenge: to improve the policy or procedure without changing the meaning.

The main purpose of this review is to check for items such as format, wording, consistency, flow, cohesion, layout, and visual appeal. These are the finishing touches that make the document read smoothly and look good.

## The Number of Edits

How many edits you go through depends largely on the document and the project. A complex, lengthy procedure requires substantially more editing than a simple one-paragraph policy.

Use the number of edits you feel is appropriate. Try breaking them down by groups: a format edit, a language edit, a style edit, and so on. This increases concentration by narrowing the scope.

Also be careful not to confuse the function of editing with the functions of verification and validation. Titles aren't that important: You can call verification an accuracy edit or validation a usability edit. Just be sure you do all of them.

## How to Edit

Good editing is a matter of knowing what you want from your document. In the case of policies and procedures, it's *readability* and *usability* (accuracy and content are addressed during verification and validation). Know your audience and your organization, and that knowledge will be your guide as an editor.

The mechanics of editing are largely a matter of organization and consistency. Use a uniform marking system. Develop a style sheet if you don't already have one. Use an insert system for major changes, and try different color pens for different drafts. Read aloud to see how the text sounds. Good editors use every trick available to keep the process organized and focused.

Approach editing with great precision. Know what you're editing for, and plan sufficient time to do it. And don't be distracted by side issues. There are always other things to spot during an edit, and it's easy to get sidetracked. If you're doing a format edit, ignore grammar.

## Level of Detail

Editing should be done with an eye to the important matters of mechanical correctness, not the trivial ones. Items such as transposed letters and

---

Elusive Editing

Editing can mean just about anything you want it to mean. Know your audience, your organization, and your document's purpose. Then look at your schedule and decide what types of edits are most essential to your document and how many you have time for.

---

typographical errors will be caught during proofreading, which is the next level of review. Unless they jump right out at you, ignore them. Concentrate on the items mentioned above.

## What to Look For

Review the page layout. Is standard information blocked out in a brief, clear form? Look at the formats. Are they the best possible options, given the nature of the material and your audience?

Consider the design elements. Is material arranged for maximum visual appeal? Study the style. Is the tone appropriate for the audience and the content?

Then scrutinize everything for consistency and logic. Look at structure: sections and groupings, headings and subheadings. Look at style: formality, tone, abbreviations, word length, sentence and paragraph length, wording. Look at design: graphics, typestyle and size, emphasis, margins.

See the Editing Tip Sheet (8-3) at the end of this chapter for details on this review.

## Proofreading

Proofreading is every bit as important as the other reviews, but for a different reason: Your audience assumes that if you let little things slip through, you've probably let some big things slip through too. The issue is credibility.

Unfortunately, proofreading has a bad reputation. It's not so much that it's boring. It's that most people consider it insignificant. Next time you're proofing and someone asks what you're doing, watch the reaction when you say proofreading. The response is usually, "Oh, then could you just help me with . . ." The assumption is that it's a nontask.

Nothing could be further from the truth. Proofreading is an exacting, demanding, time-consuming step that requires discipline, concentration, and patience. It's the final walk-through of your policy or procedure to be sure that not a single item is out of place.

---

Consider what happened to a sewing machine company when a few letters (indicated here in italics) were omitted from this statement: ". . . the built-in butt*on* holer." The issue in proofreading is the credibility of the document.

---

## The Secret to Effective Proofreading

It's called *decontextualizing*. It means that you must reverse the learned habit of reading for meaning and concepts. Take letters, numbers, and words out of context and consider them strictly as letters, numbers, and words.

This is harder to accomplish than it sounds. We all learned to read by looking for ideas, grouping words together as we moved rapidly from left to right on the page. As a result, the eye has learned to skip the details and connectors of language, words such as "of," "and," or "but."

It's also the reason so many proofreaders miss basic errors: "off" when it should be "of," "adn" when it should be "and," "tha" when it should be "the."

All proofreading techniques are an attempt to decontextualize, to fool the eye and brain into thinking about the details instead of the meaning. (Remember that you've already reviewed for meaning during verification, validation, and editing.)

## How to Proofread

There are a number of ways to proofread, all of which decontextualize in some manner. One of the most common is to read backwards. You can also read aloud, read into a tape recorder, read with a partner, or read diagonally (to check for things like hyphenation). You can turn the page upside down (to check for capitalization), photocopy it, scan it vertically, or just take frequent breaks.

---

### DID YOU SEE THAT?

As one writer says, "Proofread backwards. Proofread out loud. Proofread naked. Anything to keep yourself alert." No, this is not a recommendation that you proofread naked. But if it works for you, well . . .

---

## What to Look For

Look for every single imperfection, small or large, subtle or glaring. Look for typographical errors, punctuation, spacing, spelling, agreement, page breaks, titles, misplaced words and phrases, alignment, names, numbers, typestyle, typesize, and margins.

Be especially careful when proofing graphics. Enlarge the copy you're using so that all the details are enhanced. Make certain every number is correct, every line is plotted accurately, every item is labeled correctly, every bit of information is consistent with the text.

The most commonly missed typographical errors are transposed letters ("thier"), duplicate letters ("rotatinng"), omitted letters ("numbrs"), and substitute letters ("commemt").

In addition, all proofreaders have personal blind spots, certain words or phrases that we're never quite sure of. Should it be *affect* or *effect*? *Lie* or *lay*? Does accommodate have two *c*s and one *m*? Find a memory trick to help conquer your puzzlers, such as *accommodate: to see an M & M* (two *c*s and two *m*s). At the very least, keep a list of your personal puzzlers and their corrections handy as you begin proofing.

## Proofreading Your Own Material

Proofing is your last chance to correct the document before publication, and reviewing your own material at this stage creates even more of a challenge than normal. You may have proposed the document, outlined it, drafted it, revised it, verified it, and edited it. By this time you've read it so much you're mumbling portions of it in your sleep.

Decontextualize, decontextualize, decontextualize. Or give it to someone else to proof.

## Proofreading Fast

Time pressure can ruin you. Quick and good are not synonymous in proofreading. Detail takes time, so include adequate proofing time in the initial schedule.

Unfortunately, despite the best planning, you often face tight deadlines at this point in the project. If you're under the gun or simply out of time, have different people proof for different aspects simultaneously. You can also "free-proof": Read once, without stopping, to flag anything that catches your eye; then check and correct the flagged items only.

Just don't skip proofreading, no matter what the time constraints are.

---

### So You Don't Like Proofreading?

You're tired, and you've seen this document a million times. Do you really have to go through one more round?

Yes. A perfect 200-page manual goes out with one typo—and guess what readers see first? What's more, most of them aren't shy about mentioning it.

Make it a million and one times.

---

See the Proofreading Tip Sheet (8-4) at the end of this chapter for details on this review.

## Approval

Getting final clearance is the last leg of the journey. After checking and rechecking the document, send it to the designated approvers.

However, don't wait until this point to start communicating with the approvers. Talk to them throughout the process. Confer with them for guidance and interpretation. Consult them periodically for input, and update them on major issues as you go. If what you've written comes as a shock to them, you're in for trouble. They may balk and want the whole thing rewritten. Approvers aren't fond of surprises, so don't wait until the last minute.

---

SURPRISE, SURPRISE!

Your document is ready for final clearance, so you send it to the approver—who sends it back saying it needs to be rewritten. You can forget about meeting your deadline.

How does this happen? By not keeping approvers involved and informed during the rest of the development and writing process. Surprise them, and they may do the same to you.

---

## The Formal Approval Process

The approval process should never be haphazard, casual, or done at the last minute. It's best to create a formal procedure for approving policies and procedures. It saves time, aggravation, and confusion.

Your procedure should outline the approval cycle and time frames. Define whether clearances are required after certain review levels. A section manager may need to sign off on the technical accuracy of a policy after it's been validated, but before it's been edited and proofread.

The procedure should also encourage approvers to solicit input and comments from within their own areas. Managers, especially, can be somewhat isolated from day-to-day reality, so circulating a draft to appropriate individual users for comment is often useful.

## Getting Approvals Back

Approvals often sit at the bottom of someone's stack for days or weeks on end. It's a common problem, so don't be surprised if it happens to you. The good news is that there is a way to work around it.

Slow response is usually a time problem. Most managers who authorize policies and procedures are busy, and this is just one more administrative matter on their plates.

There's a simple way to conquer these delays: Make it so easy for approvers to respond that they're glad to take care of it and get it off the agenda. How? With a well-designed form that's fast and easy to fill out.

The time-consuming part for approvers is originating a memo with comments and a detailed response. But you can give them a good form, with limited information to fill out, to encourage fast action. See the Sample Approval Form (8-5) at the end of this chapter for an example of a good form.

If you have a lengthy document or manual, give the approver a summary memo. Include the impact of the policy or procedure (both positive and negative), implementation ramifications, cost considerations, overall rationale or need, and internal side effects such as potential fallout, controversy, and resistance.

Making it fast and easy for approvers to respond eliminates the majority of late response problems.

---

### HELP APPROVERS HELP YOU

Approvers don't like to take the time required to deal with these matters, so help them to give you what you need. Make it easy by giving them an approval form that has just a few boxes to check and a brief comments section to complete. Some reading, a few pen strokes, and they're done.

---

## Disagreement Among Approvers

Don't be disturbed by disagreements among approvers. One of the main purposes of having multiple approvers is to identify differences of opinion. It's better now than after the policy or procedure is in force.

When this happens, your job is to coordinate and communicate. Analyze the responses and look at the validity of the objections. Set up a joint meeting if appropriate and review the issues thoroughly. It may ultimately be necessary to override an objection, but it should be done only after careful consideration and discussion.

## Unofficial Approvers

Official authorizations are necessary and proper, but you also have unofficial approvers. These are the influential people who give an unofficial thumbs-up or thumbs-down to the final product. Frontline managers, group leaders, or even informal clique leaders can be your key supporters or detractors in implementation.

Don't forget them during your writing and review phases. Keep them informed of your progress. Consult with them on issues. Solicit their suggestions, advice, and viewpoints. As you near completion, keep them up-to-date on status and time frames.

Just like official approvers, the unofficial influencers dislike surprises. The difference is that they can make or break the policy or procedure because they're the ones who use it every day. Communicate with them and get them involved to avoid later problems. One helpful tool is the "Unofficial" Approvers Analysis Form (8-6) at the end of the chapter.

See also the general Approval Tip Sheet (8-7) at the end of this chapter for details on this review.

# The Critical Decision: Who Reviews?

Reviewing your own work at any of these stages is extremely difficult. You're too close to it. You don't really see what's printed on the page; you see what you thought you wrote.

It's always better to have others review your document. They'll improve it simply because they're fresher and can find things you're no longer seeing.

## Using Other Reviewers

Other reviewers bring a fresh eye and a fresh perspective with them. However, they may also bring their own marking system or their own style guide. The use of other reviewers requires that you control the process, or it may create chaos at a time you can least afford it.

Communication and coordination are the keys to using other reviewers. See the Guidelines for Using Multiple Reviewers (8-8) at the end of this chapter for details.

## Reviewing Your Own Work

Yes, it's best to have others review your work. Unfortunately, it's not always possible. Many times there is no one else available. You're it: the sole developer, researcher, writer, and reviewer all in one.

If you must be your own reviewer at any or all of the review levels,

---

REVIEWER'S SYNDROME

Are you reciting section 3 in your sleep? Can't get that seventh step out of your mind? Format getting you down?

Get help. Enlist someone else to share the work. Beg or plead if you must, but don't compromise the integrity of the document.

---

you'll have to exercise twice your normal discipline. Consciously control your physical and mental environment. Play tricks on yourself to stay fresh. It's all in the name of concentration.

Specific suggestions for techniques and tricks to use are in the Guidelines for Reviewing Your Own Work (8-9) at the end of this chapter.

## Chapter Summary

- Reviewing is the final step in the process of writing policies and procedures. It ensures accuracy in both content and writing.

- Without adequate review, the policy or procedure will contain embarrassing, costly, and sometimes dangerous mistakes. Plan sufficient time into the schedule for adequate review, and use other reviewers to share the task.

- There are five different types of review: verification, validation, editing, proofreading, and approval.

- Verification and validation are separate processes that are often done together. Verification makes sure that the policy or procedure is accurate. Validation ensures that it's both understandable and usable.

- Editing refines the document's style and tone. It ensures consistency and is concerned with making the document easy to read and easy to use.

- Proofreading catches all grammatical, mechanical, and typographical errors.

- Approval reviews give the final authorization to implement the finished policy or procedure.

# Tools and Resources
# for Chapter 8

## 8-1: VERIFICATION TIP SHEET

### Purpose

☐ Verification ensures that the document is accurate and complete. It's a process of double-checking to find any errors in the content. The more complex or technical the document, the more critical it is.

### When to Do It

☐ Right after the document is finalized. Can be combined with validation as one review in some cases.

### What to Look For

☐ Any mistakes in content or meaning. Look at all information and data for technical correctness.

### Special Considerations

1. *Err on the conservative side:* If you're uncertain about an item, mark it. Then research it for confirmation. Guessing isn't good enough.

2. *Block out all distractions:* The whole purpose of verification is to catch *everything* that may be wrong in the content of the document. One error is one too many in some policies and procedures. Verifying requires intense concentration and attention to detail, so find or make a quiet place to work.

### How to Do It

1. *Compare the final to the original draft:* If you've produced multiple drafts, go back to the original and compare it to the final version. Errors in one draft that aren't caught can become permanent features in succeeding drafts. Suppose the temperature figure was transposed from "320°F" to "230°F" in the second draft, but that mistake wasn't spotted. If you compare the third draft only to the second draft, that number will

*(continues)*

## 8-1: VERIFICATION TIP SHEET (*continued*)

|  | appear to be correct. The wrong number becomes permanently embedded in the document.<br><br>It isn't necessary to use the original as a comparison in all drafts, but do use it with the final version. |
|---|---|
| 2. *Check the final draft against the original source documents:* | You know the original source documents are correct: notes, charts, tables, reports. (Any doubts about their accuracy should have been resolved during the research phase, before drafting began.) Before final publication of critical policies and procedures, compare the final version to the source documents. If time won't permit wholesale comparison, compare only critical items or sections. |
| 3. *Check numbers, formulas, and statistical data:* | In some policies and procedures, the main accuracy concerns are statistical data. Check numbers, formulas, charts, and graphs. Be sure totals add up and measurements are properly labeled. This approach usually bypasses the narrative of the document except for references it may contain. |
| 4. *Have others review it:* | Use content experts or people with experience in the subject. Content experts can spot discrepancies faster than nonexperts. When verifying content issues that are nontechnical (as is frequent in policies such as a customer service or a vacation policy), ask someone with experience in the subject to review it to see if it conforms with standard practices or the desired end result. |

## 8-2: VALIDATION TIP SHEET

### Purpose

☐ Validation ensures that the policy or procedure is understandable and usable.

### When to Do It

☐ Prior to editing and proofreading. Can sometimes be combined with verification as one review.

### What to Look for in Policies

☐ *Is it understandable?* Does the policy make sense? Is it clear? Is anything missing? Is the information sufficient? Is the concept clear? Has ambiguity been used appropriately? Will readers have trouble following it?

### What to Look for in Procedures

☐ *Is it understandable <u>and</u> usable?* Does the procedure work? Can the user follow the steps? Can the user take the steps in the correct order? Do the steps require the reader to backtrack? Are warnings clear? Can the user take action quickly after reading?

### Signs to Watch For

☐ Excessive time spent
☐ Guesswork
☐ Hesitation
☐ Improvisation
☐ Omissions
☐ Page flipping
☐ Rereading
☐ Trouble locating equipment or parts

*(continues)*

## 8-2:  VALIDATION TIP SHEET (*continued*)

**How to Do It**

1.  *Have a user walk through the procedure from start to finish:*

Users can identify errors faster than anyone else. They can also spot practical problems others may miss: shortcuts that should have been taken (and those that shouldn't), timing difficulties, inconsistencies, contradictions, obstacles, and outright impossibilities.

2.  *Have multiple users do a walk-through:*

You'll get more information with a broader sample. Include users with different levels of experience, education, training, and receptivity.

3.  *Do a walk-through yourself:*

It's preferable to have a user do the walk-through, but the writer can also do so effectively when a user isn't available. Reserve this technique for situations where time is short and staff is limited.

4.  *Use a focus group:*

Focus groups give a broader sampling of opinions and reactions and allow the group to discuss the subject. Use a representative sampling of affected parties: users, readers, enforcers, and approvers.

To keep the group to a manageable size, some writers use the Rule of Four: two users, one senior manager, and one colleague. Be sure that whoever leads the sessions is a skilled facilitator; otherwise, the discussions can turn into personal gripe sessions.

5.  *Observe a user doing a walk-through:*

This technique combines the user's experience with the writer's knowledge. Cooperation from the user can be a problem, since none of us likes to work with someone peering over our shoulder. Explain what you're doing and why. Ask for permission. Get comments and clarification as you go. Note conditions or exceptions. Record your observations and review them with the user.

| 6. *Survey users:* | Keep questions short and to the point, but be thorough. Probe for points of confusion, errors, and omissions. Word the survey in as nonthreatening a way as possible, and encourage honest reactions. |
| 7. *Review documents and files:* | Look for records of current or past difficulties or complaints. Look for suggestions that may have been made but never acted on. |

## 8-3: Editing Tip Sheet

### Purpose

☐ Editing refines the tone and style of the document. It also creates a document that's visually appealing, easy to read, and easy to use.

### When to Do It

☐ After verifying and validating the processes. Should be done for all policies and procedures.

### What to Look For

| | |
|---|---|
| ☐ *Visual appeal:* | Indentations, margins, headings, spacing, centering, alignment, graphics, lists. |
| ☐ *Consistency:* | Numbering system, headings, format, page layout, vocabulary, style, symbols, graphics. |
| ☐ *Usage:* | Parallelism, misplacement, negatives, ambiguity, repetitiveness, transitions, absolutes. |
| ☐ *Grammar:* | Subject-verb agreement, pronouns, tense, voice, phrases and clauses, modifiers. |
| ☐ *Vocabulary:* | Jargon, acronyms, definitions, abbreviations, technical terms, clichés, sexist language, fad phrases. |
| ☐ *Punctuation:* | Hyphens, dashes, commas, colons, semicolons, lists. |
| ☐ *Organization and flow:* | Headings, subheadings, numbering system, paragraph usage, paragraph unity, transitional words and phrases. |
| ☐ *Format:* | Familiarity, clarity, speed, visual appeal. |

### How to Do It

| | |
|---|---|
| 1. *Develop a style sheet:* | Outline standards for format, layout, grammar, and other conventions you intend to use. |
| 2. *Use a uniform marking system:* | Use standard editing and proofing marks, or develop your own. Be sure everyone is using the same system. |

| | | |
|---|---|---|
| 3. | *Use an insert system for lengthy changes:* | Write the change on a separate sheet of paper and label it "Insert A." Then place a notation in the text, "See Insert A." You can use letters or numbers, but be consistent. |
| 4. | *Flag rewritten text:* | Use a question mark or other symbol to indicate that the original author should check to be sure the meaning is intact. Wording changes can accidentally alter the meaning. |
| 5. | *Use different color pens:* | Assign each reviewer a different color or designate a different color for each draft. |
| 6. | *Double- or triple-space the drafts:* | Leave enough room so that changes can be clearly marked. |
| 7. | *Label each draft:* | Stamp or mark each version with an identifying label or number: first draft, draft 1, preliminary draft, and so on. |
| 8. | *Read aloud:* | If it sounds boring, stilted, or confusing out loud, chances are that it will sound that way to the users too. |
| 9. | *Put it away for a while:* | A day or two is ideal, but an hour or two is better than nothing. Work on something else for a while. |
| 10. | *Read one section at a time:* | Create defined breakpoints and observe them. Avoid overload. |

## 8-4:  PROOFREADING TIP SHEET

### Purpose

☐ Proofreading is done to find and correct all mechanical, grammatical, and typographical errors.

### When to Do It

☐ Immediately prior to final printing.

### Common Errors to Look For

☐ Transposed letters, as in "recieve"
☐ Duplicate letters, as in "sendiing"
☐ Omitted letters, as in "numbrs"
☐ Substitute letters, as in "commemt"
☐ Personal puzzlers, as in spelling ("accommodate") or in usage ("lay" versus "lie")

### How to Do It

1. *Make several passes:* Focus on a different aspect on each pass: spelling, grammar, punctuation, typographical errors. Segmenting helps concentration.

2. *Read backwards:* There are a number of ways to do this. You can read backwards paragraph-by-paragraph, sentence-by-sentence, or word-by-word. Going word-by-word is extremely time-consuming, so many proofreaders prefer to do it sentence-by-sentence. Some proofreaders prefer to read backwards by section or page.

3. *Read out loud:* Reading aloud forces you to slow down. You must pronounce each word and observe each punctuation mark, and you are more likely to catch the small mistakes in "insignificant" words (like "of," "the," "and").

4. *Read with a partner:* It's effective for the same reasons as reading out loud, but it doubles the ability to catch mistakes.

| | | |
|---|---|---|
| 5. | *Read into a tape recorder:* | Record it, then proof as you listen to the tape. It's a nice compromise when a partner isn't available. |
| 6. | *Read diagonally:* | This helps you check for word divisions, hyphenation, and repetition. Start at the end of the line (on the right-hand side of the page) and go to the beginning of the next line (on the left-hand side of the page). |
| 7. | *Turn the page upside down:* | This helps you check for capitalization, which tends to stand out readily when the page is upside down. |
| 8. | *Scan vertically:* | This helps you check for spacing, outlining, and alignment. Look for any odd clumps of white space, including "rivers" of white. |
| 9. | *Read in three- to six-word clusters:* | Limit the amount of material the eye and brain take in at one time. It prevents the brain from looking for ideas and focuses on details. |
| 10. | *Use "free-proofing":* | This helps you catch major problems when you have limited time or large volumes of material. Read quickly, flagging anything you sense has a problem. Go straight through without stopping. Then go back and look at only the marked items in detail. |

## 8-5:  Sample Approval Form

<table>
<tr><td colspan="3" align="center">Review and Approval Form for Policies and Procedures</td></tr>
<tr><td>From:</td><td>Mail Stop:</td><td>Date:</td></tr>
<tr>
<td>To:<br>☐ Operations Mgr.<br>☐ Production Mgr.<br>☐ Personnel Dir.<br>☐ Dir., Eastern Div.<br>☐ Dir., Western Div.</td>
<td>☐ V-P, Admin.<br>☐ V-P, Finance<br>☐ V-P, Marketing<br>☐ General Counsel<br>☐ President</td>
<td>☐ _____<br>☐ _____<br>☐ _____<br>☐ _____<br>☐ _____</td>
</tr>
<tr>
<td>☐ Policy ☐ Procedure<br><br>Number:<br>Title:<br>Description:</td>
<td>Approval:<br><br>☐ Preliminary<br>☐ Final</td>
<td>Status:<br><br>☐ Revision<br>☐ New Issue</td>
</tr>
<tr>
<td></td>
<td colspan="2">Return by: _____ days from now. If you are unable to meet this deadline, please contact _____ at _____.</td>
</tr>
</table>

**Response/Approval:**
    ☐ Approved without comment
    ☐ Approved with comments below
    ☐ Approved on condition comments below or attached are resolved.
    ☐ Not approved. Reasons given below or attached.

**Comments:**

| Signature: | Date: |
|---|---|

## 8-6: "UNOFFICIAL" APPROVERS ANALYSIS FORM

1. Who will be most affected by this policy/procedure?

   _____

2. What are their main concerns likely to be?

   _____

   _____

   _____

3. Which users (individuals or departments) have the most influence with their peers? _____

   _____

   _____

4. Of these, which ones support the policy/procedure? _____

   _____

   _____

5. Which ones are neutral about it? _____

   _____

   _____

6. Who opposes it, and why?

   *Individual/Department*                    *Reason*

   _____            _____

   _____            _____

   _____            _____

   _____            _____

7. What have we done up to this point to overcome this opposition and get buy-in? _____

   _____

   _____

   _____

   _____

*(continues)*

## 8-6: "Unofficial" Approvers Analysis Form (*continued*)

8. What can we do now to get buy-in or at least defuse the opposition? _____

_____

_____

_____

_____

9. How can we use the support of those individuals/departments who favor the policy/procedure?

_____

_____

_____

_____

_____

## 8-7: APROVAL TIP SHEET

### Purpose

☐ Approvals give the writer final authority to proceed with publication and implementation of the policy or procedure.

### Types

☐ *Formal approval:* An official sign-off from a designated authority

☐ *Informal approval:* Should begin in the initial planning stages with user involvement and continue throughout the project.

### Special Considerations

1. *Develop a formal approval procedure:* Don't leave official sign-offs to chance. Have an agreed-on procedure with the approver or an official procedure, whichever seems more appropriate in your circumstances.

2. *Develop an easy-to-use form for official approvers:* A quick form that requires minimal effort on the approver's part encourages a faster return.

3. *Resolve differences between approvers:* How this is done depends on the nature of the disagreement, the subject, and sometimes the relative authority level of the approvers.

4. *Consider how to approach your informal approvers:* Identify influential users who may help or hinder the implementation of the policy or procedure. Analyze objections and strategize how to deal with them. Develop a strategy to use the influential supporters also.

## 8-8:  Guidelines for Using Multiple Reviewers

Communication and coordination are imperative when you're using other reviewers. Lack of clarity in supposedly simple matters, such as the marking system to be used, can cause endless confusion.

| | |
|---|---|
| 1. *Use content experts:* | Use grammar and format experts for proofing and editing. Use subject matter experts for verification and validation. |
| 2. *Meet with them in person:* | This elicits greater cooperation than a memo or e-mail message. |
| 3. *Assign specific roles:* | Use each reviewer's specific area of expertise. Consider individual schedules. |
| 4. *Ask for detailed, constructive feedback:* | Be specific about what you want from each reviewer on each draft. Watch out for the constant complainer. |
| 5. *Emphasize objectivity and thoroughness:* | Reinforce the fact that accuracy, readability, usability, and correctness are the issue, not personal preference. |
| 6. *Agree on deadlines:* | Everyone has demands on his or her time. Negotiate as needed. |
| 7. *Follow up before deadlines:* | This is a courtesy and a gentle reminder. |
| 8. *Ask reviewers to initial every page:* | This is especially important if content is critical or there is a significant departure from past practice. |
| 9. *Request a written list of changes:* | This is especially useful in verification and validation, and it is occasionally used in editing, seldom in proofreading. Keep it informal; a handwritten list will do. |
| 10. *Create a file for comments:* | Share the comments with other reviewers as appropriate. |
| 11. *Agree on a marking system:* | Use the same marks, the same color pens, and the same word-processing program. |
| 12. *Define the type of review:* | Is this a validation or a proofreading? A format edit or a grammar edit? |
| 13. *Give reviewers a style sheet:* | You can also develop one that everyone agrees on. The key is consistent conventions and usage. |

## 8-9: Guidelines for Reviewing Your Own Work

If you must be your own reviewer, you have to exercise twice your normal discipline. You're so close to the document that it's tough to catch omissions or errors or see possible improvements. How do you stay fresh?

The trick is largely to decontextualize (take things out of context). And it is a trick: You often have to fool the eye and the brain into thinking that they're dealing with something different.

| | |
|---|---|
| 1. *Control the physical environment:* | ☐ Take more frequent breaks.<br>☐ Adjust the temperature up or down (extremes are good).<br>☐ Exercise before starting, even if you only do a simple stretch.<br>☐ Increase the lighting.<br>☐ Sit in a comfortable chair.<br>☐ Make sure desk or table height is good for working on.<br>☐ Have reference books and marking materials handy.<br>☐ Go to a quiet place.<br>☐ Put the phone on forward or voice-mail, or take it off the hook.<br>☐ Put up a DO NOT DISTURB sign, tell everyone you're in a meeting, or issue instructions that you don't want to be disturbed. |
| 2. *Control the mental environment:* | ☐ Take defined breaks (something to look forward to).<br>☐ Take more frequent breaks.<br>☐ Set the whole thing aside for a while (a day or two is good, an hour or two is better than nothing).<br>☐ Use your personal peak times of the day.<br>☐ Use a relaxation technique to clear the mind.<br>☐ Brainstorm a list of questions before you start (this sharpens focus).<br>☐ Identify areas of confusion or emphasis before you start.<br>☐ Read reasonable amounts at one time. |
| 3. *Trick the eye and brain:* | ☐ *Photocopy the document.* A photocopy looks slightly different.<br>☐ *Enlarge it or reduce it.* This gives it a wholly different look. Enlarging is more practical. |

*(continues)*

## 8-9: GUIDELINES FOR REVIEWING YOUR OWN WORK (*continued*)

☐ *Put it on colored paper.* This is another way to make it look different. Avoid strong colors that are hard on the eye.

☐ *Move to a new location.* New surroundings feel different.

☐ *Read out of order.* Try reading back to front, pick a section from the middle, or be totally random.

☐ *Pretend it's someone else's work*—someone you really dislike.

# 9

# No One Ever Told Me About That

One of your toughest implementation challenges is communicating clearly with the users. After all, all this hard work has had one goal: to make it fast and easy for readers to get the information they need to do their jobs properly.

Yet comments such as "I didn't know!" or "Is that what that meant?" are common. And "No one ever told me. . . ." is legendary in policy and procedure circles.

## How to Notify Users

You have only three choices for notifying users about a policy or procedure. You can (1) announce it in person, (2) communicate it in writing, or (3) send it by e-mail.

Which you use is partly a matter of preference and partly a matter of circumstance. Everyone might prefer a meeting, but if half the users are 2,000 miles away, the circumstances dictate a written notice.

---

### Don't Be Surprised to Hear It

| | | |
|---|---|---|
| "No! Really?" | "I didn't know." | "Nobody ever told me." |
| "It says that?" | "You're kidding." | "Who says?" |

---

Your choice of notice method is often determined by your own organizational norms. Some organizations routinely put everything in writing, while others prefer one-on-one discussions or e-mail. Communication preferences can be strong, and deviating from them can distract or even worry users.

Whichever method you choose, remember that the purpose of notification is to get the user's attention and convey certain basic information. But the substance of the message remains in the policy or procedure itself. Even if you choose to announce it in person, users must receive a copy of the policy or procedure.

---

DETERMINING YOUR NOTIFICATION METHOD

How you notify users—on paper, in person, or by e-mail—will depend on such factors as:

- Amount of material
- Nature of the material
- Complexity of the subject
- Organization's standard

- Communication method
- Size of user group
- Urgency
- Location of users

---

## Notifying in Writing

Notifying users in writing is common because it has a number of advantages. It communicates the policy or procedure in a uniform way to all users. It can be distributed in mass and reaches users at all locations, on all shifts. It serves as legal documentation. And it formalizes and reinforces the message.

It also has some disadvantages. Remote locations and later shifts may get their copies late and feel slighted. It may sound rigid or bureaucratic. It eliminates personal contact and the ability to ask questions directly of the issuer.

The appropriate times to use a written notice are detailed in the Notification Tip Sheet (9-1) at the end of this chapter. Briefly, they are when:

- You're writing for an external audience such as an accrediting agency or customer.
- The audience is large or widely dispersed.
- The material is complex or lengthy.
- The subject is noncontroversial.
- Personal contact is unnecessary.

## Notifying in Person

Notifying in person can take several forms: group meetings, individual meetings, phone conferences, or videoconferences. Whichever format you use, conduct the meetings as quickly and as close together as possible. You don't want some users getting the news by word of mouth.

---

### IMPORTANT CONSIDERATIONS

| *Notify in writing when:* | *Notify in person when:* |
| --- | --- |
| ■ Personal contact is unnecessary.<br>■ The subject is noncontroversial.<br>■ Users are external, widely dispersed, or numerous.<br>■ The subject is complex or lengthy. | ■ The subject is sensitive or controversial.<br>■ You want to emphasize the importance or urgency.<br>■ Unofficial expectations differ from the official policy or procedure.<br>■ It requires examples or elaboration to be understood. |

---

The main advantage to notifying in person is that it gives direct contact with the issuer. That tends to increase cooperation and reduce resistance, because questions can be asked and concerns aired.

The disadvantage is that these meetings can be both hard to coordinate and unpleasant to conduct. You may have three separate shifts or multiple remote locations to cover. And users may be unhappy.

The Notification Tip Sheet (9-1) at the end of this chapter details the appropriate times to use a personal notice. Briefly, they are when:

- The subject is simple or the user group small.
- You need to convey a sense of urgency or importance.
- The policy is ambiguous and needs explanation.
- Unofficial expectations differ from official policies.
- The subject is controversial or sensitive.

The last item on this list deserves special attention. It's especially important to announce sensitive policies and procedures in person. When there's controversy, people want to voice their opinions and get

---

### Sensitive Subjects

Most of us announce controversial policies or procedures in writing because it's easier than facing a lot of unhappy users.

Unfortunately, it also undermines cooperation. Users perceive it as avoidance, cowardice, or both. Neither bodes well for successful implementation.

Facing a hostile audience is never easy but sometimes necessary. Do it in person.

---

---

### Defining What's Controversial

What's sensitive to a user is not necessarily what's sensitive to the organization, and vice versa.

When considering just how controversial an issue really is, put yourself in the users' shoes.

Anything that intrudes on what users perceive as their rights will cause controversy.

---

answers. They want to look the issuer in the eye and gauge what's really going on.

But a written notice often gives the impression that the issuer is either afraid to face users or doesn't care what they think. The result? An increase in "attitudes" and a drop in cooperation.

A good example of a controversial issue is a company's smoking policy. A number of organizations developed policies and simply issued written notices of the new smoking rules. Management considered the issue to be a straightforward matter of health and working conditions.

But many smokers were offended by what they saw as a high-handed mandate that violated their personal rights. Nonsmokers fought back, defending their perceived rights. Ill will lingered for a long time.

Other organizations dealt with the problem in person and experienced a smoother transition. The issue was aired openly, and everyone's opinion was heard. Meetings were often difficult, but smokers adjusted with minimal aftereffects.

## Notifying by E-Mail

E-mail is something of a hybrid approach. It's a written announcement in that it requires the user to read the notice and eliminates personal contact with the issuer. But like the personal notice, it permits the user to fire questions or comments back to the issuer on the spot.

Notification by e-mail is best used when (1) you have on-line policies and procedures or (2) most of the organization's communication flows through an e-mail system and users are comfortable with it.

The Notification Tip Sheet (9-1) at the end of the chapter details the appropriate times to use an e-mail notice.

## What to Put in Your Notice

Written notices, including e-mail, should always include certain basic information. Verbal notices, on the other hand, may vary widely depending on the extent of discussion desired.

## Written Notices

Paper or e-mail announcements should clearly identify the policy or procedure and give a summary of it. Include logistical information such as title and number, effective date, implementation time frame, who's covered, and whom to contact with questions or problems.

Also include a brief summary of the substance: the reasons for it, the basic provisions, user responsibilities, and the impact it will have on users.

The Notification Tip Sheet (9-1), the Sample Transmittal Memo (9-2), and the Sample Transmittal Form (9-3) at the end of this chapter outline the details on what to put in written notices.

---

### WHEN THE ISSUE IS CRITICAL

Notify users both in writing and in person when the matter is of special importance. Don't hesitate to combine methods whenever it helps.

If it's an emergency, notify users by voice-mail or e-mail and then back it up with a written or personal notice.

---

## Verbal Notices

What information you include, and how much, depends on whether you intend for this meeting or phone call to be (1) an introductory session, (2) an informational session, or (3) a training session.

The first is brief and very general, the second is lengthier and contains substantial information, and the third lasts as long as necessary and covers all operational details. Depending on the subject, you may use a combination of meeting types.

See the Meeting Work Plan (9-4) at the end of the chapter to help you prepare for your discussion.

## Special Cases

Consider users who may have special needs, such as vision impairments, language barriers, or literacy problems. As an organization, it's your responsibility to communicate clearly with all those who need the information.

Physical impairments, such as hearing, vision, or even color blindness, can usually be accommodated easily and inexpensively. For instance, you might make an audiotape for a user with a vision problem or meet individually with a hearing-impaired user.

Language barriers can be more costly to deal with, since you may need to translate both the notification document and the policies and procedures themselves. You could also enlist the services of another user who speaks that language.

Dealing with literacy problems is a special challenge. Users who are unable to read or to read well are usually embarrassed. In fact, they're often unwilling to even acknowledge the problem. Exercise discretion and diplomacy. Constant personal contact and communication may be required until full understanding of the policy or procedure is reached.

## Notifying Managers First

Managers are the frontline people who interpret and enforce your policies and procedures. They're the key to successful implementation, and you need them.

Just remember that managers hate surprises. Meet with them before you issue a general notice to all users. Let them voice their concerns and work through the issues without pressure from the watchful eyes of staff. If you want their support, help them.

Conduct these meetings quietly and discreetly, and require confidentiality. Then make the general announcement as quickly as possible so users don't find out through word of mouth.

---

### CAUGHT OFF-GUARD

Imagine this scenario: A manager and her staff are called to a meeting to hear about a new policy or procedure for the first time. The manager has some doubts about what she's hearing, and despite her best efforts, her face and body language show it.

Her staff members are watching to see what her reaction is. When they see that she has reservations, they get the impression that since the boss doesn't like the new policy, they don't have to take it too seriously either.

Failure to notify managers first can embarrass and alienate them. It also undercuts your efforts to gain cooperation from their staff members.

---

## Multiple Notices

You may occasionally find it helpful or necessary to issue more than one notice to users. If a policy or procedure is especially complicated, advance notice of the impending change forewarns and forearms them. This is also true of highly charged or controversial issues that users may need time to adjust to.

Grace periods (see Chapter 10), which allow a gradual transition prior to full implementation, usually require three separate notices. Each succeeding notice adopts a firmer stance on compliance.

## Chapter Summary

- Notifying users can be done in writing, in person, or by e-mail. Your notice method is dictated by both circumstances and organizational norms as noted on the next page:

- Written notices are best used when the audience is large or widely dispersed, the material is complex, personal contact is unnecessary, legal documentation is required, or the subject is noncontroversial.

- Personal notices are best used when the subject is sensitive to users, the policy is ambiguous, or the unofficial expectation differs from the official policy or procedure.

- E-mail is best used when policies and procedures are on-line, or when it's the standard means of communication within the organization.

- Accommodate users with special communication needs, such as physical impairments, language barriers, or illiteracy.

- Enlist managers' support by notifying them first.

# Tools and Resources for Chapter 9

## 9-1: NOTIFICATION TIP SHEET

### Methods

- ☐ *In writing.* Via memo, letter, transmittal form
- ☐ *In person.* Via group or individual meeting, phone, or videoconference
- ☐ *By e-mail.*

### Information to Include

- ☐ Applicability (who's covered)
- ☐ Contact information
- ☐ Effective date
- ☐ Filing instructions
- ☐ Impact (what it does to or for the user)
- ☐ Implementation time frames
- ☐ Reasons for implementation
- ☐ Reference number
- ☐ Summary of basic provisions
- ☐ Title
- ☐ Urgency, if any
- ☐ User's responsibilities

### Special Considerations

- ☐ Users with communication impairments
- ☐ Multiple notices
- ☐ Giving bad news

### When to Notify in Writing

☐ *When it's hard to get everyone together physically:*   Schedules are difficult, and you may be dealing with remote sites, multiple locations, or international users. Meetings or conference calls can be expensive and hard to coordinate. However, do consider occasional personal visits or calls. Late shifts and remote locations can start to feel isolated or abandoned, and that's when compliance slips.

*(continues)*

## 9-1: NOTIFICATION TIP SHEET (*continued*)

| | |
|---|---|
| ☐ *When you're distributing massive quantities:* | In most cases it's impractical to personally notify hundreds, or thousands, of users. The exception is major changes of critical importance, which should always be done in person. |
| ☐ *When it's for external use:* | Accrediting agencies, customers, or other users outside the organization usually want notification in writing. |
| ☐ *When you need legal documentation:* | A written notice is additional proof that every reasonable effort to communicate was made. |
| ☐ *When you want to formalize the message:* | Putting it in writing reinforces the seriousness and official nature of the message. |
| ☐ *When it's detailed, complex, or lengthy:* | Complicated or technical material is hard to get into. The same is true of large volumes of material. A written notice helps get the reader's attention and start the concentration process. |
| ☐ *When personal contact isn't necessary:* | Sometimes a policy or procedure merely formalizes what everyone is already doing in practice or clarifies a routine matter. Many users prefer not to waste time in meetings if the situation can be handled with a brief memo or e-mail. |
| ☐ *When the subject is noncontroversial:* | Written notification is usually all that's needed for noncontroversial matters. However, remember that controversial means controversial to the *user,* not to you. What you consider a routine business matter may in fact be a sensitive issue to users. |
| ☐ *When the organization routinely puts everything in writing:* | Organizations have communication styles and preferences. Observe them whenever possible. Deviating from them may distract or even worry users. |

## When to Notify in Person

☐ *When the subject is controversial, sensitive, or potentially intrusive:*

Users have strong feelings about rules that impinge on what they believe to be their rights. Telling people what they can and can't do on break periods, for example, can cause a storm of protest. Dress codes, nepotism policies, and others may seem like matter-of-fact business issues to the organization, but to users these can be sacred waters. The most effective way to deal with strong feelings and opposition is in person. This way, users can question the issues and vent their feelings.

☐ *When personal contact is needed:*

Any time users (especially employees) start to feel ignored, you're in trouble. They may want the courtesy of a personal appearance. They may be flooded with memos and need some extra motivation to pay attention. There may be lots of routine questions. It may have been a while since anyone talked to the folks on the third shift. Or you may just think people will respond better to a personal notice.

☐ *When the organization routinely communicates verbally:*

Again, every organization has its own communication style and preferences. Stick with them whenever possible.

☐ *When you want to emphasize the urgency or seriousness:*

There's nothing like an intense, face-to-face discussion to drive home a point. In fact, you may want to use both written and personal notices when the subject is critical.

☐ *When unofficial expectations differ from the stated policy or procedure:*

Policies and procedures frequently have exceptions or set a minimum standard only. What if the policy sets a maximum reject rate of .5 percent, but the supervisor's real goal is zero? Such variations are normal but hard to explain in writing.

☐ *When a policy is ambiguous:*

Policy statements are often broadly worded and require elaboration or examples to be understood. Your customer service policy may say that you'll do whatever it takes to satisfy the customer, but users need to know what

*(continues)*

## 9-1:  NOTIFICATION TIP SHEET (*continued*)

that means in practice. You can get hopelessly bogged down trying to explain it in writing.

### When to Notify by E-Mail

☐ *When your policies and procedures are on-line:*

Users of on-line systems expect the notification to be on-line also.

☐ *When users routinely communicate by e-mail:*

People who routinely communicate electronically and are used to it tend to think that other modes of communication are out-of-date. They usually don't pay as much attention to other forms of notification.

## 9-2: SAMPLE TRANSMITTAL MEMO

Here is a sample transmittal memo sent to employees to inform them of a new procedure. It describes the procedure, gives the effective date, and explains the reasons for its implementation. Notice that the writer gives a brief background and explains the benefits of the new procedure.

**Date:** September 3, 1997

**To:** All Warehouse Employees

**From:** Bernie Jenks, Warehouse Supervisor

**SUBJECT:** *New Monthly Inventory Procedure*

Attached please find a copy of the new monthly inventory procedure. It becomes effective on November 1.

Background —— As you know, we've been working on this for the last six months and have reported to you on the project's status at staff meetings. Your input was instrumental, and we appreciate all of your comments.

We undertook this project because our inventory —— Reasons procedures were inadequate. They took too much time and gave false product counts. The informal manual process we've used for years simply couldn't cope with our rapid growth.

The process has now been computerized. Monthly —— Summary of impact inventories will still have the same start dates, but will be completed in 3 days instead of the current 16 days. Daily shipping information will also be logged into the system, and you'll receive a daily inventory list.

Benefit —— It's a tremendous stride forward. The next time a sales rep wants to know if we have an item in stock, you can tell them within minutes instead of hours. No more back-breaking searches or apologetic phone calls.

*(continues)*

## 9-2:  SAMPLE TRANSMITTAL MEMO (*continued*)

Please read the new procedure carefully. We intro-
duced some of the steps in the last few staff meetings, and you've been notified of the training
sessions. It's your responsibility to come to the
training fully prepared.

File the procedure in the Inventory section of your
departmental handbook.

If you have any questions, call me at ext. 107. If necessary, we'll set up a time to discuss your concerns.
All of us working together will make this a success.

Reader's
responsibility

Instructions

## 9-3: SAMPLE TRANSMITTAL FORM

You may prefer a standardized transmittal or notice form to a memo. List key issues in the Summary section. Emphasize items of special interest or urgency in the Special Notes column.

| **Notice of** ☐ **Policy** ☐ **Procedure** | | |
|---|---|---|
| Number and Title: | | |
| Applies to: | Effective Date: | ☐ New |
| | | ☐ Revised |
| Filing Instructions: | | |
| Contact Information: | | |
| Summary | | Special Notes |
| | | |

## 9-4: Meeting Work Plan

### Meeting Planning Form

Date of meeting: _____

Time of meeting: _____ to _____

Conducted by: _____

Attendees:

_____

_____

_____

Location(s): _____

1. What's the policy/procedure to be discussed? _____

_____

_____

2. Will anything else be discussed at this meeting?

      ☐ **Yes**   ☐ **No**

   If yes, what effect will that have on concentration/attention? _____

_____

_____

3. How much time should we allot?_____

_____

4. Will the time allotted be sufficient? Is it possible that additional meetings will need to be scheduled? _____

_____

_____

5. Are there other sites or shifts to consider? _____

_____

   If so, what dates/times would be good for those meetings? _____

_____

_____

6.  What's the basic message we have to get across? _____

    _____

    _____

    _____

    _____

7.  How detailed do we need to be (information versus training session)?

    _____

    _____

    _____

8.  What documents or backup material should we take to the meeting?

    _____

    _____

    _____

    _____

9.  What questions are people likely to have? _____

    _____

    _____

    _____

    _____

10. What objections are people likely to have, and how will we respond to them?

    | *Objection* | *Response* |
    | --- | --- |
    | _____ | _____ |
    | _____ | _____ |
    | _____ | _____ |
    | _____ | _____ |
    | _____ | _____ |
    | _____ | _____ |
    | _____ | _____ |

(*continues*)

## 9-4: MEETING WORK PLAN (*continued*)

11. Are there any intense feelings or strong opposition? Is hostility or con-frontation likely?

☐ **Yes**   ☐ **No**

If yes, use the following to prepare.

**Controversial or Sensitive Issues**

12. How controversial is it?

☐ **Extremely**   ☐ **Moderately**

13. To whom (individuals or groups) is it most sensitive?

_____

_____

_____

14. What are their complaints or tactics likely to be, and how will we respond?

| *Complaint* | *Response* |
| --- | --- |
| _____ | _____ |
| _____ | _____ |
| _____ | _____ |
| _____ | _____ |
| _____ | _____ |
| _____ | _____ |
| _____ | _____ |
| _____ | _____ |
| _____ | _____ |
| _____ | _____ |

15. What strategy can we pursue to get their cooperation? _____

_____

_____

16. What will we do if the meeting deteriorates or gets out of hand? _____

_____

_____

**Meeting Follow-Up**

17. Was the meeting successful?

☐ **Yes**   ☐ **No**

If no, why not? _____

_____

_____

18. What issues remain unresolved? _____

_____

_____

_____

_____

19. What follow-up action is needed?

| *Action* | *Person Responsible* |
|----------|----------------------|
| _____ | _____ |
| _____ | _____ |
| _____ | _____ |
| _____ | _____ |
| _____ | _____ |

20. How quickly is action required? _____

_____

_____

21. Is another meeting necessary?

☐ **Yes**   ☐ **No**

If yes, when should it be scheduled? _____

_____

_____

# 10

# But That's Not the Way We've Always Done It

Brace yourself. Because no matter how well you've done your job as a policy and procedure writer, there's always going to be someone who says:

*"Here we go again."*

*"You're kidding, right?"*

*"That's the stupidest policy I've ever seen."*

And of course there's always the classic:

*"We've never done it that way before."*

You may be tempted to offer a somewhat less than diplomatic reply ("Tough!"). All that work and effort, all that striving to meet the readers' needs and the organization's needs. Is it really all for nothing?

## Don't Give Up

It's not as bad as it may seem. Do you know that what you're running into is completely normal? Unpleasant, perhaps, but normal.

You've worked hard to keep your feet on the ground as a writer. You've tried to be realistic and practical. Don't give up now. There's no need to be discouraged.

Realists know that change is hard, sometimes excruciating. Besides, you have a slight advantage over the rest of these folks. You've been working with and thinking about this issue for a while. They're just tuning in.

What you're seeing is nothing more than the initial shock. Again, don't be discouraged, and don't give up. There are things you can do. But you have to start at the beginning.

# Dealing With Resistance

As you involve users, bear in mind that most resistance to change stems from fear: fear of the unknown, fear of looking foolish, fear of being taken advantage of, fear of failure, fear of losing face. The list is endless.

You can't conquer other people's fear for them, but you can provide them with tools to chip away at it. And those tools are found in the communication process.

There are six basic steps you can take to help users manage the change: (1) involve, (2) explain, (3) listen, (4) enforce, (5) reinforce, and (6) evaluate. These are the basis for the early communication, continuing education, and final notice processes discussed below. Use the Resistance Tip Sheet (10-1) at the end of this chapter for details on these six steps.

## Early Communication

Remember this: Early communication reduces later resistance. The single most important thing you can do to combat negativity is to involve users up front. Don't end with involvement. Start with it.

We recognized back in the planning process (Chapter 2) just how important it is to talk to people early on. For one thing, their perspective and their information are invaluable to the good decisions and the good writing you have to produce.

But early communication also serves two other critical purposes. It's both (1) an early detection system and (2) an advance preparation system. So don't end with involvement. Start with it.

### Early Detection

You're likely to encounter a lot of skepticism in the beginning. That's normal. Users may have been through similar situations before and think it will somehow either (1) fade away or (2) end up to their disadvantage. Open, honest communication as the project develops will address many of these concerns.

However, there are some concerns that you know won't go away. Maybe the new policy or procedure will require more work or more time from users. Maybe it really will be to their disadvantage. The earlier you get these issues out in the open, the better chance you have of reducing them to a manageable level.

Early detection also reveals the hard-core resisters. Skepticism is one thing, but cynicism is quite another. Identify those who appear to be engaged in a personal campaign to undermine the whole process. They may have a genuine reaction based on fear or disagreement. On the other hand, it may be gamesmanship by someone who just likes to be disruptive.

There are no quick fixes for hard-core resisters. You usually know who your cynics are from past experience, and it's beyond the scope of this book to deal with the psychology of cynicism. However, forewarned really is forearmed. If nothing else, you'll know when and with whom to take a firm stand.

### Advance Preparation

There's no mystery to the fact that people who are consistently involved are also more cooperative users. They've had time to work through the issues. The whys and the wherefores are out on the table for everyone to see. In cases where objections or disagreements can't be resolved, they've had time to come to grips with that fact.

None of this means that they will necessarily like the result any better. Disagreements, strong ones, may continue. But people are amazingly resilient. Most can deal with disagreements so long as they're included in the process and their voices have genuinely been heard. Forewarned *is* forearmed.

## Continuing Education

As the process continues, keep talking to people. There's a tendency to start out on the right communication foot and then lose steam.

Run ideas by users. Update them on the status periodically (even if nothing is happening). Solicit their continued input. Ask their opinions, and listen to them carefully. Test possible approaches on them.

This is not, repeat not, a waste of valuable time. It's a vital ingredient in successful implementation. If you want to see an explosion, all you have to do is shut people out of the process and then drop it on them at the end. Fireworks are guaranteed.

What's more, constant communication with users—continuing education of them—strengthens your final product. Their continued input and participation helps you pinpoint weaknesses and errors. Ultimately, users will help you improve both your decisions and your writing.

## Final Notice

The final notice of implementation will come as no surprise if you've communicated early with users and educated them continually. Strong disagreement may continue, but the shock waves disappear.

Acknowledge continuing disagreements and hot spots. Don't ignore them simply because everything is final. If sensitivities still exist, they will remain a powerful emotional force for the users.

Hone your listening skills. Keep the door open to those who want to talk it over. Take a genuine interest in the problems they're pointing out. It doesn't mean you agree with them. It means you respect their right to have a different point of view.

Use the supporters among the group. There will be some who are feeling positive about it by now or are at least willing to give it a try. Mobilize them. Ask them to explain to others how they'll approach it or why they're willing to try it.

However, this is also the time when you may have to put your foot down firmly. Those hard-core resisters you identified during early detection may still be hard at work. Meet with them individually and reinforce the necessity for them to adapt. The reality is that they must learn to live with the change.

You can discuss ways to do that with them, but if they ultimately refuse, remember that it's their decision. Do what you can, but don't expect too much. Just be sure they understand the consequences of noncompliance.

## Grace Periods

Grace periods are an excellent way to deal with any resistance or disagreement that still exists at this point. They allow a gradual transition prior to full enforcement.

In reality, a grace period is nothing more than additional preparation time. It's especially useful when the policy or procedure is controversial, complicated, or represents a major change from current practice.

The first notice usually introduces the policy or procedure, along with an explanation of what's expected from users. It also explains that (1) there is some flexibility during the initial period and (2) full enforcement begins at a later date.

Follow-up notices are then given as the date for full enforcement draws closer.

---

### FEELING INTIMIDATED?

Hard-core resisters are strong-willed and persistent people. What's more, they're good at it. Many of them work hard at being obnoxious and cynical. Some have spent years at it.

Don't be intimidated. Yes, they have the right to be heard. And yes, their voices should be respected and listened to like those of other users. But they don't have the right to dominate the process. And they don't have the right to refuse to abide by the organization's final decision. Make that clear, and stand firm.

---

### THE VALUE OF GRACE PERIODS

Grace periods recognize realistic learning curves. The pressure is turned down a notch, making users more comfortable and giving them time to adjust. As a result, they usually adapt more quickly to the new requirements.

---

## How to Use a Grace Period

How do you use a grace period? Let's say the new monthly inventory procedure starts in October. But because it's significantly different from current practices, you know it will take several months to iron things out.

The first notice announces the procedure and informs users that procedural discrepancies in the October inventory will be handled informally. The supervisor will discuss problems with the individuals involved.

However, the November inventory is expected to improve significantly. The second notice informs users that if they fail to follow the procedure in November, they'll receive a formal reminder.

Finally, full enforcement starts with the December inventory. The final notice makes it clear that infractions in December will result in disciplinary action.

## Delivering Bad News

What if the policy or procedure you're about to announce is just plain unpopular? Visions of endless complaints dance in your head. You see resistance and even sabotage on the horizon.

Don't try to change unpopular to popular in the blink of an eye. It takes planning, preparation, and patience.

Your first and greatest weapon is the communication that's already occurred. If you've involved users, sought their continued input, and kept them informed, you're halfway home. It's likely that they trust you enough to listen seriously, even if they don't like the message.

The other half of the question is what to do now. The Guidelines for Delivering Bad News (10-2) at the end of this chapter lists seventeen different steps you can take to help everybody get through this. Two of the most important are preempting and taking the heat, and you should master both.

## Preempting

Preempting is a way to defuse resistance. Before the meeting at which the new policy or procedure will be discussed, analyze the objections you think will be raised. Then present those objections to the group yourself, with a diplomatic but definite rebuttal. By being the first to raise the objections, you steal the objector's thunder.

---

### HOW TO PREEMPT OBJECTIONS

You know Sue will raise a fuss about the new inventory procedure. Analyze what her objections are likely to be and prepare a factual response. Then raise the matter yourself in the meeting. It might sound like this:

> *Now, there are certainly objections that can be raised to this new procedure. Someone might say, for instance, that our current inventory procedure works just fine and we don't need a new one. It's easy to say that, but the fact is that we're unable to account for more than $4,000 worth of product every month. This new procedure will help us locate that "lost" inventory.*

You've made it difficult for Sue to insist that the new procedure isn't necessary. If she does, she's undermining her own credibility.

---

## Taking the Heat

Those who make policies and procedures must be willing to accept responsibility for them. The hard fact is that some will be unpopular no matter what you do. People have a right to feel strongly about things that affect them or their jobs, so don't be offended by forceful reactions.

Be patient when users resist, be calm when they get upset, and be tolerant when they object. If you have planned your strategy, are prepared, and exercise patience, you will eventually get your message across.

See Guidelines for Receptivity (10-3) at the end of this chapter for suggestions on being patient and receptive when faced with complaints.

---

### CHECKING YOUR EGO AT THE DOOR

It's not easy to listen to constant carping or intense complaining. It requires skill, discipline, and patience. What's more, a writer's ego often gets in the way. And before you say, "Who, me," think about how long and hard you've worked on that policy or procedure. Along comes an uncooperative user with a criticism, and suddenly you're thinking, "What does this guy know, anyway? He's just a troublemaker." It happens to the best of us. The trick is to recognize and deal with it.

---

## Here Comes Trouble

There are certain things that are guaranteed to cause trouble when you're dealing with policies and procedures. Sometimes they're unavoidable. Many times we're simply oblivious to them in the rush to get the policy or procedure done.

There are fourteen different indicators that spell trouble. They range from differing expectations to what users see as hypocrisy. The policy or procedure may violate what users think of as an inherent right. It may be too restrictive or hard to use. It may just seem unfair.

Some of the key issues are summarized below. The Guidelines on Resistance Factors (10-4) at the end of the chapter examines all fourteen and helps you deal with them.

### Unfairness

This is a major issue for users. Nobody likes to be treated unfairly. Unfortunately, users often cry "unfair" when what they really mean is "unreasonable from my point of view." Don't react emotionally to the charge of unfairness.

Explore whether or not the policy or procedure is reasonable given all the circumstances. And be sure the implementation process is reasonable, too. If you make that new smoke-free workplace policy effective immediately, those three-pack-a-day people simply can't cope. It would be reasonable to give a few months' notice or offer some type of assistance.

This old-fashioned rule is a good one: Look at it from the other guy's point of view.

## Negativity

Don't do this, don't do that. Negativity is a turnoff. It reminds us of our parents and principals. This is a writing trap that most of us fall into unconsciously. We're thinking "don't" and so it's easier to write "don't." But "Don't take extended breaks" could become "You must observe the scheduled break times." Although readers still may not like the message, it's easier to swallow.

Keep your eyes peeled for these trouble signs. You can control some of them through the communication and writing processes. You may not be able to control others, but at least you can be prepared to cope with them.

## Hypocrisy

Suppose an organization talks about empowerment and encourages people to develop an entrepreneurial spirit. But the policy says that any expenditure over $25 has to be approved by a supervisor and a purchasing agent.

The real message is that the organization is afraid to let go. So the organization's talk about empowerment isn't enough. The substance of the policy or procedure must support the talk. Words and actions that are in conflict are perceived by users as hypocritical.

## Pointlessness

Does the policy or procedure really do something, or does it end up making people jump through hoops for nothing? Help them see the value. Show them the end result. Impress on them why it's important.

The first thing users look at is what the policy or procedure will do to them or for them. It often requires more time, more effort, and more hard work on their part. That can be an initial problem, but most people will go along if they understand that it is not pointless and will truly *accomplish* something.

See Chapter 4 for details on how to avoid negative wording.

## Unworkableness

A lot of users think policy and procedure writers live in never-never land. And there's sometimes good reason for their skepticism. A ham radio maker tested its procedures on children, on the theory that if a kid could follow them, anyone could. The company rarely received any complaints during testing with the children. But adult users, in the real world, hated the procedures.

Remember the three keys to workability: accuracy, completeness, and testing. Does it work in the real world that users inhabit?

## Restrictiveness

Policies and procedures are rules, and most people aren't fond of other people's rules. They want to do things their way. Maintaining the proper balance between control and flexibility is a constant struggle.

Team leaders may have been told that they're trusted and empowered. They then expect to exercise their professional judgment. But what if all they ever get is detailed procedure after detailed procedure that leaves no room for discretion? They don't feel very trusted. In fact, they feel like robots. They were just looking for guidelines.

On the other hand, handing out broad guidelines when people are looking for detailed how-tos creates the opposite problem. It's not restrictive enough. That can create confusion, inconsistency, and danger.

Write every policy and procedure with a firm eye on the balance between control and flexibility.

## When the Writer Is the Resister

Don't be so surprised. You may have written this policy or procedure, but you're still human. Sometimes you're the one who strongly disagrees with it.

Address your own concerns the same way you would anyone else's: Listen and consider. Be sure to write your concerns down. (Talking to yourself is often useful, but in this instance it's more likely to turn into a gripe session.) Write down what you really think of the policy or procedure. You may think it's stupid, trite, wrongheaded, poorly thought out, unnecessary. Say so.

Then write down the reasons for the policy or procedure and the circumstances that are driving it. Explain it on paper the way you would to a resister sitting in front of you. Pull out every good writing technique you know. Focus on facts.

Read your own explanation carefully, then set it aside and come back to it later. Give it time to sink in.

Now go back and throw away that first piece of paper listing your concerns. Recognize that this is the organization's decision, and until such time as that changes, everyone needs to understand and abide by the policy or procedure—including you.

Keep yourself focused forward and quit rehearsing how much you hate this policy or procedure. Concentrate on *do* statements. *Don't* statements, of which you have plenty, have a tendency to turn into "yuck" statements under these circumstances.

---

### WHEN YOU DON'T LIKE IT ANY BETTER THAN THE USERS

It's perfectly OK to express disagreement yourself. And it's OK to fight for changes that you believe are important. Put your case together and present it to the appropriate people.

But recognize that like other users, you have an obligation to abide by the organization's rules. If the final decision goes against you, be gracious. Be professional. Use your best writing and formatting skills the same way you would if you agreed with the policy or procedure. And make a genuine effort to help others overcome their resistance.

---

## Chapter Summary

- Don't give up when you encounter resistance. It's normal, and there are things you can do about it.

- The basic process is one of early communication, continuing education, and final notice. Understanding that fear is the real cause of most resistance to change helps you take the right steps at each stage. Observe the fundamentals of good communication: involve, explain, listen, enforce, reinforce, and evaluate.

- There are special rules for breaking bad news that you know will be unpopular. Among the most important are learning to preempt objections and being willing to take the heat.

- Certain signs spell instant trouble. Users will resist instinctively if they think a policy or procedure is unfair or unworkable, if they perceive that their rights have been violated, or if they find it negative, too restrictive, or not restrictive enough.

- And finally, watch for one resister you'd never suspect: yourself. When you don't agree with the policy or procedure, be the ultimate professional. Fight for changes you think are needed, but design and write the same way you would if you agreed.

# Tools and Resources
# for Chapter 10

## 10-1: Resistance Tip Sheet

### The Main Problems

☐ Lack of involvement
☐ Fear (of the unknown, of losing face, of failure, and of a dozen other things)

### The Main Strategies

☐ Early communication (early detection, advance preparation)
☐ Continuing education
☐ Final notice
☐ Grace periods

### Special Situations

☐ Unpopular subjects and bad news
☐ Resistance on the part of the writer

### Factors That Guarantee Resistance

☐ Changing cultural norms
☐ Differing expectations
☐ Difficulty in use
☐ Hypocrisy
☐ Incomprehensibility
☐ Inconsistency
☐ Negativity
☐ Outdatedness
☐ Pointlessness
☐ Punitiveness
☐ Restrictiveness
☐ Rights violations (real and perceived)
☐ Unfairness
☐ Unworkability

### Communicating for Reduced Resistance

1. *Involve:*   Involve others in the planning, research, early communication, and continuing education phases. The

*(continues)*

## 10-1: Resistance Tip Sheet (*continued*)

going can get rugged, and you may be tempted to stop. Don't.

Be sure you involve everyone: the most competent and the least competent, the old hand and the new kid, the official supervisor and the informal leader everybody looks up to, the cheerleaders and the whiners, senior management, quality control people, subject matter experts.

They all have something to bring to the party. The most competent people can educate you. The least competent can tell you what you have not provided. The old hand gives you the history, and the new kid gives you the vision.

The drawback is that all this takes time. It's worth it. Acceptance and implementation are much less painful for everyone when you help the change process along.

2. *Explain:*    One of the big mistakes we make in implementing policies and procedures is thinking that people don't want long-winded explanations. It's true that they don't want them on paper, in the policy or procedure. But they do want the explanation.

How many times have you had a user ask, "Why?" Why should I do this? What's the point? What's the benefit? Who benefits? Not me. So why should I work myself to death? Tell me why.

Your failure to explain makes people feel like robots. It's like saying, "Just do what we tell you to do. Trust us. We know what's best." Most organizations don't do this intentionally. It happens because we don't want to take the time for these discussions. And sometimes it happens because we don't want to take the heat. Either way, it kills cooperation. Give people a reason to comply.

You can sometimes do this in the policy or procedure itself. Putting a "purpose" section in the page layout is one way (see Chapter 5). Careful wording is another. Consider this example from a hygiene policy:

*Your fellow employees, as well as the guests, have a right to expect cleanliness from you, as you do from them.*

|   |   |   |
|---|---|---|
| | | Point out the benefit to the user, and you're more likely to get cooperation. |
| 3. | *Listen:* | Listening is about being open. Face the issue squarely, no matter how unpleasant or unpopular. Be willing to hear the tough things people have to say. Facing an angry crowd of users isn't on anyone's top ten list of favorite things to do, but it comes with the job. |
| | | Encourage questions. Few people like to be the first to ask a question, especially in a tense situation. If you're in a meeting and dead silence is all you hear, ask a few questions of your own. |
| | | You might start by saying, "When I first looked at this issue, I wanted to know . . . . " Develop your own wording, but come prepared with a few questions you think users will have. Another favorite starter is, "I've heard a couple of concerns . . . . " |
| | | And then be willing to listen to the answers. People will have doubts and disagreements. They may be angry, confused, or frustrated. Let them vent. They want to be heard. |
| | | This requires patience and sincerity. Don't interrupt, cut people off, or nod your head condescendingly. Remember that most people have a built-in sincerity meter and can spot a phony listener a mile off. |
| 4. | *Enforce:* | If you don't take you own policies and procedures seriously enough to enforce them, why should anybody else? On the one hand, you're telling people to comply. On the other, you're telling them it's OK not to. It's as if you were saying, "Please comply, but if you don't, nothing will happen." |
| | | Make the consequences of noncompliance clear. Let the users know what exceptions will be made and by whom they can be made. Tell them who the enforcer is and to whom the rule applies. |
| | | And be sure that the standards for compliance are clear. Some people may honestly believe they're complying when they're not. |
| 5. | *Reinforce:* | Repetition is how most of us learn. And it's how all of us retain, comprehend, or believe. If you see something once, you may say, "I don't believe it." See it a dozen times and you start believing. |
| | | The same is true in policies and procedures. Tell |

*(continues)*

## 10-1:  RESISTANCE TIP SHEET (*continued*)

users once and they may smile and nod their heads. But chances are that many will go back to business as usual. Tell them every day for the next month, talk about it in staff meetings, send out an occasional reminder memo, and they begin to get the message.

It isn't just formal communication that counts, either. Post a notice of the change on the employee bulletin board. Mention it in the hallway. Drop a one-sentence reminder at break.

Be sure that your other organizational systems support the policy or procedure. Provide training where necessary. Hold users accountable—in performance evaluations, for instance. And above all, make certain that managers and supervisors support the changes with their daily actions and words.

6. *Evaluate:*   When the whole process is over, take a break. Relax and enjoy. But remember that this is just a vacation, not a divorce.

After a well-deserved rest, look at how things are going. Ask yourself one key question: Is it working?

Is it doing what we intended it to do? If not, why not? There may be one small glitch that's causing major problems. There may be a major glitch that no one foresaw. Or things beyond your control may have changed just two days after you implemented the policy or procedure (a new technology, a market change, or new management).

There is no rest for the policy and procedure writer. Organizations are changing rapidly in today's world, and the rules have to change with them.

## 10-2: GUIDELINES FOR DELIVERING BAD NEWS

Follow these steps when delivering news you know will be unpopular.

| | | |
|---|---|---|
| 1. | *Listen carefully:* | These are adults (most of them), and they're good at what they do. They want to be treated with respect. |
| 2. | *Consult with key staff members:* | Win the support of key users, and they'll influence others. |
| 3. | *Anticipate objections:* | What objections and complaints are likely? Are they valid? From whom will they be likely to come? |
| 4. | *Preempt objections:* | In the meeting or memo in which you discuss an unpopular policy or procedure, present the objections yourself. It defuses and deflates them. |
| 5. | *Train them:* | When users are busy concentrating on the "how to," they have less energy for the "I object." |
| 6. | *Hold multiple discussion sessions:* | Let people vent. But require those with objections to offer constructive solutions or suggestions as well. |
| 7. | *Position users' interests first:* | Wherever possible, point out the benefit to users first and the benefit to the organization second. |
| 8. | *Phase it in:* | Implementing objectionable rules gradually makes them more palatable. Allow a grace period where possible. |
| 9. | *Give advance warning:* | Forewarned is forearmed. It gives users time to adjust. |
| 10. | *Be willing to take the heat:* | Those who make the rules must be willing to accept the responsibility for them. It's part of the job. |
| 11. | *Create a complaint system:* | It allows implementation to go forward without cutting off the dialogue. |
| 12. | *Be prepared to meet one-on-one:* | Be available for questions, or designate someone who will be. |

*(continues)*

## 10-2:  GUIDELINES FOR DELIVERING BAD NEWS (*continued*)

13. *Explain the reasons thoroughly:*

Then have the patience to explain them over and over again until they sink in. Acceptance takes time.

14. *Don't expect them to like it:*

Be a realist. It's naive to think that all users will be happy about this. They have a right to be upset or concerned.

15. *Use data and facts to establish the background:*

Be prepared. Use facts and logic to back up what you're saying.

16. *Be honest:*

It's the only choice. If you fabricate facts, make up reasons, or withhold information, they'll see right through it.

17. *Don't delay:*

Bad news travels fast. Putting it off encourages rumor and gossip. Attitudes will only harden.

## 10-3: Guidelines for Receptivity

It's all well and good to talk about listening to people's complaints and being patient with resistance. But the truth is that it's awfully hard to do. Patience isn't infinite, and neither is time. An odd form of reverse resistance develops, in which the writer resists any more input or criticism from users and reviewers. These guidelines can help you be more receptive when faced with complaints and resistance about the policy or procedure you've worked so hard on.

### Understanding Reverse Resistance

☐ Users aren't the only ones who resist change. Writers sometimes find it hard to accept changes suggested by users or by reviewers. We sometimes think like this: *All this research, writing, and design—all this hard work—and now someone thinks they're going to carve up my document? Destroy my procedure? Reword it? I'm in charge of this. I know best.*

Oops. This isn't really you. It's just writer's ego trying to derail the process of improving the document. It slipped in the back door while you were busy. Usher it right back out and bolt the door.

### Paying the Price of Ego

☐ No writer thinks of everything. That means that other people, be they users or reviewers, have something you just might have overlooked. If you reject suggestions or criticism, chances are you're missing something that could make you look better when the document is finished. That's a high price to pay for the fleeting satisfaction of ego. It isn't worth it.

### Putting Your Cards on the Table

☐ Every writer finds a unique way of dealing with the ego question. But it's always wise to be honest. Let people know that you're really committed to a certain policy, writing style, or format—but you'll try very hard to keep an open mind. Get it out in the open.

### Having a Heart-to-Heart with Yourself

☐ Have an honest conversation with yourself, just as you would with any other troublemaker. (You're creating your own trouble here.) Ex-

*(continues)*

## 10-3:  GUIDELINES FOR RECEPTIVITY (*continued*)

amine the facts of the project. Ask yourself whether the critiquer is really out to lunch or whether you just might have a little too much ownership in this.

You may be responsible for the project, but think about this: That policy or procedure belongs to everybody. What's more, it's probably those other people (including the critiquer) who will be the ones to make or break it. It might be worth it to listen a bit longer.

### Handling Criticism of Your Work

☐ Watch out for that old catchphrase, "constructive criticism." What a silly idea! Who really considers criticism constructive? Nobody I know. The minute people say they want to offer a critique, defenses go up. There are four things you can do to keep those defenses down:

1. *Separate your writing from you.* The reviewer or user is assessing your work, not you.

2. *Don't interrupt the critiquer.* That just makes you seem combative. Wait until the reviewer has finished.

3. *Use normal body language.* Don't look down or away. Don't fold your arms and grit your teeth. Don't sit back and clench your jaw. Instead, make eye contact and lean forward a bit. Be as normal as possible. As long as your body language says you're still listening, you can even tell the critiquer you don't like what's being said.

4. *Ask for specifics.* Don't let critiquers get away with vague, general comments. "It's hard to read" doesn't tell you anything. You may be thinking that you've used the very best format available, but the critiquer may actually mean that the sentences are too long. Ask questions until you get specific answers.

## 10-4: GUIDELINES ON RESISTANCE FACTORS

Sometimes resistance is unavoidable, but sometimes we're simply oblivious to trouble in the rush to get the policy or procedure done. Note each of these potential troublespots and use the accompanying questions to decide where you stand.

### Changing Cultural Norms

- ☐ Does the policy or procedure go against tradition?
- ☐ How long-standing is the tradition?
- ☐ How strongly do users feel about the tradition?
- ☐ What's the best way to wean users away from that tradition?

### Differing Expectations

- ☐ What is the organization's perspective on the issue?
- ☐ What is the user's perspective on it?
- ☐ How large is the gap?
- ☐ How can we close the gap?
- ☐ Are users expecting something different from what they'll get? Where did this impression come from? How can we conteract it?

### Difficulty in Use

- ☐ Are the formats reader-friendly?
- ☐ Is the document well designed and produced?
- ☐ Is information hard to find?
- ☐ Is there an index or table of contents?
- ☐ Does everyone who needs the information have a copy or quick access to one?

### Hypocrisy

- ☐ Does the policy or procedure match the management style?
- ☐ Does it jibe with stated goals?
- ☐ Is it consistent with the way things really work around here?

*(continues)*

## 10-4:  Guidelines on Resistance Factors (*continued*)

### Incomprehensibility

- [ ] Will people take one look at it and groan?
- [ ] Are users likely to be overwhelmed by the technical matter?
- [ ] Are there any readers who may be afraid they can't cope with it?
- [ ] Are there any readers who may be afraid to try?
- [ ] Is the document written at the proper reading level?
- [ ] Is it well written (short, concise, uses common language)?

### Inconsistency

- [ ] Does the policy or procedure contradict any other policy or procedure on the books?
- [ ] Does it contradict any unwritten policy or procedure?
- [ ] Is it consistent with what users are told informally?
- [ ] Is it consistent with what managers and supervisors actually do or expect?

### Negativity

- [ ] Is this a "don't" policy or procedure?
- [ ] Is it written for offenders?
- [ ] Is there any way to word it to tell people what *is* expected instead of what is *not* expected?

### Outdatedness

- [ ] Is the policy or procedure consistent with current technology?
- [ ] Is it in sync with current practice in the field or industry?
- [ ] Is there a revision or update system?

### Pointlessness

- [ ] Does the policy or procedure actually *accomplish* something? Precisely what?
- [ ] Does it make the user's job easier? Will it take less time? Will it take less effort? Will it take less money?
- [ ] Does it make the user's life easier? Will it reduce confusion? Will it reduce frustration? Will it increase satisfaction?

## Punitiveness

- ☐ Is the policy or procedure a reaction to a few isolated incidents?
- ☐ Is it aimed at one or two violators?
- ☐ Does it address an issue that affects most users?

## Restrictiveness

### Users

- ☐ Does the policy or procedure permit the user to exercise some knowledge, judgment, or discretion?
- ☐ If not, is there a good reason why not (health and safety, legalities, consistency)?

### Enforcers

- ☐ Does it allow supervisors or team leaders to lead (as opposed to mindlessly enforce)?
- ☐ Do they need general guidelines or specific how-to's, and which are they given?

## Rights Violations (Real and Perceived)

- ☐ Does the policy or procedure violate any laws (health, safety, privacy, antidiscrimination, and so on)?
- ☐ Does it tread on sensitive issues that users may perceive as a right (privacy, personal choices such as speech or appearance)?

## Unfairness

- ☐ Is the policy or procedure reasonable, given the combination of circumstances and user expectations?
- ☐ Will users see it as reasonable? If not, why not?
- ☐ Have we given users a reasonable amount of time to adjust?

*(continues)*

## 10-4: GUIDELINES ON RESISTANCE FACTORS (*continued*)

**Unworkability**

- ☐ Is the policy or procedure accurate?
- ☐ Is it complete?
- ☐ Does it tell users everything they really need to know?
- ☐ Have we devoted sufficient time to research?
- ☐ Have we tested it to the degree possible?
- ☐ Have we tested it in realistic conditions?

# 11

# We Haven't Used That Procedure in Years

The courts hold you responsible for notifying users about changes in a clear and timely manner. But users are an even tougher taskmaster than the courts.

They're ruthless in their criticism of policies and procedures that are obsolete or unworkable. And you won't have any trouble spotting their displeasure: complaints, jokes, sarcasm, rolling eyes. Sometimes, it can develop into far more serious trouble such as demotivation or unsafe practices.

There's practical and legal danger in allowing policies and procedures to become old and faded. People begin to ignore the irrelevant ones, and soon they're ignoring all of them. Guesswork becomes prevalent. Errors, some of them serious, start to occur. And right behind that comes legal trouble.

Make a commitment from the beginning to establish a clear and regular review process. Policies and procedures require maintenance or they begin to deteriorate.

## When to Revise

There are numerous opinions about when and how often you should revise your policies and procedures, but there are no firm rules. The best approach is to find the proper balance of two methods:

1. Regularly scheduled review and revision
2. As-needed review and revision

The best balance for your organization depends both on content factors (legalities, critical nature of the topic, last revision date, condition

---

THE ENDLESS CYCLE

Revision is an ongoing process that never stops. It requires you to become actively involved in the maintenance process and to continually monitor how well the policies and procedures are working.

---

of current policy or procedure, urgency) and on logistics (staff and re-source availability, schedules and time frames).

## Regularly Scheduled Reviews

The ideal is to review and revise your policies and procedures once a year. Put it on the calendar and do it.

If this isn't possible (and it isn't for many of us), create a realistic schedule that will work in your organization with your own time frames. Once every two or three years is better than once every five years.

It sometimes helps to consider the consequences of not reviewing. If you forgo an annual review of safety procedures, could health and safety be at greater risk? If you forgo an annual review of quality assurance procedures, could your ISO accreditation be in question?

Time may be at a premium, but you might decide that you can't afford to skip that annual review. Then you face other trade-offs, such as what projects you'll have to reschedule or what assistance you'll have to request.

Deciding on the right schedule and frequency is a matter of clarifying priorities. Weigh the consequences of delay against the demands of the process. And be realistic about it.

Use the Sample Review Schedule Form (11-1) and the Sample Review Planning Form (11-2) at the end of this chapter to plan and schedule your reviews.

### Rolling Reviews

Rolling reviews are a good way to work regular revisions into your schedule with a minimum of disruption, and they're simple to do. Just schedule different groups of policies and procedures for review periodically. Then as each review is completed, roll another group into the schedule. Example 11-1 illustrates sample rolling schedules.

**Example 11-1.** How to do a rolling review.

---

Rolling reviews can help you work regular revisions into your overall schedule with a minimum of disruption.

Break your schedule down into months or quarters. Then break your policies and procedures down into small groups of related topics.

Finally, schedule one group for review during each successive time period. As each review period is completed, add another period and topic to the schedule.

A typical rolling schedule might look like this:

| | |
|---|---|
| *1st quarter:* | *Billing Procedures* |
| *2nd quarter:* | *Accounts Payable Procedures* |
| *3rd quarter:* | *Collection Procedures* |
| *4th quarter:* | *Financial Reporting Procedures* |

Or it might look like this:

| | |
|---|---|
| *January:* | *Billing—New Accounts* |
| *February:* | *Billing—Existing Accounts* |
| *March:* | *Billing Adjustments* |
| *April:* | *Credit Policy and Procedures* |
| *May:* | *Payables Processing* |
| *June:* | *Payment Requests* |
| *July:* | *Vendors* |
| *August:* | *Past Due Accounts* |
| *September:* | *Outside Collections* |
| *October:* | *Monthly Closeout* |
| *November:* | *Quarterly Report* |
| *December:* | *Annual Reports* |

Or it might look like this:

| | |
|---|---|
| *1998:* | *Health and Safety Manual* |
| *1999:* | *Maintenance Manual* |
| *2000:* | *Employee Handbook* |
| *2001:* | *Accounting Manual* |
| *2002:* | *Sales Handbook* |

It doesn't matter how small the groups are or how long each review period is (weekly, monthly, annually). The key is to establish a discipline of regular revision. With rolling reviews, revision is under way at all times and becomes part of the ongoing process of managing your policies and procedures.

## As-Needed Reviews

Regularly scheduled reviews won't necessarily catch everything that needs attention. You may have reviewed a policy two months ago, but a relevant new law has just been passed. Revision is needed when:

- A significant number of changes have been made to the documents.
- Content changes, such as operational or legal, occur or are pending.
- Certain types of problems or behaviors increase.

---

### A CHANGING STANDARD

A quick rule of thumb used to be that manuals and handbooks should be revised every five years. However, in today's organizations, that may not be sufficient to keep up with rapid changes. Consider a complete revision every two to three years.

---

### Accumulated Changes

When a number of changes have been made over a period of time, policies and procedures start to resemble a patchwork quilt. You can only fix pieces of a document so many times before you must fix the whole of it.

If you've issued a significant number of changes to a document, consider a complete revision. It ensures that nothing has accidentally slipped by or been overlooked.

Some writers use the 25 percent rule: If approximately 25 percent of a given policy or procedure has been changed, it's time for a complete review. The same rule may be applied to a manual or handbook.

### Content Changes

Existing policies and procedures need adjustment anytime you have new equipment, new programs, or new products, procedures, and policies. The same is true if you have new management or a new philosophy of operation. Be especially alert for changes in legal or regulatory requirements.

Anytime you attend a meeting or have a conversation in which someone suggests doing something differently, think "policy and procedure review." Make notes. If the change is authorized, put the review on your schedule. If no change is authorized, keep the notes on file for use at the next regularly scheduled review.

### Significant Clues

Pay attention to the things going on around you. Listen to daily conversations in the hallway and break area. Be alert to the side comments in meetings. They could be telling you something.

Users often express their frustrations to everyone except the writer. They complain to others. They try to struggle through somehow. They become confused and make errors. They get frustrated and quit trying.

Complaints increase. More time is taken up with questions, many of which are repetitive. There are numerous deviations and unique "interpretations."

---

### CLUES THAT IT'S TIME FOR A CHANGE

A significant number of or increase in:

- Accidents
- Complaints
- Questions
- Confusion

- Errors
- Deviations
- Rejection rates
- Corrective actions

Comments, such as:

*"Oh, we don't do that anymore."*

*"Don't worry. Nobody wears those safety goggles."*

*"Yeah, that's what the manual says, but let me show you how it's really done."*

---

If any of these conditions or significant clues exist, it's time to review and revise.

## When *Not* to Revise

Your information clearly shows that the policy or procedure isn't working. Should it be revised?

Not necessarily. Ask that favorite question of good investigators: "Why?"

Why isn't it working? Could it be that users need more training? Was communication insufficient or unclear? Is it normal resistance that just requires time and patience to overcome? Has enforcement been lacking?

Don't rush to revision. The policy or procedure may not be broken. It may be the implementation process instead.

---

### THE ELUSIVE CLUES

Increasing confusion, complaints, and other clues aren't always easy to spot because they seldom jump out at you. In the daily rush of things, it may just seem like a bad spell.

Stay alert for the signs of gradual deterioration. How long has this bad spell gone on? Are people confused consistently, not just occasionally? Have complaints become the rule instead of the exception?

If you spot a pattern developing, it's more than a temporary bad spell.

---

## How Much to Revise

The goal is to change as much as is necessary and as little as is possible. Exactly how much you have to revise depends on the nature and degree of the changes themselves. You can change:

- A portion of an individual policy or procedure
- All of an individual policy or procedure

- A section or related group of policies or procedures
- An entire handbook or manual

If you make significant changes in a portion of a policy or procedure, group, or handbook, it may be wise to review the entire document and reissue it. This reassures users that the policy or procedure has been examined in its entirety and that conflicts or contradictions have been eliminated.

---

### REMEMBER THAT INDEX

If you're revising a manual or handbook, or a significant portion of one, don't forget to change the front and back matter as well. It's easy to overlook the table of contents, the appendices, and the index.

---

## How to Revise

The revision process is much the same as the process you followed in the original development of your policies and procedures.

Research the topic, organize the information, format it, and draft it. Review and edit it, then get it approved. What's important is that you exercise the same meticulous care in all these steps as you did when you wrote the originals.

In addition, though, you must take some extra steps. The Revision Tip Sheet (11-3) at the end of the chapter has a detailed outline of steps, but in brief they are:

1. *Develop a follow-up mentality.* Watch out for the old "I'm glad that's done!" feeling. Your work is *not* done. You're just switching from the development phase to the maintenance phase. Gear up for it.

2. *Check and double-check related documents and cross-references. Then check again.* A planned change can have an unplanned effect on some other policy or procedure. If there are cross-references or other connections between your document and another one, check for accuracy. Anything can change, from content to page numbers.

3. *Create a formal mechanism for users to give feedback.* Develop a simple form on which users can report problems or observations as they

happen. Make it easy for them to tell you what's good and what's not. Use the Sample Notice of Policy/Procedure Discrepancy Form (11-4) and the Sample Input Form (11-5) at the end of this chapter.

4. *Continually solicit information, formally and informally.* Make it a habit to ask how things are going. Use scheduled meetings or informal hallway conversations. Ask, "Is it working? Is it doing what we wanted it to do?"

5. *Keep a file for suggestions and ideas.* Comments and suggestions will start right away, probably the very day the change is issued. Don't groan and ignore them. Instead, record them and file them. Your memory isn't likely to last until the next revision rolls around.

6. *Keep records of all revisions.* Keep a copy of each version and a record of its effective date for documentation purposes. There is sometimes a legal or a practical need to refer back to older versions. Use the Sample Revision Record Form (11-6) at the end of this chapter.

## How to Clarify the Changes

Make it as easy as possible for the user to see what, and how much, has been revised. You have several options, which may be used separately or together:

- Visually highlight the changes on the page.
- Use clear, descriptive wording in your transmittal document.
- Summarize the changes.

### Highlighting

With the advent of computers, you have lots of choices in highlighting. You can shadow, bracket, or block the relevant sections. You can use

---

### A Tip for Quick Revisions

Use the "pink pages" method to make quick revisions. Issue a temporary revision on colored paper. (Pink paper was originally used to indicate temporary status, but you can use any color you want. Blue is common.) Anytime users see a revision on that color paper, they know it's immediate and temporary and that further changes will be coming.

---

**Example 11-2.** How to highlight changes.

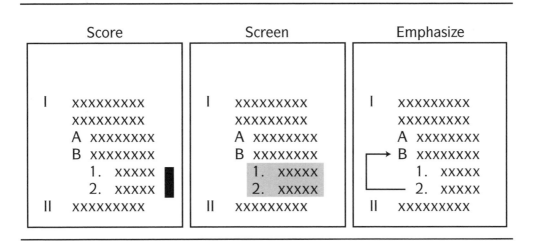

marginal notations of some type. You can use a different typeface or ink color, although these may get confusing in daily use.

The trick is to highlight the changes so that they are immediately obvious to the user. Stay with a simple method that gives the user an immediate visual cue. Readers hate searching. Example 11-2 illustrates several techniques.

## Using Clear Wording

A revision can mean just about anything, so make it clear in your transmittal document exactly what you've changed. Use words or phrases such as:

- Added
- Canceled
- Changed
- Deleted
- Modified
- Repealed
- Replaced
- Rescinded
- Supplemented

Use common, everyday words wherever possible. And use all those wording techniques from Chapter 4 so that your message is direct and clear. The goal is to make it fast and easy for the reader to tell what's changed.

In some cases your attorneys may have a specific legal reason for complex-sounding wording. But if not, stay with the clearer, more common variety.

---

### KEEP IT SIMPLE

Keep your language as direct and simple as possible. Avoid complicated and legal-sounding wording:

*Policy MM-1 is officially rescinded effective July 3 and is super-seded by this policy.*

It would be better to say:

*This policy replaces Policy MM-1. The change is effective on July 3.*

---

### DANGEROUS CONTRADICTIONS

The revised billing procedure says that bills of lading will now be processed on the first of the month, but the existing shipping policy still says the fifth.

Contradictions are an invitation to trouble. If users have a choice between two opposing directives, they'll choose the one they think is best—which is usually the one they like most.

---

## Summarizing

Readers want the message fast and clear. If the cover memo says that a revised policy is attached, but there are five pages, how do you know what's changed in the policy and what hasn't?

You don't. You would have to line up the old and new documents side by side and compare them to really find out. Readers don't have the time or patience for that, and they'll take shortcuts. They'll skim it, skip it, or ask a buddy. All can lead to serious misunderstandings.

Give a brief summary of the major changes in the transmittal document. Tell readers:

- What areas are affected
- How extensive the change is

- The reason for the change
- The impact on the bottom-line

## How to Hold Users Responsible

Probably the most frequent problem with revisions is that there's always someone who says, "But I never got it!" And that claim is often made months later, after using the old procedure has landed him or her in trouble.

The solution? Use a notification system that forces users to share responsibility for updating their document(s).

---

### THE "I NEVER GOT IT" GAME

Copies do get lost in transit, but most of the time this claim turns out to mean that the user misplaced it, ignored it, or never got around to reading it. You must impress on users the fact that they are just as responsible for successful implementation of changes as the organization is. Hold them accountable or the games will continue.

---

A shared responsibility system is fairly easy to construct. In fact, its effectiveness lies in its simplicity.

1. Users are given a revision index form on which they record all revision notices in the order of receipt.

2. All change notices are clearly numbered in an obvious and easy-to-identify manner so that any missing numbers can be spotted immediately.

3. Users are instructed that it is their responsibility to record all change notices in their revision indexes *and* to notify the appropriate person if any are missing.

4. A summary of all the change notices issued is periodically sent to users. Users are instructed to compare this summary to their revision indexes and report any missing notices immediately.

This system is straightforward and simple, yet highly effective. If clearly communicated and properly enforced, users find it difficult to claim they were unaware of the changes to policy or procedure.

The Action Memo system outlined below is a good example of such a system. Use it as a basis for developing your own system, suitable to your organization or unit. Numbering, for example, can vary widely depending on the complexity and sheer volume of your policies and procedures. Keep it as simple as possible.

In addition, some organizations require users to acknowledge in writing that they have received policy and procedure revisions. This is particularly important if (1) the change is major or (2) the change could have a serious impact on the user's job or employment status. See the Sample Acknowledgment of Revision Form (11-7) at the end of this chapter. Then consult your attorneys for precise wording applicable to your organization.

Whatever notification system you choose, be sure it makes clear to users that (1) they have obligations in the change process and (2) they will be held accountable for meeting those obligations. You must hold users responsible for mistakes arising from the use of old policies and procedures.

## Shared Responsibility: The Action Memo System

Here are the steps in the Action Memo system:

1. Label your transmittal document an "Action Memo."

   - "Action Memo" indicates that the user is required to take some action, such as removing an old document and replacing it with a new one. You can also use other terms, such as "change notice" or "revision notice." See the Sample Action Memo (11-8) at the end of this chapter. A variation of this transmittal document, the Sample Revision Notice Form (11-9), is also available at the end of this chapter.

2. Number each Action Memo in sequential order.

   - Make sure the sequence is obvious enough that the eye can spot a discrepancy immediately. Clear numbering is the key to this system.
   - A simple "1, 2, 3. . . ." may not be sufficient if you have lots of changes or many different categories. Some people use a yearly numbering system, such as "97-1." Others use subject matter designators as a prefix to the number, such as "ER-1" (for an emergency room procedure). Develop your own numbering system.

**Example 11-3.** Abbreviated example of a Revision Index.

Record all Action Memos immediately on receipt and check to be sure they're in numerical sequence. If not, you are missing a change notice. Contact your supervisor immediately for a replacement copy. *This is your responsibility.*

| Action Memo | Subject | Revision Date | Effective Date | Page Number(s) |
|---|---|---|---|---|
| PR - 1 | Outside vendors | 3-1-00 | 6-1-00 | 32 |
| PR - 2 | Gifts | 6-3-00 | 7-1-00 | 36 |
| PR - 5 | Expenses | 10-1-00 | 10-15-00 | 210 |

3. Give each user a "Revision Index."

- Divide a sheet of paper into five columns: Action Memo, subject, revision date, effective date, and page number(s). See the partial index in Example 11-3 and the full worksheet in the Sample Revision Index Form (11-10) at the end of this chapter.
- In manuals or handbooks, insert the Revision Index at the front.

4. Instruct users that it is their responsibility to record each new Action Memo in the Revision Index as it's received.

- Missing items are immediately obvious because of the clear numbering system. If it jumps from "ER-3" to "ER-5," it's obvious that ER-4 is missing.

5. Instruct users that it's also their responsibility to notify you if they're missing any Action Memos.

- You can designate any appropriate party, such as their supervisors or a central authority.

6. Every six months, send out a list of all Action Memos that have been distributed during that period (more often if the volume of changes is high).

7. Instruct users that it's also their responsibility to check the summary list against their Revision Index and report any missing items immediately.

8. If readers claim they never got the new one, ask to see their Revision Index (see Example 11-3). If it clearly shows that one is missing, ask them why they didn't report it. Ask if they got the summary you have been sending out every six months and whether they checked it against their Revision Index. If not, why not?

## Chapter Summary

- Policies and procedures require maintenance or they deteriorate. Both users and the courts hold you responsible for the currency and accuracy of your documents.

- Revisions should be done both on a regular schedule and as the need arises. Watch for signs that change is needed.

- On the other hand, don't rush into revisions. Look at the implementation process first to see if improvements are needed there instead.

- Use much the same process in revision as you did in the original writing. Use the same meticulous care as well. The main difference between the two processes is that revision is a never-ending process of monitoring and communication.

- Develop feedback systems and solicit input. Use every possible method of clarifying the changes. Use a notification system that forces users to share responsibility for updates.

# Tools and Resources
# for Chapter 11

## 11-1: SAMPLE REVIEW SCHEDULE FORM

| REVIEW SCHEDULE FOR POLICIES AND PROCEDURES | | |
|---|---|---|
| Policy/Procedure Handbook | Last Review Date and Type* | Next Scheduled Revision Date and Type* |
| | | |
| | | |
| | | |
| | | |
| | | |
| | | |
| | | |
| | | |
| | | |
| | | |
| | | |
| | | |
| | | |
| | | |
| | | |
| | | |
| | | |
| | | |
| | | |
| | | |
| | | |
| | | |
| | | |
| | | |
| *Total, partial, or minor. | | |

## 11-2: SAMPLE REVIEW PLANNING FORM

| Policy/Procedure/ Handbook to Be Reviewed | Review Date* | |
|---|---|---|
| | Desired | Realistic |
| | | |
| | | |
| | | |
| | | |
| | | |
| | | |
| | | |
| | | |
| | | |
| | | |
| | | |
| | | |
| | | |
| | | |
| | | |
| | | |
| | | |
| | | |
| | | |
| | | |
| | | |
| | | |
| | | |
| | | |
| | | |
| | | |
| *Projected date or review cycle (monthly, quarterly, yearly). | | |

## 11-3: REVISION TIP SHEET

### When to Revise

☐ At regularly scheduled intervals
☐ As needed

### Things to Watch For

☐ Increases in complaints, errors, or accidents
☐ Significant or frequent deviations and creative "interpretations"
☐ Numerous questions
☐ Comments such as "We don't do that anymore" or "Nobody really does it that way"

### When *Not* to Revise

☐ When the implementation process, not the policy or procedure, is at fault. Consider more or better:
- Training
- Enforcement
- Communication
- Time and patience

### How to Revise

1. *Develop a follow-up mentality:*

   You're finally finished! You've developed and written that quality assurance manual. You give a sigh of relief and move on to the next project.

   Watch out for the "I'm glad that's done" syndrome. Your work is *not* done. You must now switch from the development phase to the maintenance phase. Gear up for it.

2. *Plan your review process:*

   Create a regular schedule for revising all documents. You may not be able to review them as often as you'd like, but the discipline of periodic review is important. Use the Sample Review Schedule Form (11-1) and the Sample Review Planning Form (11-2).

*(continues)*

## 11-3:  REVISION TIP SHEET (*continued*)

3.  *Decide how much should be revised:*

    You can review a portion of a policy or procedure or the entire document. You can review groups of documents, sections, or entire manuals. Plan the amount of change or one thing will lead to another and, before you know it, the project will be twice its original size.

4.  *Triple-check for cross-references and contradictions:*

    One of the biggest problems in revising is that a planned change can have an unplanned effect on some other policy or procedure. If there are cross-references between your document and another one, check each scrupulously. Everything from content to page numbers can change.

    Above all, ask yourself, *If we make this change, what other areas of operation could be affected? What policies or procedures do we have in those areas, and have we coordinated all of them?*

5.  *Create a feedback mechanism for users:*

    Develop a simple form on which users can report problems or observations. Make sure users understand that the information they give is important because it will be used in the next revision process. Keep all forms in a central file and analyze them for emerging patterns. Use the Sample Notice of Policy/ Procedure Discrepancy Form (11-4) and the Sample Input Form (11-5) at the end of this chapter.

6.  *Actively solicit information:*

    Make it a habit to ask how things are going. Use official meetings and informal hallway conversations. Keep tabs on the results. Ask everyone, "Is it working? Is it doing what we wanted it to do?"

7.  *Keep a file for comments and suggestions:*

    The day the new policy comes out, you may get a phone call from a user with a complaint or suggestion. Don't groan and ignore it. Record it and put it in the file. Comments and other input frequently start right away. They won't stop until a revision occurs and sometimes not even then. It's part of the natural organizational process. Just don't rely on your memory come revision time.

8. *Have a system for handling questions:*

Be realistic. Any change creates some confusion and resistance, especially if it involves long-standing practices. Be prepared to respond to users' questions and complaints.

9. *Make it easy for users to understand the changes:*

Use every possible trick to tell users what the changes are. Summarize the key areas and impact in the transmittal memo (see the Sample Action Memo at the end of this chapter). Explain the reasons for the change. Use plain, clear language. Visually highlight the revised portions of the document with screening, brackets, or other devices. And provide detailed instructions to users (use the Sample Revision Notice Form as a template).

10. *Force users to share responsibility for updates:*

Adopt an Action Memo or similar system that requires users to record each revision and report missing documents. The key to this system is a clearly identifiable gap in the sequence of change notices, so keep the numbering system as simple as possible.

Issue summaries once or twice a year, with instructions for users to check their own documents. Hold users accountable, or the "I never got that" problem becomes an epidemic. See the Sample Revision Record Form (11-6) and the Sample Revision Index Form (11-10) at the end of this chapter.

11. *Use a distribution list:*

Since you're responsible for notifying users of changes, it's important that no one be overlooked. Develop a list, study it, and make additions or corrections. Distribution is too often a last-minute, haphazard affair.

12. *Get a signed acknowledgment:*

Any significant changes, or any changes in significant policies or procedures, should be acknowledged in writing by the recipients. The acknowledgment statement can be a separate page or part of the transmittal document. It should state that the user has (1) read, (2) understood, and (3) agreed to abide by the changes. See the Sample Acknowledgment of

*(continues)*

## 11-3: REVISION TIP SHEET (*continued*)

|  | Revision Form (11-7). Also, check with your attorneys for the preferred wording. |
|---|---|
| 13. *Include revision date and effective date:* | Users need to know when the revision takes effect. The courts want to know both the revision date and the effective date. |
| 14. *Use a notation system that clearly identifies revisions:* | Users need to know which version of a document they're looking at. There are many different notations, such as "Rev. 5" and "Revised 3/98," and they are usually placed in the page header or footer. Sometimes the notation is part of the numbering system, such as "ER - 3.2 [R-5]." |
| 15. *Use loose-leaf binders:* | Revisions often get lost or misplaced after distribution for the simple reason that it's a hassle to insert the new pages. Eliminate that problem. If you anticipate many revisions, choose a binding system that's fast and easy, like loose-leaf binders. |
| 16. *Keep a record of all revisions:* | For legal and practical purposes, you may occasionally have to refer back to an old policy or procedure. Keep a master copy of each version along with a record of its effective date. Also keep a copy of the transmittal document. In addition, you should retain source material and artwork. |

**Comments**

☐ Good revision follows much the same process as the original development and writing work. You must plan, research, analyze, and organize. That's followed by drafting, editing, and implementation.

The main difference lies in the fact that revision is an ongoing process that never stops. It requires the writer to become actively involved in the maintenance process and to continually monitor how well the policies and procedures are working.

## 11-4: SAMPLE NOTICE OF POLICY/PROCEDURE DISCREPANCY FORM

| NOTICE OF POLICY/PROCEDURE DISCREPANCY |
|---|

**Policy/Procedure/Handbook name:** _____ **Number:** _____

**Step number:** _____

**Other:** _____

(table, illustration, graphic, etc.)

**The problem appears to be:**

☐ Incorrect  ☐ Unclear  ☐ Omitted
☐ Duplication  ☐ Contradictory  ☐ Incomplete
☐ Wrong reference  ☐ Out of sequence  ☐ Other _____

**Please describe the problem:**


**Please suggest ways to improve/correct it:**


**Reported by:** _____ **Date:** _____

**Action taken?**

☐ **Yes** ☐ **No**

If no, why not?



If yes, what action?



Action taken by: _____

Date:_____ Authorized by: _____

Communicated back to reporting party on: _____

## 11-5: SAMPLE INPUT FORM

---

### POLICY AND PROCEDURE INPUT FORM

Use this form to record any observations or problems you have with a company policy or procedure, and return it to your supervisor or other appropriate manager. Your input as a user is important. We will review your comments and either (1) take action or (2) keep them on file until the next revision takes place. Attach as many additional pages as you need.


To: _____

From: _____

Date: _____

Re Policy/Procedure/Handbook: _____

---

### OBSERVATIONS or COMMENTS




---

### WHAT WOULD YOU LIKE TO SEE DONE?

## 11-6: SAMPLE REVISION RECORD FORM

| REVISION RECORD | | |
|---|---|---|
| for: _____ | | |
| (policy, procedure, or handbook) | | |
| *Date of Revision* | *Effective Date* | *Nature and Extent of Changes* |
| | | |
| | | |
| | | |
| | | |
| | | |
| | | |
| | | |
| | | |
| | | |
| | | |
| | | |
| | | |
| | | |
| | | |
| | | |
| | | |
| | | |
| | | |
| | | |
| | | |
| | | |
| | | |
| | | |
| | | |
| | | |
| | | |
| | | |
| | | |
| | | |

## 11-7: Sample Acknowledgment of Revision Form

Users should acknowledge in writing their receipt of all revisions, using a form like the one below. (*Note:* This sample contains suggested wording only. Check with your attorney before finalizing your own acknowledgment statement.)

---

ACKNOWLEDGMENT STATEMENT

I have received a copy of the revision(s) to _____
_____. I have read the
revision(s) and understand that it is my responsibility to fully
understand and implement them. I agree to abide by these
changes, as prescribed by the company.

Signed: _____

Date: _____

---

## 11-8: Sample Action Memo

Transmittal notices such as this memo need to be clear and must indicate what action is required.

Start with specifics.

Give reason for the change.

Give filing and recording instructions.

Tell what the new document does.

> ## Action Memo No. AF-17
>
> **To:**   All staff members
>
> **Date:**   December 3, 1997
>
> **Notice of Change to:**   Policy and Procedures on Outside Collections
>
> Policy ACO - 4.0 on the use of outside collection agencies has been changed. A new procedure, "Reporting Requirement," has been added to section 4.2 and is effective on January 1, 1998.
>
> The new section spells out procedures for reporting complaints of inappropriate or illegal activity by a collection agency that is acting on the company's behalf. Although such complaints are not common, we have seen a rise in the number of them in recent months. The new procedure is necessary to track and control problems that may arise with our outside agencies.
>
> Please insert the new pages into your handbook immediately, and record the change in your Revision Index. Remove and destroy old pages 42 through 45.
>
> Read the new section carefully, then sign the acknowledgment statement and return it to Maria Collins by December 15.

Put the acknowledgment statement on the memo itself or on a separate page.

Give instructions for acknowledgment statement.

## 11-9: Sample Revision Notice Form

| | |
|---|---|
| **Action Memo No.:** _____ | |
| REVISION NOTICE | |

**Manual:** _____ **Date:** _____

Add ☐　　　　Delete ☐　　　☐ Modify

| **Items to Be Removed** | **Items to Be Inserted** |
|---|---|
| | |

**Disposition of Items Removed:**

Throw away ☐　　　Shred ☐　　　Return ☐

Other: _____

## 11-10: SAMPLE REVISION INDEX FORM

| | REVISION INDEX | | | |
|---|---|---|---|---|
| Record all Action Memos immediately on receipt and check to be sure they're in numerical sequence. If not, you're missing a change notice. Contact your supervisor immediately for a replacement copy. This is your responsibility. | | | | |
| *Action Memo* | *Subject* | *Revision Date* | *Effective Date* | *Page(s)* |
| | | | | |

# 12

# We're Thinking About Going On-Line

On-line policies and procedures are becoming more common, and their use will continue to increase as readers become more and more computer-literate.

But the decision to go on-line, like any decision, has advantages and disadvantages, costs as well as benefits. Weigh them all carefully before you jump in. Going on-line shouldn't be a leap of faith. It should be a thoughtful, deliberate decision.

## What It Means to Go On-Line

First and foremost going on-line is not a magic cure that will remedy your policy and procedure woes. It does not guarantee instant understanding or proper application.

On-line documentation is simply a different method of communicating your final product to users. In the past, we were restricted to verbal or written policies and procedures. Now we also have the option of sending them electronically.

### What Does Not Change

The content of your policies and procedures doesn't change when you go on-line. Your development process doesn't change. Neither do your

---

THE THREE METHODS OF COMMUNICATING WITH USERS

1. Verbal
2. Written
3. Electronic

---

writing, review, editing, or content revision processes. You still face the challenges of careful decision making, careful planning, and careful writing.

---

### ON-LINE DOCUMENTATION

| *Is* | *Is Not* |
|---|---|
| A different method of communicating your policies and procedures | A panacea that will suddenly make your policies and procedures understood and used |

Going on-line is simply a different way of delivering your policies and procedures to the user. The format and design will change, but the way in which you develop and write them won't.

---

## What Does Change

What does change is the method by which you communicate the finished policy or procedure to the user. There is no physical product, so you no longer have to print, copy, and mail a piece of paper. You send your message electronically, through cyberspace.

In essence, going on-line simply means that you're using a different delivery system.

## The Advantages and Disadvantages of Going On-Line

Like all delivery systems, being on-line has its advantages and disadvantages.

## Advantages

The advantages of being on-line can be significant. Going on-line is faster and more efficient than a paper system, delivering the message instantly and simultaneously to hundreds of users. Information is disseminated rapidly, and no one's copy arrives a week late.

Once installed, on-line systems also tend to be less costly to maintain. There are no paper revisions to issue or binders to wear out.

They save vast amounts of storage space in both user and central files. A 120mm optical disk can hold at least 200,000 pages of text, and it has a longer storage life than paper.

---

### ADVANTAGES OF GOING ON-LINE

| *Logistical* | *Informational* | *Motivational* |
|---|---|---|
| ■ Lower maintenance costs<br>■ Faster<br>■ More efficient<br>■ Instant distribution of originals and revisions<br>■ Space-saving<br>■ Easier access for disabled users | ■ Can link related facts or documents together in a way that gives users faster access. Done through the use of hypertext (the ability to click on a word or phrase and call up related items) or by searches.<br>■ Can jump quickly from one document to another. | ■ Less intimidating to users who are familiar with computers<br>■ Easier and faster than picking up a 300-page manual |

---

There are also fewer deadline pressures for the writer, who no longer has to worry about printing deadlines.

And most important of all is what it can do to make life easier for users: They can find related documents and information faster through the use of searches or hypertext (highlighted words the user can click on to instantly call up related or supplementary material).

For those who are computer-literate and are comfortable using computers, it can also be less intimidating to turn to the machine than to pick up a 300-page manual. And disabled users gain new access with the ability to magnify text, "turn" pages, and even adjust the style, pace, or order of the text as needed.

## Disadvantages

On the other hand, going on-line is not a panacea. It has some significant disadvantages as well.

Users who aren't especially comfortable with computers can be intimidated by on-line systems and may revert to paper copies. Going on-line requires a major commitment from the organization to supply the time, training, and even empathy that are needed to make users fully comfortable.

It can also require a significant budget. New hardware or software may be necessary for a large number of users. You might use sophisticated graphics, but the resolution of the users' display screens may be so poor that the images are grainy and unreadable. In addition, it can be costly to convert text and graphics and to develop or buy appropriate software.

Readability is less than that of a paper document. A display screen is harder on the eye and is therefore harder to read. Concentration suf-

---

### DISADVANTAGES OF GOING ON-LINE

| *Logistical* | *Informational* | *Motivational* |
|---|---|---|
| ■ Need for training<br>■ Requires major organizational commitment of time, money, and resources<br>■ Small screen size (as opposed to a piece of paper)<br>■ Higher initial costs for design and development and possibly equipment<br>■ Format limitations<br>■ Lower readability | ■ Fast access or ability to compare data can be hindered by inadequate software or hardware.<br>■ Format limitations tend to lend themselves more to short documents. Can encourage readers to skim or skip longer documents.<br>■ Some users may not have access to a terminal.<br>■ If the system crashes or is down for maintenance or other reasons, information is unavailable. | ■ Peering at a screen is difficult and tedious.<br>■ Users may be intimidated by the system or the mere use of the computer.<br>■ Some users just prefer a hard copy. |

---

fers, and lengthy documents are difficult for users to follow. Eyestrain can be a serious problem with lengthy documents, manuals, and handbooks, which require a lot of viewing.

The small size of the screen also creates a visual problem. If the user opens a window to compare two documents, each may be too small to read. It would be much easier to take two paper documents and line them up side by side. Other display features may limit users' ability to cross-reference and compare different pieces of information.

Format in general is a problem because of readability. Blocks of text, for instance, must be smaller to keep the reader's visual attention. Colors and emphatic techniques must be limited and graphics kept simple.

It can also be hard for users to distinguish between a "page" and a "screen." Most of us still think of a page as being a sheet of paper at least 8 1/2″ × 11″, while a screen holds only a portion of that amount. Users might read just three or four screens, think they've read several pages and that's enough, and fail to scroll through the entire document.

And finally, there is the fact that the system may not always be available. What happens if the computer crashes or if the system is tied up for maintenance or other reasons? What if the user is away from the computer, perhaps in the field where one isn't accessible? What if it's a shared computer that's busy at the moment?

---

QUESTIONS TO ASK WHEN GOING ON-LINE EXTERNALLY

- How experienced and comfortable are users with computers?
- What kind of equipment do they have?
- What kind of software do they have?
- Do they have ready access to a terminal (at their workstation, around the corner, ten minutes away)?
- What format(s) are they used to working with and do they prefer?
- What's their environment like (difficult, conducive, indifferent)?
- Are their organizations supportive (providing training, time, empathy)?
- Will they really check the system regularly for updates?
- How can they be made to acknowledge receipt?

---

## The Case of External Users

On-line systems for external users, such as customers, present special challenges. This stems from having:

- A widely, and sometimes wildly, divergent group of external users
- Limited knowledge of, and no control over, external users' equipment or environment

For instance, do all potential users know how to operate a computer? Are they comfortable with it? Do they have access to a terminal? You may have some who are experts and some who are afraid to lay a hand on a computer. And you can't train all external users.

How much do you know about their equipment and the environment in which they'll use it? Is their software sophisticated enough to handle the system? Is the hardware adequate? Are the surroundings conducive to use (lighting, physical proximity, and so on)? Do they have to take a five-minute walk just to reach the terminal?

Your ability to investigate and analyze these factors when dealing with external users is often extremely limited, and you may end up relying on guesswork.

If you must proceed but don't have much information, assume that equipment, conditions, and comfort levels are minimal. Then develop your system for the lowest common denominator.

---

### ON-LINE DESIGN CONSIDERATIONS

#### Visual Ease

- Use small blocks of text.
- Limit the number of colors on the page to two.
- Limit highlighting and other visual devices used for emphasis.
- Use simple graphics.
- Use lots of white space.

#### Ease of Use

- Use hypertext (click-on capability) or searches.

#### Clear Operating Instructions

- Indicate page, document, or file size on the screen.
- Differentiate between "page" and "screen."
- Use a CONTINUED notation at the bottom of the text.
- Create screen headers and/or footers, and be sure to keep them simple.
- If not using hypertext, include information on how to find related or supplementary information.

---

## Designing an On-Line System

The unique nature and limited readability of the computer screen create certain design considerations. The format and design of your documents must necessarily be different from that of a traditional paper system.

As you design your on-line system, remember that a computer screen is visually harder to see and concentrate on than a piece of paper. Many of the design guidelines are aimed at eliminating visual clutter and keeping the reader's attention. Others deal with the need to maintain control of the revision and notification process.

The four design factors to keep in mind are:

1. Visual simplicity
2. Ease of use
3. Clear operating instructions
4. Adequate conversion of elements such as acknowledgments and revisions

See the On-Line Tip Sheet (12-1) at the end of this chapter for a full explanation of all these factors.

---

CONVERTING THE ACKNOWLEDGMENT AND REVISION PROCESS

- Require an electronic or written acknowledgment.
- Ensure that revisions are instantly recognizable.
- Create a notification method that allows you to issue immediate changes when emergencies arise.
- Review changes verbally and in writing, as well as electronically.
- Require that users periodically check the system for changes.
- Create an electronic version of the Revision Index (see Chapter 11).
- Make sure users are still held responsible for reading, understanding, and using the material.

---

## Chapter Summary

- Going on-line is not a magic solution for policy and procedure woes. It's simply a different method of delivering the final product to the user.

▪ The development and writing processes remain the same. What changes is the format and design of your system.

▪ Going on-line has a number of advantages, including speed of distribution, simultaneous distribution, faster access to material, and lower maintenance costs.

▪ It also has disadvantages, including readability problems, user discomfort, higher initial costs for design and development, and the need for a significant organizational commitment.

▪ As you design your electronic delivery system, counter its disadvantages. Plan and design your system carefully.

# Tools and Resources
# for Chapter 12

## 12-1: On-Line Tip Sheet

### User Preference

☐ Preferred by users who are fully computer-literate and have access to a computer in their own work area. Currently used mostly by fully automated organizations such as engineering, design, or certain manufacturing companies. Will become more common as computer literacy and equipment availability increase.

### When to Go On-Line

☐ When the benefits to both organization and users outweigh the development and training costs and the difficulties of implementation.

### Major Issues

☐ *Create readability:* A screen is visually much more challenging than a piece of paper. It's smaller, contains less information, is harder to read, and can cause eyestrain. Reading lengthy documents on-line is tedious work, partly because it's hard on the eye and partly because the user's body posture is rigid and unnatural. (We don't normally concentrate by staring straight ahead for long periods of time.) Physical and visual strain sets in quickly.

☐ *Give clear operating instructions:* On a small screen, it's easy to lose track of the size of the document you're reading. Without a stack of paper to physically touch or look at, there is no constant reminder of how much material needs to be covered. Users can easily get careless and think they're done when they're not. They also need to know how to find related materials and how to revise their documents.

☐ *Convert the control and revision systems:* In a traditional system, revisions and acknowledgments are controlled by a physical piece of paper. On-line systems must retain control of these elements in some manner. You can integrate them into the software, retain a paper system, or use a combination of the two.

*(continues)*

## 12-1:  ON-LINE TIP SHEET (*continued*)

### Planning Considerations

1. *Get a commitment from your organization:*

   Designing and developing the software for the system can require substantial time and money, as can training users. And you may need to buy new equipment.

2. *Decide how extensive the system should be:*

   Decide whether the system will apply to all policies and procedures throughout the organization. It might make sense to go on-line in one area only, if the people in that area are already using computers for most of their work and have both the equipment and the training to use an on-line system.

3. *Work with users from the beginning:*

   Start communicating with end users right away. Tell them what you're doing and why. As you finalize parts of system, introduce them briefly to the users. Don't add to the natural resistance by springing a full-blown system on users overnight.

4. *Consider the hard-copy dilemma:*

   If the on-line system is well planned and implemented, users can be weaned from hard copies. But there is an initial reluctance to give them up, so expect some users to hold on to them. Also consider whether some users need to retain hard copies. A field engineer or an installation or repairperson may not be able to carry, operate, or access a computer. Users also need the capability to make copies of documents, but printing out massive numbers of hard copies defeats the purpose of going on-line.

5. *Consider the need for new hardware:*

   If screen size, resolution, or color is inadequate, it will discourage the use of the system. Assess the state of your users' current equipment.

### Design Considerations

1. *Use small blocks of text:*

   Scrolling through screen after screen of unbroken text makes it seem as if the policy or procedure is endless. The same is true for pieces of paper, but the effect is exaggerated on a screen. Keep your sentences and paragraphs even shorter than normal. Use short, simple words.

2. *Use lots of white space:* In addition to small blocks of text, leave plenty of white space in margins. Separate graphics and text distinctly. Because the screen is harder on the eye than a piece of paper, you have to work harder so the reader can use it without straining.

3. *Limit colors to two:* Ignore the Rule of Three in an on-line system. Too many colors overwhelm the eye in the small space of a screen. Limit colors to two in both text and graphics.

4. *Keep graphics simple:* The contradiction here is that you can create wonderfully complex graphics on the computer, but you can't use them in your on-line system. They create visual clutter. Simplicity is the key to keeping the readers' attention.

5. *Clearly label the size of the document:* Make it impossible for readers to ignore how large the document is and where they are in it. Give any or all of the following: the page or screen number, the total number of pages or screens, the document or file size.

6. *Use a notation system that shows that the text is continued:* It's easy to scroll through a few screens and think you're done. Make sure readers know there's more. You can use a statement such as "CONTINUED" or even "DON'T STOP HERE." Place it at the bottom right-hand corner of the text, so that it falls in the eye's natural sightline.

7. *Create headers or footers:* These serve the same purpose as they do in a traditional paper system: to give the user needed information (title, number, effective date, and so on). Try to use one or the other but not both. Keep them as simple as possible to avoid visual clutter.

8. *Limit the use of emphasis:* It's best to use emphasis sparingly even on paper, as noted in Chapter 6. It's even more true on the screen, where you risk totally overwhelming the eye.

9. *Use hypertext:* Hypertext is the ability to click on a highlighted word or phrase and instantly access related or supplementary material. It's a tremendous improvement over thumbing through hundreds of

*(continues)*

## 12-1:  On-Line Tip Sheet (*continued*)

pages of a manual or even poring over an index or table of contents.

10. *If not using hypertext, give clear instructions on how to find related material:*

Hypertext is ideal, but your system may not have that capability. If it doesn't, tell users exactly how and where to find related material. Can they type in a word or phrase and do a search? Do they have to scan the index or table of contents? Each system is different, so be sure instructions are clear.

11. *Differentiate between a "page" and a "screen":*

A "page" usually refers to a standard piece of paper. Decide whether to keep this definition or make "page" and "screen" synonymous in your system. Either way, you'll have to train users and continue to reinforce the training. The tendency to equate "page" and "screen" is hard to overcome.

### Considerations Regarding Aknowledgment and Revisions

1. *Get an acknowledg-ment signature:*

It's easy to overlook this since you're communicating electronically. Some systems require users to respond electronically by a given date. Others still require a paper confirmation. Whichever way you do it, remember that this is a legal issue.

2. *Create a process to inform users that a revision has been made:*

Notice of revision is commonly sent by e-mail, instructing users to check their system for the announced change. But a problem develops if users don't check their e-mail regularly. Make them responsible for doing so. Some organizations use paper as a confirmation. You might choose to use both paper and e-mail for critical or major changes.

3. *Create an electronic version of the Revision Index:*

Require users to periodically check the system, and make it easy for them to do so. (See Chapter 11.) Allow them to go to one central electronic location where all changes have been recorded. Make them responsible for checking their documents against the central list.

4. *Create an emergency notification process:*

There may be occasions when there is an urgent need for an immediate change. Incorporate some type of notification method into the system, whether it's an electronic alert, a paper notice, a verbal directive, or a combination of the three.

5. *Review changes periodically:*

Issue an electronic summary of changes every few months, then reinforce those changes in staff meetings or memos. No communication system is perfect, and you sometimes need to use every available means to get the message out.

# Index